The Swoose

Odyssey of a B-17

The Swoose

Herbert S. Brownstein

SMITHSONIAN INSTITUTION PRESS
Washington and London

This book was edited by Initial Cap Editorial Services.
Production editor: Jack Kirshbaum
Designer: Janice Wheeler

Library of Congress Cataloging-in-Publication Data
Brownstein, Herbert S.
The Swoose : odyssey of a B-17/ Herbert S. Brownstein.
p. cm.
Includes bibliographical references and index.
ISBN 1-56098-196-2
1. Swoose (Aiplane) 2. World War, 1939–1945—Aerial operations, American.
3. World War, 1939–1945—Campaigns—Pacific Area. I. Title.
D785.U63B76 1993
940.54'4973—dc20 92-41888

Printed in the United States of America

99 98 97 96 95 94 93 8 7 6 5 4 3 2 1

∞ The paper used in this publication meets the minimum requirements of the American National Standard for Permanence of Paper for Printed Library Materials Z39.48-1984.

Publisher's note: The descriptions of otherwise undocumented personal incidents and the recollections of episodes and persons are entirely the author's. Every effort has been made to verify details and ensure correctness; inaccuracy if it occurs is regretted.

Contents

Acknowledgments

The long and tortuous trail in search of the Swoose's story led me to many people and organizations who contributed generously and enthusiastically by providing information or suggested sources. Many read early drafts and made helpful comments or made themselves available to answer my questions. In the truest sense, this work represents the cooperative efforts of many without whose assistance it would not have been possible. Their contributions provided the museum with the factual story of an airplane that proved its fame.

Members of crews who flew the Swoose and contributed to all aspects of the research are listed below in alphabetical order:

Jack J. Crane, a pilot during its assignment in Panama and who supervised its overhaul and modification;

Colonel Henry C. Godman, USAF (Ret.), who was assigned to the airplane in Hawaii and piloted it across the Pacific to the Philippines and later into combat;

Colonel Frank Kurtz, USAF (Ret.), who took command of the airplane in Australia when it was assigned as the area commander's flagship and in "The Swoose" established five trans-Pacific records, breaking the Australian Sir Charles Kingsford-Smith's previous records. Colonel Kurtz also made several transcontinental flights during the Swoose's stay in the United States and flew it to Panama from where he made flights to the Caribbean and South and Central America. Through his subsequent intervention the Swoose was saved from the wrecker's torch; ultimately he flew it from Los Angeles to the museum's storage facility in Chicago;

Charles W. Nall, the last known assigned pilot, who flew the airplane back to the United States;

Richard S. Saxe, the last pilot to fly the Swoose;

Colonel Harry J. Schreiber, USAF (Ret.), navigator of the Swoose for much of the time it was under the command of Frank Kurtz;

Colonel John A. Wallach, USAF (Ret.), bombardier while the airplane was commanded by Henry C. Godman.

The following former crew members of the Swoose were kind enough to furnish information and or photographs: Alfred J. Chappel, assistant crew chief in Panama; John H. Crawford, engineer and crew chief in Panama; Carl Epperson, navigator for Henry Godman; and Homer C. Rogers, a copilot in Panama.

I am indebted to the following survivors of crew members who supplied records and memorabilia: Lt. Gen. Devol Brett, USAF (Ret.), who provided his father's scrapbook; and Sharon Gay Smith, Sandra G. Holmes, and Linda C. Young, the daughters of Weldon H. Smith who contributed his sketches, diary, and mementos.

The following whose lives were touched by the Swoose provided background and files on its movement: Maj. Gen. Eugene L. Eubank, USAF (Ret.), commander of the 19th Bombardment Group that ferried the Swoose and its sister aircraft to Hawaii in May 1941 and subsequently commanded the group during the early days of World War II; Paul E. Garber, Historian Emeritus, National Air and Space Museum, who was instrumental in obtaining the airplane for the museum; and Col. Francis J. Fitzpatrick, USAF (Ret.), assistant to Maj. Gen. George H. Brett in Panama and later his foreign liaison officer.

Staff specialists in the museum's Information Division provided expert assistance in searching, acquiring, and evaluating documentation and photographic evidence associated with the Swoose. I am indebted to the following who gave of their patience and expertise: Mark Avino, photographer; Dana Bell, archivist; Daniel Hagedorn, research technician; Allan Janus, photographic technician; Mary Pavolich, librarian;

Mark Taylor, film archivist; and Lawrence E. Wilson, research technician

The Center for Air Force History through M. Sgt. Roger A. Jernigan was most helpful in searching the Air Force archives for official records. Claudia Anderson, archivist, and Philip Scott, audiovisual archivist, at the Lyndon Baines Johnson Library generously furnished documentation and photographs pertaining to the ill-fated flight to Port Moresby and across Australia.

The Aeronautics Department staff at the National Air and Space Museum and my fellow volunteers made themselves available in all phases of the work. Without their constructive suggestions, guidance, and stimulation, I could not have undertaken and completed the work. I am especially indebted to the following: Francis R. Cappellitti, volunteer and former member of the 19th Bombardment Group; William T. Hardacker, volunteer and World War II naval aviator; Russell E. Lee, curatorial assistant; Robert C. Mikesh, senior curator; Dominick A. Pisano, associate curator; F. Robert Van Der Linden, associate curator; and Howard S. Wolko, special adviser. A special thanks to Anita Mason, lead secretary in the department, who cheerfully prepared the voluminous letters and supporting documentation in spite of her other official duties.

My profound gratitude goes to Jeffrey L. Ethel, the respected aviation historian who reviewed the draft manuscript and gave it his enthusiastic support; Tom C. Crouch, chairman of the Aeronautics Department, Felix Lowe, director of the Smithsonian Institution Press, and Jack Kirshbaum, project editor, for their confidence, support, and guidance in this project. The manuscript was edited by Therese D. Boyd. Her suggestions and alterations were significant contributions to the tale of the airplane and I am deeply indebted to her for her patience and professional skills.

The manuscript used for determining its potential as a Smithsonian Institution Press publication would never have seen the light of day had it not been for the members of my family. My son, Barry J. Brownstein, labored for long hours in structuring the draft material and electronically processing the information. My nephew, Jon J. Shure, and his wife, Janice Conklin, used their unique skills and spent many evenings editing a draft. My wife, Sylvia, did much of the early typing and, while enduring my anxieties and doubts as well as the interruptions in our daily routine (even on vacations), continued to radiate the glow of enthusiasm for the work and her confidence in my ability to see it through.

The Swoose

Introduction

Like a ghost out of the past, the old four-engine World War II propeller-driven bomber was flying in the jet age, headed for its last landing on December 5, 1953. The only surviving U.S. combat airplane on active duty throughout the war had fought the Japanese in the Philippines, Java, and Australia.[1] It had also seen service as a military transport in Australia, and had made four historic trans-Pacific crossings. This oldest surviving B-17 had then served out the war operating out of the Panama Canal Zone.

The battle-scarred airplane struggled to maintain flight as, one by one, two of its four engines failed as it neared its final destination. The crew had maintained a flight path over the river below, should the remaining engines fail and a crash landing become necessary. Carefully they flew on, taking the last right turn as their third engine failed. Finally, the oldest surviving bomber of World War II, with but one engine still operating, touched down at Andrews Air Force Base, outside of Washington, D.C.[2]

Thus ended the last and probably the most harrowing flight in the 4,000-flying-hour career of B-17D Serial Number 40-3097, now known as "The Swoose." This last mission began almost five years earlier when it departed the Los Angeles Municipal Airport (Mines Field) on January 22, 1949. While its final destination was the Smithsonian Institution in Washington, D.C., it spent time in temporary storage areas in Chicago, and Pyote, Texas.[3]

The airplane finally arrived in Washington to join other historically significant airplanes in the collection maintained today by the National Air and Space Museum of the Smithsonian Institution.[4] This B-17D, the Swoose, together with the B-29 Enola Gay and the B-26 Flak Bait, are the only U.S. aircraft in the collection to have actually flown in combat during World War II.

Designed originally as a weapon of defense,[5] the B-17 evolved into America's primary strategic offensive air weapon in the battle for Europe, where it was to fly previously unheard of distances over enemy territory to drop its bombs from stratospheric heights. Its defensive armament grew from the meager five .30-caliber machine guns installed in the first model to the formidable array of thirteen .50-caliber guns in the G series, the last of the B-17 models.

Today, few visible scars remain from World War II. In time, like most wars, that great conflict will fade into the history books. The efforts of our countrymen will be forgotten by all but historians. Only in the attics and museums will relics remain to remind us of the holocaust suffered in war by man at the hands of man.

One such relic is the Swoose, a B-17 survivor of World War II. The airplane never dropped bombs in the strategic battles against cities and civilians, as did so many of its contemporaries that saw action in the vast 1,000-plane raids over Europe. The Swoose is a reminder of a different part of the war—those dark days shortly after the Japanese attack on Pearl Harbor, when a handful of men in their early model B-17s fought in a vain effort to halt the advance of the invading Japanese army and navy that ultimately would overwhelm many of the islands and nations of the Pacific.

When war broke out in 1941, most Americans were unfamiliar with the geography of the hemisphere covered by the Pacific Ocean and its adjoining seas. Naturally, the public's attention was drawn to events in Europe, where there were familiar ancestral countries and cities. Most of the war correspondents' reports came from the European Theater, where the might of U.S. industrial production and fighting forces were gathered. Americans and their Allies in the Philippines and the Southwest Pacific were fighting what became known as the "backyard war" because the Allied governments had decided that the war in Europe would get top priority.

The early battles in the Pacific were waged with little notice in the public media. Defeat after defeat at remote places with strange names were but briefly noted. The weary soldiers of the Allied forces in the Pacific, armed with obsolete equipment, were left to fight delaying battles and forced to improvise and cannibalize their machines in a desperate effort to get replacement parts while more modern war materials and reinforcements went elsewhere. In spite of these conditions, during the first forty-four days of the war, the Swoose and its counterparts in the 19th Bombardment Group shot down fifty enemy fighters and sank or damaged sixty surface ships.[6]

The Swoose was first brought to the attention of the American public in press releases from Australia in 1942 and in the book *Queens Die Proudly* by William L. White, published in the same year. The book described the Philippine and Netherlands East Indies adventures of Frank Kurtz, then the pilot of the Swoose, and his crew. While the book documented some of the airplane's days in Australia as a "flagship," no one wrote of its role in combat before that time. Some uninformed authorities flatly stated that the Swoose never flew a combat mission.[7]

B-17D 40-3097 was part of the 19th Bombardment Group (Heavy) stationed in the Philippines, the first U.S. Army Air Corps unit to go into offensive action against the Axis forces. In 1943, when the Group was disbanded, it was the most decorated organization in the U.S. Army, holding four World War II decorations.[8] On December 9, 1941, they attacked the onrushing tide of Japanese ground, sea, and air forces that would ultimately drive the United States and its allies from their Pacific island bases and threaten the invasion of Australia. The Swoose and the other planes of the 19th fought that backyard war heroically. And, though scarred, the Swoose managed to survive. Many pilots and crews flew the Swoose, and many more maintained the airplane and kept it flying for so many years. Now, more than fifty years later, few of the airmen who fought with the Swoose remain.

The records of those early days of World War II vividly demonstrate the heroic ability and daring of the combat and maintenance crews of the 19th Group and the ruggedness of their B-17s. Exhausted crews with inadequately maintained aircraft, operating out of makeshift airfields without proper communications and adequate information on enemy movements, flew with small bomb loads in order to achieve greater distance, often through tropical storms, to make bombing runs on moving targets.

Without the protection of fighter escort and outnumbered, they would often strike out singly against the well-equipped and -trained Japanese forces. During December 1941 and the early months of 1942, they fought this retreating war in a makeshift attempt to delay the enemy's advance southward across the islands of the South Pacific to Australia.

Apparently, only the Swoose is left of the airplanes that fought on the very first day of the Japanese attack on Pearl Harbor and the Philippines. Not only did the Swoose survive these battles, but it went on to leave its mark in aviation history and to serve in other military and diplomatic missions halfway around the world until the war ended.

Henry C. Godman, one of the early pilots of the airplane that would later be known as the Swoose, described the events of these first few months of the war in the Southwest Pacific: "We flew every mission we were told to fly, even though we felt we were on a treadmill to death. There didn't seem to be an end until all of us were killed, wounded, taken prisoner, or there were no more planes to fly."[9]

When B-17D 40-3097 was delivered to the National Air Museum in December 1953, it lacked its historical records. Attempts in the intervening years to find them were unsuccessful. In the days before the onset of hostilities, the crews kept daily track of their airplanes' flights on special forms (AAF Form 1) that were used to log the time flown and to record the pilot's comments on the aircraft systems. After the war began in the Philippines, aircraft flight records became unimportant in light of daily events and even the early records were lost.[10]

In those early days of the war, with missions being constantly flown, it was humanly impossible to keep track of events as they occurred. Communications between bases were very poor, even after the evacuation to Australia. Many of the records that were created were lost with the fall of the Philippines; either they were destroyed by enemy action (such as the bombing of Clark Field) or by the retreating forces to keep them from falling into the hands of the advancing Japanese.

Over the intervening years, various combat histories and organizational and personal diaries have surfaced that permit some reconstruction of the history. According to those who fought the air war in the Philippines during December 1941, the official combat histories were often reconstructed long after the actual events took place. The 19th

Chapter 1

Birth of a Veteran

The Boeing B-17 Flying Fortress was probably the most famous of World War II combat aircraft. This beautiful but deadly war machine was described by Gen. Henry H. "Hap" Arnold as the "backbone of our worldwide aerial offensive." The development of this airplane was unique in aviation history. With the marriage of the U.S. Navy's Mark XV Norden bombsight and the high-altitude long-range B-17, a new and novel precision-bombing platform came into being.[1] During World War II, B-17s dropped a total of 640,036 tons of bombs on European targets alone, compared to 452,508 tons dropped by B-24 Liberators and 463,544 tons dropped by all other U.S. aircraft. The Fortress is credited with shooting down 23 enemy aircraft on a single 1,000-plane raid. A total of 4,750 B-17s were lost on combat missions.[2] Because of its role in the destruction of strategic targets in Europe, the Flying Fortress became the symbol of victory over the Axis powers.

The history of the B-17 actually began when the prototype Boeing Model 299 first flew on July 28, 1935. That prototype was followed by thirteen Y1B-17s (the "Y" designated the aircraft for service test and evaluation, while the "1" indicated that a special government procurement provision was used that provided for "limited acquisition of experimental aircraft without open competition"). A fourteenth Y1B-17, designated the Y1B-17A, was built for experimental purposes, primarily for the installation and test of General Electric exhaust-driven turbo superchargers. When Germany attacked Poland in September 1939, only the thirteen Y1B-17s had been delivered to the Air Corps.

The precursor of the B-17 was the experimental four-engine XB-15. In spite of being underpowered, the XB-15 broke several weight-carrying records. Oddly, the design of the XB-15 was started before the B-17, but did not fly until October 15, 1937, more than two years after the B-17 had flown. As it was designed to be a research tool, only one aircraft was built.

On July 17, 1935, the giant Model 299 rolled out of the Boeing hangar in Seattle, Washington. It had been designed to meet an Army requirement for a multi-engine airplane capable of carrying a 2,000-pound bomb load 2,200 miles at a top speed of 200 miles per hour. (In those days the word *multi-engine* was usually considered to mean twin engines. However, Boeing was assured that it could also be interpreted to mean four.) Equipped with four 750-horsepower Pratt and Whitney "Hornet" radial engines, the Model 299 had a wingspan of 103 feet and 9 inches, was 68 feet and 9 inches long, and provided accommodations for a crew of eight. Enclosed in the fuselage were five machine guns capable of covering many angles of attack. This was considered a formidable array of armament and caused Dick Williams, a reporter for the *Seattle Times,* to refer to it as a "15-ton flying fortress."[3] Later, Boeing had the name "Flying Fortress" registered as a trademark.

On August 20, 1935, the Model 299, known as the "Mystery Bomber," was flown from Seattle to the Army Air Corps facility at Wright Field outside of Dayton, Ohio, for a design competition with other aircraft manufacturers. The 2,040-mile flight was made in nine hours at the then-amazing speed of 227 miles per hour.[4]

The Model 299 easily outperformed the other two entries in the competition, twin-engine Douglas and Martin airplanes. However, on October 30, shortly before completion of the 299's final performance flight, the airplane crashed when an Army pilot attempted takeoff with a control surface gust lock engaged. The Boeing model was disqualified; Douglas won the competition as well as the Army's order for 133 B-18s.[5]

In spite of its disqualification, the Air Corps was impressed enough with the Model 299 to award Boeing a contract for thirteen aircraft designated YB-17. This model was designated 299B by Boeing, with the single major difference from its predecessor the four 850-horsepower Wright R-1820-39 "Cyclone" engines capable of delivering 1,000 horsepower for takeoff. Other less significant changes were made in the armament and landing gear, and the crew was decreased from eight to six.[6] Because the money used by the Army to procure the YB-17 was obtained from a separate budget category, on November 20, 1936, the Air Corps designation was changed to Y1B-17.[7]

The first Y1B-17 was flown on December 2, 1936. Five days later, the Army's chief test pilot stood the airplane on its nose following a landing with the brakes locked, but by January 2, 1937, it was back in service. The first B-17 delivered to a tactical organization, YB-17 Number 36-150, arrived at Langley Field, Virginia, on March 1, 1937, the first anniversary of the Army's establishment of the General Headquarters, Air Force.[8]

The last of the thirteen Y1B-17s were delivered to the Army on August 5, 1937. A fourteenth Y1B-17 had been ordered for static testing. However, an earlier Y1B-17 was subjected to such extreme aerodynamic forces during a violent thunderstorm that the need for a static test model was waived and the fourteenth airplane was delivered as a flight model. The Army designated it as a Y1B-17A (Boeing's designation was 299F).

The Y1B-17A was first flown on April 28, 1938, and was used in the development of the turbo supercharger for the Wright R-1820-51 engine. Exhaust-driven superchargers were installed on the top of the engine nacelles but were moved to the underside of the wings for all subsequent B-17s. Following completion of the supercharger development program, the airplane was delivered to the Army on January 31, 1939.[9]

Use of the turbo supercharger had a significant impact on the performance of future aircraft. In addition to its use on subsequent models of the B-17, the supercharger was also used on the four-engine Consolidated B-24 Liberator, the Republic P-47 Thunderbolt, the Lockheed P-38 Lightning, and, later, the Boeing B-29 Superfortress.

The engines of the Y1B-17 delivered 775 horsepower at 14,000 feet; the maximum speed at that altitude was 256 miles per hour. The Y1B-17A's exhaust-driven, turbo-supercharged 1820-51 engines delivered 800 horsepower at 25,000 feet and a maximum speed of 295 miles per hour at that altitude.

The first of the thirty-nine B-17Bs to be produced was delivered on July 29, 1939, and the last on March 30, 1940. These aircraft incorporated a number of improvements. The B-17B was the first model to provide for a full-time navigator as a member of the crew.[10] The navigator was positioned in the nose section, on the left-hand side of the aircraft, immediately behind the bombardier.

The nose of the B-17B was shortened by six inches and a new, clear nose cone was installed that incorporated a flat glass aiming window for the bombardier (previously located in a notch below the airplane aft of the nose). The gun blister in the nose was eliminated and replaced with a socket mount for a .30-caliber gun in the upper right side of the new nose. An astrodome was installed to the right of the center line of the fuselage above the flight deck, for use by the airplane commander. A new, larger rudder was installed. The pneumatic system for operating the main landing gear brakes was replaced with a hydraulic system. An improved Wright R-1820-51 engine delivering 1,200 horsepower for takeoff was installed. The B model was equipped with constant-speed full-feathering Hamilton Standard propellers. The oxygen necessary to sustain human life at high altitude was distributed through an interconnected manifold and delivered to crew members through rubber hoses placed in their mouths.[11]

A total of thirty-eight B-17Cs followed, twenty of which were sent to Great Britain in the spring of 1941. Although the B-17C was not built to defend itself in a war situation, the first B-17 to fly in combat was the C model. On July 8, 1941, three B-17Cs, named "Fortress I" by the British, were flown on a trial bombing mission by the Royal Air Force (RAF). These aircraft were equipped with the Army's Sperry bombsights, which proved inferior to the Norden product.[12] The major design changes in the Model C were gun mountings at the waist positions and a large ventral gun enclosure, resembling the bottom of a bathtub, just aft of the wings, on the underside of the fuselage.

As a result of the operational experience with the C model, all Cs operating in the United States were modified in 1941 to B-17Ds. In addition to the modified Cs, forty-two B-17Ds were built. While a number of significant changes were introduced in the D models, the only outward difference between the C and D models were the newly incorporated cowl flaps designed to improve engine temperature control. Crew accommodations were increased from eight to nine.[13]

Boeing built 512 B-17Es, the first of which flew on September 5, 1941. Among the major changes in the E were a longer fuselage, increased vertical fin area, dorsal and ventral power turrets, tail-gun position, and increased nose armament. All thirteen machine guns were changed from .30- to .50-caliber.

In the spring of 1942, the F replaced the E on Boeing, Douglas, and Lockheed production lines. The F model incorporated more than 400 changes, the most obvious being the one-piece clear plastic nose, newer ball turret, and new "paddle" propellers.

The last production model of the B-17 series were the Gs, which were merely late-production Fs retrofitted with a remote-controlled two-gun "chin" turret. Later G models included redesigned side-nose gun mountings, and enclosed waist and tail guns. The last B-17 was rolled out of the Boeing Seattle facility on April 9, 1945.

On August 17, 1942, at Rouen, a German rail center, 87 miles northwest of Paris, U.S.-manned Flying Fortresses made their first strike in the European Theater. In broad daylight, twelve B-17Es came in at 25,000 feet and bombed the freight yards, trains, and roundhouses, while others carried out diversionary raids on Cherbourg and Dunkirk. All these B-17s returned safely to their bases in England.[14]

Its remarkable ability to withstand punishment made the B-17 a legend. Many came back from bombing missions over enemy territory with fuselages riddled with bullet and flak holes, with one or two engines dead, with large pieces of wings and tail surfaces torn or missing. In spite of its reputation for being close to indestructible, more B-17s were lost in the European, Pacific, and African theaters of war than any other Allied aircraft that fought simply because there were more of them to lose.

The B-17's record for shooting down enemy fighter planes over Europe surpassed that of its escorting fighter protection. Enemy fighter planes were unable to stop the massive formations of 1,000 Flying Fortresses which destroyed twenty-three attackers on average while the protective escorts were limited to eleven kills on the average raid over Europe.

In the summer of 1941, the Air Force initiated a unique arrangement to produce the large quantities of B-17s required by the United States and its allies. While the Boeing Company would continue to produce the B-17, the Douglas Aircraft Company and the Vega Aircraft Company (a subsidiary of Lockheed) would also produce the airplane using Boeing's blueprints and Boeing-designed and -furnished tools and jigs. The B-17F was the first model built by the triumvirate. Boeing built 2,300 of that model while Douglas built 605 and Vega 500. By the time the last B-17 rolled out on the production line, 12,731 would be produced—6,981 by Boeing, 3,300 by Douglas, and 2,750 by Vega.[15]

One of those 12,731 B-17s built was a model D, Serial Number 40-3097, manufactured by Boeing at a cost of $252,144, as part of Contract W-535-ac-13257. Government-furnished equipment, such as propellers ($10,360), engines ($35,256), ordnance ($3,042), radio ($9,250), and miscellaneous other items ($37,000), made the total cost about $347,000.[16] Received by the U.S. Army Air Corps on April 28, 1941, 40-3097 was flown for about seven hours and ten minutes while at the Boeing factory in Seattle, and to its first assignment with the 19th Bombardment Group at March Field near Riverside, California, 70 miles east of Los Angeles.

B-17D 40-3097 was one of the group of forty-two B-17s designated at the time of manufacture as D models delivered between February 3 and April 29, 1941. The B-17D introduced self-sealing fuel tanks. A revised fuel system removed the permanently installed refueling lines of the C model. A 24-volt electrical system was introduced. The old leaky high-pressure oxygen system that was vulnerable to catastrophic damage from gunfire was replaced with a low-pressure system. It was the last model of the Flying Fortress to be without a tail gun and tail gunner's compartment, power-operated top turret, and semi-retractable ball turret in the underside of the fuselage.[17]

While the C model carried a single .50-caliber gun in its "bathtub" or "dust bin," located on the underside of the fuselage just aft of the radio compartment, and a single .50-caliber gun in the ceiling of the radio compartment just aft of the bomb bay, the D model had twin .50-caliber guns in those positions. Like the C model, the D had single .50-caliber guns located on each side of the rear compartment in the waist of the aircraft.[18] These waist guns were fired through oval openings in the aircraft, where windows were removed to permit operation of the guns.

Completing the armament was a single .30-caliber gun positioned so that it could be fired from gun ports in the bombardier's compartment in the nose. Additional guns recovered from wrecked aircraft were sometimes installed in the nose by combat crews. These early B-17s could adequately protect themselves from attacking fighters only when flown in full squadron formation and in level flight. During the early part of the war, a flight of one, two, or three attacking enemy ground and sea targets was exceptionally vulnerable.

When the B-17D was introduced into the Air Corps inventory, it and other new aircraft were procured without spare parts. The government pushed the airplane manufacturers for more planes, forcing the manufacturers to neglect the production of spares. This shortage would frustrate attempts to maintain operational combat aircraft and prematurely remove many otherwise operational aircraft to the junkyard because of cannibalization.

The D's greatest weakness was that it had no protection from attacks from the rear. Accordingly, pilots fish-tailed the aircraft to give the waist gunners a chance to fire at the attacker and keep attacking aircraft away from the blind spot in the tail.[19] Following their evacuation from the Philippines, the first combat crew assigned to 40-3097 partially overcame this deficiency by modifying the plastic tail cone under the rudder and installing a .30-caliber machine gun that was operated by a cable running to the waist gunner positions.[20] The gun was mounted loosely so that it had a wide firing pattern.

In January 1941, the beginning of the last year of peace in the United States before the Japanese attack on Pearl Harbor, the 19th Bombardment Group participated in the inauguration ceremonies held for Pres. Franklin D. Roosevelt in Washington, D.C. From their base at March Field, California, the 93rd Squadron flew their B-17Bs to El Paso, Texas, to Fort Benning, Georgia, to Langley Field, Virginia, and from there over the Capitol during the ceremonies being held there.[21]

As fast as the B-17 C and D models were coming off the production lines in Seattle, they were flown to March Field to strengthen the 19th Group and fully equip them with the late-model aircraft. The flow of men and material to support the operation of the new B-17s of the 19th Group increased significantly so that personnel could be trained in flying and maintaining the heavy bombers. Many of the navigators were still aviation cadets, yet to be commissioned as officers. Tactics were developed to train gunners in combat methods and pilots trained in long-distance formation flying to make maximum use of the airplane's combat capability. Methods to wring the most out of the B-17's performance were accomplished by experimenting with various engine power settings to maximize flight range. Later that year, the training program would overwhelm the facilities at the field in California, and on June 14, 1941, they moved their base of operations to Albuquerque, New Mexico.[22]

A great amount of discussion had taken place in planning councils of the War Department regarding the possibility of flying these modern long-range bombers to Hawaii to reinforce and extend the range of the patrol forces stationed there. However, there was great fear of public reaction in the event of failure to successfully fly the overwater mission. The reluctance of the War Department's Plans Division was overcome on April 11, 1941, when the secretary of war, Henry L. Stimson, wrote the secretary of the Navy to ask for naval surface force support for a flight of B-17s. In that same month, the 19th Bombardment Group began intensive training in preparation for the pioneering overwater mission.[23]

Chapter 2

Beginning of the Pacific Sojourn

The war in which 40-3097 would soon take part was well along by the time the aircraft was delivered to the U.S. Army Air Corps. Japan had invaded China in 1937 and in 1939 began its movement of conquest southward by occupying Hainan Island off the southern coast of China. With the fall of France in 1940, the Japanese stationed troops in French Indochina. Later that year they joined forces with Germany and Italy in an arrangement by which it was agreed that each would provide the other with assistance if attacked by a power not then at war (obviously the United States). In 1941, Japan was poised for further moves southward into Malaya, the Philippines, and the Netherlands East Indies.

By New Year's Day of 1941, an open clash with the Japanese seemed inevitable to many in the American government. After Japanese forces moved into Indochina in September 1940, the United States imposed embargoes that cut off all vital war materials, with the exception of petroleum, to Japan.

Against this backdrop of events in the Pacific and the advances of the Axis powers in Europe and North Africa against the British and French, the United States, having reinforced its Atlantic defenses, developed plans to reinforce its air forces in the Pacific. In the past, such outlying forces were supplied with obsolete equipment; the more modern aircraft were reserved for those operating in the United States.[1]

The Territory of Hawaii (T.H.), the American gateway to the Pacific and home to the U.S. Pacific Fleet, is 2,400 miles west of the mainland. Because relations with Japan were declining, Gen. George C. Marshall suggested that the Air Corps in Hawaii have some "big bombers" (B-17s) to protect the islands from potential air attack. At the time, the United States had sixty-four pilots and ninety copilots qualified to fly these four-engine bombers. The plan was to provide the capability to interdict an enemy force 750 miles outside its striking range.[2] One of the justifications for building the B-17 had been its ability to protect and reinforce Hawaii.

By 1941, the 2,400-mile barrier between the mainland of the United States and Hawaii, soon to be removed by the B-17, had been breached, but only on a small scale. Improvements in aircraft design resulted in a succession of crossings that began with the first attempt by a U.S. Navy seaplane in 1925. A better appreciation for the B-17 flight can be obtained by reviewing those early crossings.

The first recorded attempt to reach Hawaii from the mainland began at San Pablo, California, on August 3, 1925, in a PN-9-1 twin-engine seaplane built by the U.S. Navy. After flying 25 hours, the pilot was forced to land at sea when the plane ran out of fuel about 300 miles short of its goal. After nine days at sea, the aircraft was spotted 15 miles off the Hawaiian island of Kauai on September 10 by a U.S. submarine, which towed the craft and crew the remaining distance to shore. Although that early flight ended short of its Hawaiian destination, it set a record for nonstop, heavier-than-air flight of 1,730 nautical miles and ushered in subsequent attempts that were fully successful.[3]

The ocean barrier was completely breached for the first time two years later when, at 6:29 A.M., Wednesday, June 29, 1927, the first flight to the Territory of Hawaii from the U.S. mainland ended at Wheeler Field, on Oahu, T.H. Two Army pilots in a modified Fokker C-2 trimotor monoplane made the trip in 23 hours from the Oakland, California, airport.[4]

On July 14, 1927, the first civilians to fly the Pacific, Ernie Smith and his navigator Emory Bronte, made the crossing from Oakland to a crash landing on the island of Molokai, T.H., in 25 hours and 36 minutes. This flight was made in a modified single-engine Travel MA.[5]

At 8:54 A.M. on May 31, 1928, Charles Kingsford-Smith, the legendary Australian aviator, and his crew of three others took off in a Fokker F-7 Southern Cross trimotor from Oakland for Hawaii on the first leg of their 7,388-mile trans-Pacific flight to Australia. Twenty-seven hours and 25 minutes later, they landed at Wheeler Field.[6]

On January 10 and 11, 1934, six U.S. Navy P2Y-1 Consolidated flying boats made the 2,400-mile flight from San Francisco Bay to Pearl Harbor in 24 hours and 45 minutes. This marked the first time naval aircraft had been successfully flown to Hawaii from the mainland. At the time, this flight was also the longest nonstop mass flight in history, and the longest nonstop flight for a seaplane.[7]

A later trans-Pacific record set west-to-east by Sir Charles Kingsford-Smith in 1934 would remain unbroken until 1942, when B-17D 40-3097 challenged and broke it. On October 20, 1934, Kingsford-Smith and his copilot/navigator P. G. Taylor became the first to speed across the air bridge from Australia to the U.S. mainland in a single-engine Lockheed Altair monoplane. Their first stop was made in the Fiji Islands, 1,760 miles from the jumping-off point in Brisbane. The second stop was made in Honolulu, 3,150 miles from the departure point in the Fijis. The final leg in the long, unmarked route across the Pacific to the United States was 2,408 miles to the airport at Oakland where they landed on November 4, 1934.[8]

The second trans-Pacific flight from Hawaii by a land plane to the mainland of the United States, and the first to be flown solo, was made by Amelia Earhart. On January 12–13, 1935, she accomplished the sensational feat by covering the distance in a single-engine Lockheed Vega especially equipped for the long flight. Her flying time from Wheeler Field to Oakland was 18 hours and 16 minutes.[9]

On April 16–17, 1935, Pan American Airways made what was considered the most notable flight of that year in world aeronautics. A survey flight from Alameda, California, to Pearl Harbor (Honolulu) was made in 18 hours and 9 minutes. A specially outfitted Sikorsky S-42 four-engine flying boat surveyed the route for the first scheduled trans-Pacific air mail service that would be inaugurated on November 22, 1935, by a four-engine Martin M-130 flying boat called the "China Clipper." Passenger air service was started a year later by Pan American on October 21, 1936, making stops at Honolulu, Midway, Wake, and Guam islands en route to Manila.[10]

Other flights between the mainland of the United States and Hawaii were made and noted in the record books. On March 17, 1937, Amelia Earhart made the flight with her navigator Fred Noonan and two others. Starting on a planned around-the-world flight, they departed on the first leg from Oakland. After a recordbreaking 15 hours and 47 minutes, the airplane landed at Wheeler Field. Unfortunately, the intended around-the-world flight came to an abrupt end when the Lockheed Electra was wrecked during the subsequent takeoff for Howland Island on the second leg of the journey. (Earhart's more famous unsuccessful attempt at flying around the world began months later, heading east from Miami.)[11]

In 1937, the U.S. Navy began a series of nonstop flights to Hawaii from the mainland, exercising the capability of their new long-range Consolidated patrol flying boats. These flights provided naval forces in Hawaii with a new operational capability of long-range air reconnaissance. On January 28–29, twelve new PBY-1s made the 2,553-mile nonstop trip from San Diego to Pearl Harbor in 21 hours and 31 minutes. On April 12–13, 1937, twelve PBY-1s flew the new air bridge to Hawaii in 21 hours and 35 minutes. Eighteen more aircraft made the flight on January 19–20, 1938. With the advent of the faster PBY-4, the time was reduced to 17 hours and 17 minutes by seventeen aircraft on September 8–9, 1939. The prewar airlift of seaplanes to Hawaii came to a close on June 27–28, 1939, when fifteen PBYs made the U.S.-Hawaii flight in 16 hours and 39 minutes.[12]

As part of a spectacular around-the-world 81-day flight on October 3, 1938, Clyde Pangborn and Hugh Herndon Jr. flew from Samisbiro Beach, Japan, to Wenaatchee, Washington, in a special Bell single-engine monoplane. Thus they became the first to fly nonstop 4,558 miles across the Pacific.

The trans-Pacific air bridge was apparently unused in 1940, except by Pan American Clipper flying boats on their scheduled trans-Pacific crossings. However, by 1941, the threat of war in the Pacific brought a significant increase in air traffic. On February 22, 1941, thirty-six USAAC P-36 aircraft took off from the deck of the aircraft carrier *Enterprise* and landed at airfields in Oahu. Over the next two months, fifty-five Curtiss P-40 reinforcements arrived in Hawaii by the same mode of transportation. All of these aircraft had been previously hoisted aboard carriers at the North Island Naval Station, San Diego.[13]

Land-based U.S. Army Air Corps fighters took off from a carrier deck in an operational theater for the first time in June 1942 when the carrier

Saratoga ferried the 23rd Fighter Squadron of the Seventh Air Force's 318th Group to Midway. By the following January, navigation technique, pilot ability, and aircraft performance had improved so much that fighters could make the 1,300-mile flight from Hawaii to Midway under their own power.

While smaller, shorter-range airplanes could be transported by ship and assembled at their destination or flown from aircraft carriers, the much heavier B-17 bombers had to be flown to Hawaii from the U.S. mainland. Although no standard land-based aircraft had ever attempted the trip and only the U.S. Navy flying boats with their water-landing capabilities had ever made a mass flight over the route, the War Department ordered the Air Corps to prepare twenty-one B-17s for the flight to reinforce the Hawaiian Air Force. The Air Corps had planned to send thirty-five of the airplanes but inadequate facilities in Hawaii caused them to hold the remaining B-17s on the West Coast pending the completion of adequate facilities.[14]

Procurement of the B-17 had been justified initially on the basis of coastal defense, where it would be required to interdict approaching enemy surface vessels, but as with many high-altitude bombardment aircraft, it was woefully inadequate for bombing moving targets.[15] Its principal role under such circumstances would prove to be long-range high-altitude reconnaissance, a role it later performed for both the Army and the Navy in the Pacific. Accordingly, the B-17's effectiveness in defending Hawaii was relegated to a reconnaissance role rather than high-altitude interdiction of a mobile surface force.

The 19th Bombardment Group at March Field, Riverside, California, was fully outfitted with B-17Cs and Ds when twenty-one of its aircraft were ordered to reinforce defenses in Hawaii. The aircraft were to be replaced one by one as new B-17s came off the production line at Boeing.[16] In preparation for this pioneering mass flight of land-based military aircraft to an overseas station, Lt. Col. Eugene L. Eubank, commander of the 19th, carefully chose the crews that would participate from the 30th, 32nd, and 93rd bombardment squadrons and the 38th Reconnaissance Squadron. B-17D 40-3097 was one of the airplanes selected for transfer to Hawaii.

Navigating the trackless sea miles was an important concern during preflight planning. The B-17 was the first Army combat aircraft to provide for a full-time navigator. Long-range navigation in the Army Air Corps had not been a primary consideration before the Flying Fortress became operational. Prior to 1941 Army aircraft had limited range and navigation was left to the pilot, who used radio signals for fixing his position when he could not observe surface features on the ground. Flight over water added to the navigational difficulties, since there were no unique surface observations that could be used to check location. The navigational problem dictated an upper limit of four degrees error from the center line of the course from the mainland in order for the pilot to still be able to reach Hawaii.[17]

The paucity and unreliability of radio signals made their use impractical for such a flight. Only celestial navigation techniques could be relied upon. The Air Corps had a number of its pilots and future navigators trained by Pan American Airways personnel who were experienced in using such techniques in their ocean-crossing, passenger-carrying flying boats. In January 1941, B-17 flight crews at March Field started training to qualify as celestial navigators. The final qualification required a 2,400-mile night flight from March Field to the East Coast. Using only the celestial navigation techniques that would be used on the overwater flight, the crews recorded engine power settings and fuel consumption to develop cruise control data for the B-17.[18]

Without announcement to the public, on the morning of May 13, 1941, the 19th Bomb Group flew from March Field to Hamilton Field near San Rafael, California, with twenty-two B-17s. Since weather conditions were excellent, twenty-one of the twenty-two aircraft left that same evening on the first mass flight of land-based aircraft to Hawaii, while the spare airplane returned to March Field.[19] (Appendix A lists the names of the 189 men who made that historic flight.) Shortly before takeoff, Lt. Gen. Delos C. Emmons, the commanding general, General Headquarters, Air Force, arrived at Hamilton Field and announced that he was making the flight with the 19th. However, he assured Lieutenant Colonel Eubank, commanding officer of the 19th, that he would only be a passenger. Eubank assigned him to Crew No. 2.[20]

The aircraft took off at five-minute intervals. Each crew navigated by dead-reckoning and celestial fixes. After traveling over 2,400 miles in 13 hours and 10 minutes, they landed in Hawaii on the morning of May 14, 1941, in the order of their takeoff, with a variation of less than six minutes in the flight time of any airplane. All crew members were awarded the Distinguished Flying Cross for this historic achievement.[21]

To support this first mass flight of land-based aircraft from the mainland to Hawaii, the Navy stationed four Ocean Station vessels at 500-mile intervals along the flight path and all naval vessels in the vicinity were asked to transmit weather information. Commercial radio stations in the vicinity of San Francisco and Honolulu provided homing signals by broadcasting continuously throughout the night of the flight.[22]

On the morning of December 7, 1941, the radio station in Honolulu once again played music all night for a homing signal as it had for every B-17 flight from the mainland. However, in addition to guiding B-17s of the 38th and 88th reconnaissance squadrons of the 7th Bombardment Group en route from the United States to the Philippines, the same homing signal from Honolulu radio station KGMB was also used by the attacking aircraft from the Japanese carrier task force steaming for Pearl Harbor.[23]

Operations in Hawaii

First Lieutenant Henry C. Godman, who was later to be the pilot of 40-3097, arrived at Hickam Field on March 13, 1940, and was assigned as operations officer to the 23rd Bomb Squadron of the 5th Bomb Group in the Hawaiian Air Force. He was flying a twin-engine Douglas B-18A when the twenty B-17s landed at Hickam Field on May 14, 1941, following their remarkable flight from San Francisco.[24]

Born in Philadelphia on April 13, 1914, Henry Godman was the son of World War I pilot Lt. Louis K. Godman, who was killed on September 28, 1918, while flying over a Liberty Bond parade in Columbia, South Carolina. The younger Godman, a graduate of Stanford University, became an aviation cadet at Randolph Field in July 1936, and completed his flight training at the Army Air Corps flying school at Kelly Field in San Antonio, Texas, in June 1937. He was first assigned to the 36th Pursuit Squadron at Langley Field in Hampton Roads, Virginia. Godman flew the Consolidated P-30 (PB-2A) for about a year before transferring to the 2nd Bombardment Group, also at Langley.[25]

The 2nd Bombardment Group at Langley received the first twelve Y1B-17s to be produced. Since only majors and captains were allowed to sit in the left seat and pilot these precious aircraft, Godman was assigned as a "copilot-bombardier" and accumulated 365 hours in that capacity.[26] The 2nd Bombardment Group flew a number of history-making flights with these early B-17s, flying more than 9,000 hours without a serious accident while demonstrating the airplane's operational potential.

Godman participated in the second spectacular Goodwill Mission flight by B-17s to South America. These flights pioneered the use of airplanes as tools of diplomacy. They were intended to show friendship to U.S. neighbors to the south while demonstrating an ability to defend the hemisphere. Seven B-17s took off for South America from Langley Field on November 10, 1939, and landed at Bolling Field outside Washington, D.C., on November 26, after flying more than 10,000 miles. From Langley they had flown to Albrook Field, Panama Canal Zone, to Asunción, Paraguay, and on to Rio de Janeiro. On the flight north they flew along the Atlantic coast to Maracaibo, Venezuela. The remainder of the trip to Bolling was made nonstop in 11 hours over the 2,150-mile course.

Because of his experience with the Y1B-17 at Langley, Lieutenant Godman was assigned duties as the squadron instructor to train the flight crews in Hawaii who were to make the transition from the twin-engine B-18 to the four-engine B-17. When the new B-17s arrived, Godman climbed into the left side (pilot's seat) for the very first time and began familiarizing himself with the airplane from that perspective. Fifteen members of the ferrying crews had remained in Hawaii in order to train people who had never before flown or maintained heavy bombers. A crew member "checked out" Godman in the airplane in one day after three or four landings. At that point Godman and the other fifteen instructors began instructing the new crews in the art of taking off, landing, and navigating these large four-engine airplanes.[27]

Although the pilot's seat was occupied by the pilot being checked out and the instructor sat in the copilot's seat, it was a thrill for this first lieutenant to have been assigned such a prestigious position.[28] The new crews made two- or three-hour training flights to practice setting up cruise conditions, and to familiarize the bombardier, radio operator, crew chief, and gunners with the airplane. To prepare them for long-range missions, Godman taught every pilot and copilot in the squadron dead-reckoning and celestial navigation and sent them on four- or five-hour flights over water to remote islands to practice making accurate landfalls.

On May 12, 1941, in cooperation with the Navy, the Hawaiian Air Force launched a mammoth war exercise. A force of defending bombers simulated an attack on mythical enemy aircraft carriers several hundred miles away that were assumed to be approaching the Hawaiian Islands. The exercise reached its climax when, early on May 24, a strike force including a Navy patrol squadron and the newly arrived B-17s located and "bombed" the carriers.[29]

B-17D 40-3097 flew about 50 hours in May 1941, including the war exercise just described. The airplane was used to locate the "invading" aircraft carriers and to drop 100-pound practice bombs on surface targets towed by the U.S. Navy.[30] In June it flew more than 50 hours for crew training and proficiency. In July it flew almost 35 hours, and about 49 hours more in August, apparently preparing for the upcoming, unprecedented flight to the Philippines.

All during this time of preparation, the likelihood of U.S. involvement in the war grew closer. On June 22, 1941, Germany invaded Russia.

Across the Pacific

The 14th Bombardment Squadron (H) (Provisional) was organized as part of the 11th Bombardment Group of the Hawaiian Air Force's 18th Bombardment Wing. Nine of the newly arrived B-17s, including 40-3097, were assigned to this squadron. The commander was Maj. Emmett C. ("Rosy") O'Donnell Jr., who would eventually have one of the most distinguished careers in the history of the U.S. Air Force before retiring as a four-star general. O'Donnell's war-time exploits included leading the first land-based bomber raid on Tokyo on November 24, 1944, when he led 111 B-29s that set out from Saipan in the Marianas for that 3,200-mile round-trip mission.[31]

In July 1941, the Army Air Corps decided that there was an urgent need for heavy bombers to defend against a growing Japanese threat on U.S. bases in the Philippines. It was felt that a strike force of B-17s would deter Japanese advances southward, and would strengthen the U.S. position in the Far East. While waiting for the 19th Bomb Group to receive its full complement of B-17s, Gen. Hap Arnold and his staff decided that the 14th Bombardment Squadron and its nine B-17s should make the first flight of land-based bombers across the Pacific on an 8,050-mile trip to Clark Field, located about 65 miles north of Manila. There, at Fort Stotsenburg, was America's oldest overseas military base. The flight plan was based on the Pan American Clipper route to Midway and Wake islands. The flying boat route to Guam could not be used because there was no airfield on the island.[32]

In preparation for the flight to Clark Field, two Air Corps lieutenant colonels were sent ahead to New Guinea and Australia aboard two of the U.S. Navy's PBYs of Patrol Squadron 22, stationed in Hawaii. These officers were to arrange for communications, 100-octane fuel, and servicing facilities for the B-17s. The PBYs flew the mission by way of Canton Island, the Fiji Islands, Noumea, Rabaul, Port Moresby,

Darwin, and Townsville, before returning to Hawaii. (One of the PBYs was commanded by Navy lieutenant Thomas Moorer, who as an admiral in 1970 would become chairman of the Joint Chiefs of Staff.)[33]

On September 2, 1941, in preparation for the trip to the Philippines, the 14th Squadron's manpower was augmented by transferring a number of men (see Appendix B) formerly assigned to the 5th Bombardment Group (H), as well as the 42nd and 26th bombardment and the 50th reconnaissance squadrons of the 11th Group. Henry Godman was one of those transferred in from the 5th Group.

On the morning of September 5, 1941, men of the 14th and the nine B-17s lifted off from Hickam Field, en route to Midway Island, the first leg of their flight to Clark Field in the Philippine Islands, on what was the longest overseas flight yet attempted by the Army Air Corps (see Appendix C). Twelve B-17s remained at Hickam to defend Hawaii, but half of these aircraft were out of commission, having been cannibalized to provide parts for the nine that departed for the Philippines.[34]

The airplanes took off at five-minute intervals and were piloted by Major O'Donnell, Maj. Birrell Walsh, Lt. Walter R. Ford, Lt. Sam Maddux (later commanding general of the Air Training Command), Maj. William P. Fisher, Lt. Edward C. Teats, Capt. Colin P. Kelly, and 1st Lt. Weldon H. Smith (who would later give 40-3097 its now-famous name).[35]

Lieutenant Henry C. Godman was at the controls of 40-3097 that morning, the last of the nine airplanes to leave Hawaii. The aircraft carried the squadron number 21 on its tail. Lieutenant Robert S. Clinkscales (later killed over Yawata, Japan, in a B-29), was copilot and Lt. Carl Epperson was the navigator. They landed at Midway after covering the 1,132 nautical miles in 7 hours and 10 minutes.[36]

After a night's rest, during which some of the crews slept under the wings of their airplanes, they took off at 4:45 the next morning for Wake Island, some 1,035 miles distant. The squadron arrived at 11:20 the same morning and began preparing for the next and longest leg of their journey: from Wake Island south to Port Moresby, New Guinea.

The aircraft took off from Wake Island on a war footing, with machine guns armed and orders to be ready for action. To avoid detection while passing over the Japanese Mandate Islands in the Carolines, this portion of the flight commenced at midnight and was flown at high altitude. The aircraft flew without running lights and maintained radio silence. Although they encountered a heavy rainstorm, the pilots kept their assigned positions as they approached Rabaul, then flew on over

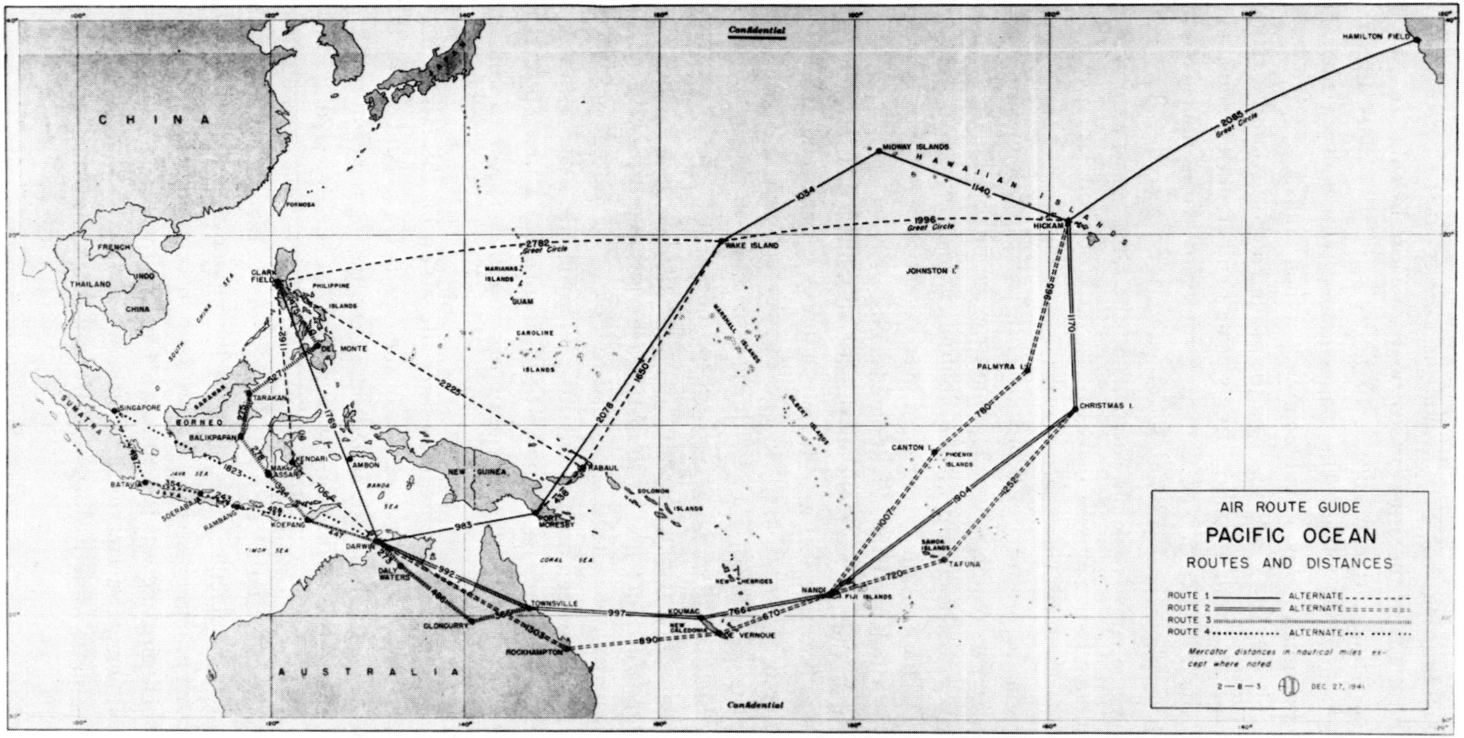

Routes across the Pacific as shown in the "U.S. Army Air Forces Air Route Guide" published by the War Department on February 15, 1942. In an accompanying memorandum, it was noted that large areas had fallen to the Japanese since the guide went to press and that Route 1 westward from Hawaii had been cut.

the mountain ranges of New Britain on a direct line to Port Moresby. The nine B-17s of the 14th landed on Port Moresby's dirt runway at noon local time on September 8, 13 hours and 2,176 miles after the takeoff from Wake Island. The planes landed with between two and two and one-half hours of fuel remaining in their tanks.[37]

September 9, 1941, was spent on the ground at Port Moresby, refueling the aircraft from 50-gallon drums using hand-cranked pumps operated by the tribesmen of New Guinea. It took almost four hours to refuel each airplane with about 3,200 gallons of gasoline. The next morning, the crews took off downhill on the tilted runway for the six and one-half hour, 934-mile flight to a Royal Australian Air Force training field at Darwin, Australia.

Early on the morning of September 12, each aircraft took off from Darwin at five-minute intervals, bound for the final destination, Clark Field at Fort Stotsenburg on the Philippine island of Luzon. On the flight to Clark, the squadron passed over Zamboanga on the southwestern tip of Mindanao in the Philippine Islands.

Due to an unexpected typhoon, the last 300-mile leg of the flight into Clark was flown at 100 to 200 feet. Before penetrating the storm, the crews noted a distinct black line in the sky between the clouds and the rain beneath them. They let down to within 100 feet of the water and at times could see only two or three miles ahead and, as an island would loom up, veered the aircraft to the right or left. Finally, they picked up the shore line of the Manila harbor entrance.[38] The B-17s were flying so low that the crews had to look up to see the barracks on the island of Corregidor in Manila Bay. Following the eastern shore line of the Bataan peninsula, Godman flew the airplane at treetop level to Clark Field, where on the evening of September 12, in low visibility, he landed.

Never having spotted any of its sister aircraft during this last leg of its long journey, 40-3097 was the last of the nine B-17s to land on the turf runway at Clark. The 14th Squadron, in completing the eight-day trip, had set the record for the longest mass flight of land-based aircraft. (In March 1946 a B-29 Superfortress would make the first nonstop flight from Hawaii to Clark Field in 21 hours and 49 minutes.[39]) Despite the navigational problems brought about by flight over long stretches of open water, primitive servicing facilities, and inaccurate weather briefings, not a single airplane was lost en route. One B-17 was damaged immediately following the landing at Clark, when its tail section struck a parked aircraft while taxiing. (On December 8, when the Japanese at-

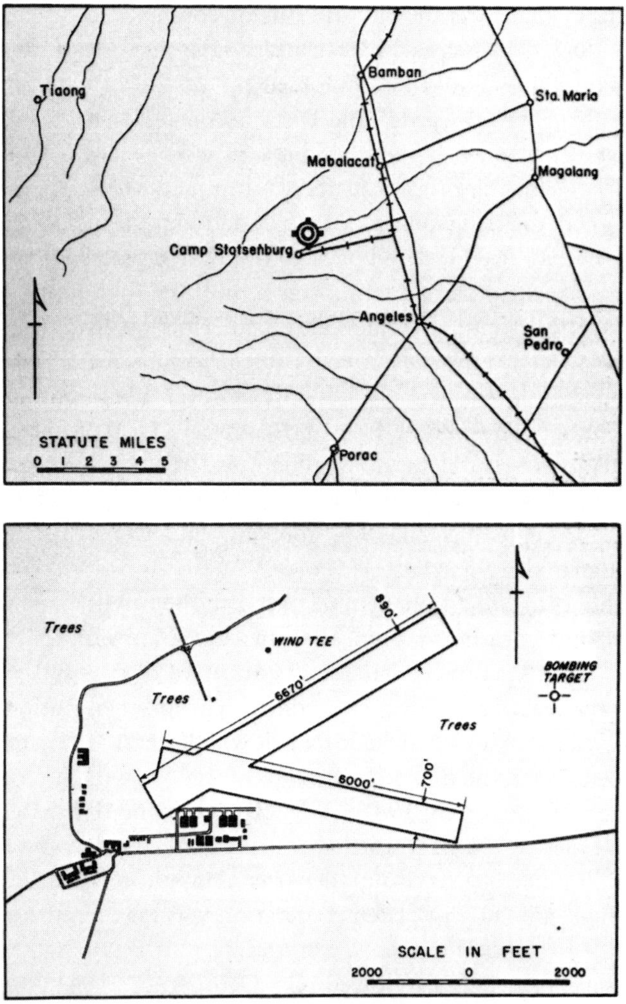

Layout of Clark Field as shown in the "U.S. Army Air Forces Air Route Guide." The facility was located 509 feet above sea level just east of Fort Stotsenburg on the north side of the highway to Doa and about 50 miles northwest of Manila. The two landing strips were composed of "sandy soil with very good drainage." The guide noted that "a special canvas can be placed along the landing strip to be used" and "pilots should land to the right of and opposite 'T.' "

tacked Clark, that aircraft was still out of commission.) This historic flight, conducted in secrecy, blazed new trails in aviation and proved that the Philippines could be reinforced by air. All of the crews of the 14th Squadron were awarded the Distinguished Flying Cross for their accomplishment.[40]

At Clark Field, the officers of the 14th Squadron (see Appendix D) were assigned to living quarters that had been evacuated by military families who had been ordered back to the United States. Operating out of Clark Field, in spite of a fuel shortage, the 14th Squadron immediately began tactical training in high-altitude formation flying, navigation, and bombing and gunnery missions. According to Air Corps records, Godman and his crew flew 40-3097 about seven hours during September and October. Gasoline was in short supply until October, at which time the tempo of readiness training increased.[41]

Meanwhile, organizational changes were underway as the war approached. On September 20, 1941, the Philippine Department Air Force was redesignated the Far East Air Force.[42]

Since the 14th Squadron demonstrated the feasibility of reinforcing the Philippines with heavy bombers flown from Hawaii, on September 18, 1941, the Air Corps ordered a second wave of twenty-six B-17s to duplicate the feat. The 19th Bombardment Group, then stationed at Albuquerque, New Mexico, which had flown the first B-17s to Hawaii, was given the assignment.[43]

Starting on October 16, 1941, under the command of Lt. Col. Eugene Eubank (leader of the May 13 flight to Hawaii), the 30th Squadron of the 19th Bombardment Group departed Hamilton Field, California, with the first nine aircraft. Their destination was Hawaii, the first leg of their journey to the Philippines. On October 20 at 10:30 P.M. the remaining seventeen B-17s followed. On October 22, 1941, the twenty-six airplanes of the 19th Bombardment Group left Hawaii.

To avoid overwhelming the servicing facilities en route, these twenty-six B-17Cs and Ds flew separately over the same route that had been flown just a month before by 40-3097 and the other B-17s of the 14th Squadron. Within one week, the first eight aircraft arrived at Clark and by November 6, twenty-five of the original twenty-six aircraft had landed. The last B-17 was delayed at Darwin because of engine changes; however, it ultimately arrived safely in the Philippines. (Appendix E lists the names of those who participated in the trans-Pacific flight of the 19th Bombardment Group.)

Although the American public knew nothing of the historic flights made by the 14th Squadron and the 19th Bombardment Group, all members of the participating crews were later decorated for the achievement.

Clark Field Operations

In the autumn of 1941, Clark Field was a turf-covered airdrome adjacent to Fort Stotsenburg on Luzon Island in the Philippines. The field lay in open country 12 miles east of an unmistakable landmark, the singular peak of an extinct volcano rising up from the plain, the 3,867-foot Mount Arayat. It was also the only available base in the area capable of handling the needs of the large heavy B-17s. The only other field in the Philippine Islands that could possibly be used as a base of operations for these airplanes was a natural meadow about 600 miles to the south, on the Del Monte pineapple plantation in Mindanao. The new B-17 air base under development here was being built to accommodate additional B-17s that were to be flown from the United States. Unfortunately, these aircraft never arrived; en route to the Philippines, they arrived in Hawaii on December 7 as the Japanese attack was underway.

Much of the ground surrounding the runway at Clark was too wet to support the heavy B-17s and so it was not possible to properly disperse the parked aircraft. Where possible, the airplanes were parked and maintained in the hangar area. Those parked along the edge of the field were arranged so that not more than two were in a line. Some B-18s and pursuit aircraft were parked on the north side of the field and the remainder, including observation, training, and pursuit types, were dispersed east of the hangar area.[44]

Camouflage painting of airplanes was directed on April 8, 1941, with the issuance of Technical Order 07-1-1. All aircraft were to be painted as soon as possible by activities in the field that had the necessary equipment to accomplish the camouflage work. The urgency was so great, the directive suggested, that the work should be accomplished out of doors if climatic conditions were satisfactory. However, all of the B-17s arrived at Clark in their natural silver aluminum finish. On a clear day the glow of the sunlight reflected from the parked airplanes could be spotted by approaching pilots from a distance of 25 miles or more.

All of the B-17s at Clark Field were scheduled to be painted in two hangers to be used exclusively for that purpose; maintenance of the Flying Fortresses would be accomplished in the open. Only one of the B-17s was ever camouflaged at this facility.[45]

On November 1, 1941, the 14th Bombardment Squadron, to which B-17D 40-3097 was still assigned, officially became part of the 19th Bombardment Group under the command of Colonel Eubank.[46] The thirty-five B-17s were divided among the 14th, 28th, 30th, and 93rd squadrons. B-17D 40-3097, with Godman and his crew, remained with the 14th under O'Donnell's command.

During November the 19th Bombardment Group (and B-17D 40-3097), operating from Clark Field, began flying reconnaissance missions north of Manila. The area for reconnaissance was divided into pie-shaped sections, one approaching the tip of Formosa, another covering northern Luzon, small islands to the north, and then running up the east coast.[47] B-17D 40-3097 flew more than 24 hours during November.

John A. Wallach, the bombardier on 40-3097, would recall these prewar reconnaissance missions forty-six years later. He remembered the Japanese ships plowing through the sea south of Formosa and the low-level flights the B-17s had made in an attempt to detect Japanese submarines.[48]

Since there was a shortage of replacement engines for the B-17s, the routine 400-hour changes were not made.[49] To conserve engines, training missions were consolidated so that several training objectives could be achieved on one flight. Training missions were flown using three aircraft in formation with a navigational assignment in which the crews had to locate a specific reef. There they would drop practice bombs and fly back to Clark by another route.

Pilots, navigators, and bombardiers had become skilled in operating in this new flying environment. As always, there was a general shortage of spare parts and a limited supply of oxygen for high-altitude flying. However, except for the one B-17 damaged on its initial landing at Clark, maintenance crews kept all of their assigned aircraft in operating condition.

The Move to Del Monte

On November 24, 1941, the War Department notified the Pacific commanders that hostile action was possible at any moment. On November 28, General Arnold, commanding general of the Army Air Corps, suggested that all units take immediate action to protect themselves.[50]

American forces at Clark knew that it was only a matter of time before they would be attacked. A single Japanese bomber came over

Manila every night and frequently flew over Clark Field to have a look. Sometimes the searchlights on the ground would illuminate the lone intruder. Smoke could be seen from Clark, rising in the sky some miles away, and was suspected to be a Japanese reference point for locating the airfield.[51]

At Clark Field on December 1, 1941, Gen. Lewis H. Brereton, commander of the Far East Air Force under Gen. Douglas MacArthur, briefed the 19th Bombardment Group on Japanese movements. General Brereton informed the men that despite the absence of shooting they were to consider themselves at war with Japan.

As suggested in General Brereton's briefing, Clark Field was put on a war footing. Bulldozers were used to build earthen revetments around the B-17s, in hopes that they would provide some protection to the aircraft should Clark Field be attacked. The crews also dug trenches near the aircraft using hand shovels. Blackouts were initiated and bamboo aircraft decoys were placed at several locations on the field.

On Wednesday night, December 3, 1941, orders were received to move the B-17s of the 14th and 93rd squadrons 600 miles south to the airfield at Del Monte. This move of two squadrons was intended to make room at Clark for the additional B-17s scheduled to be ferried from the United States. The crews being sent to Del Monte expected to return to Clark in three or four days, and therefore took with them only the personal gear that would fit in their flight bags.[52]

The move to Del Monte began on the night of December 5, 1941; the 14th Squadron under command of Major O'Donnell and the 93rd Squadron, commanded by Maj. Cecil E. Combs, began taking off singly from Clark for the flight to their new base. Lieutenant Godman and his crew flew 40-3097.

In very rugged country much like that of Hawaii, Del Monte was a partially completed 7,000-foot dirt landing strip, formerly part of a golf course on the Del Monte pineapple plantation. It had no more than a bare minimum of housing and aircraft servicing facilities. Communications with the outside were unreliable, with only one radio available with the range necessary to reach Clark.[53] Field lights had been installed, but there were no shops or hangars. All takeoffs had to be started at the upper end of the dirt runway that slanted downhill toward the bay.

Since none of the barracks at Del Monte had yet been completed, the crews had to live in tents with cots, blankets, rations, and whatever

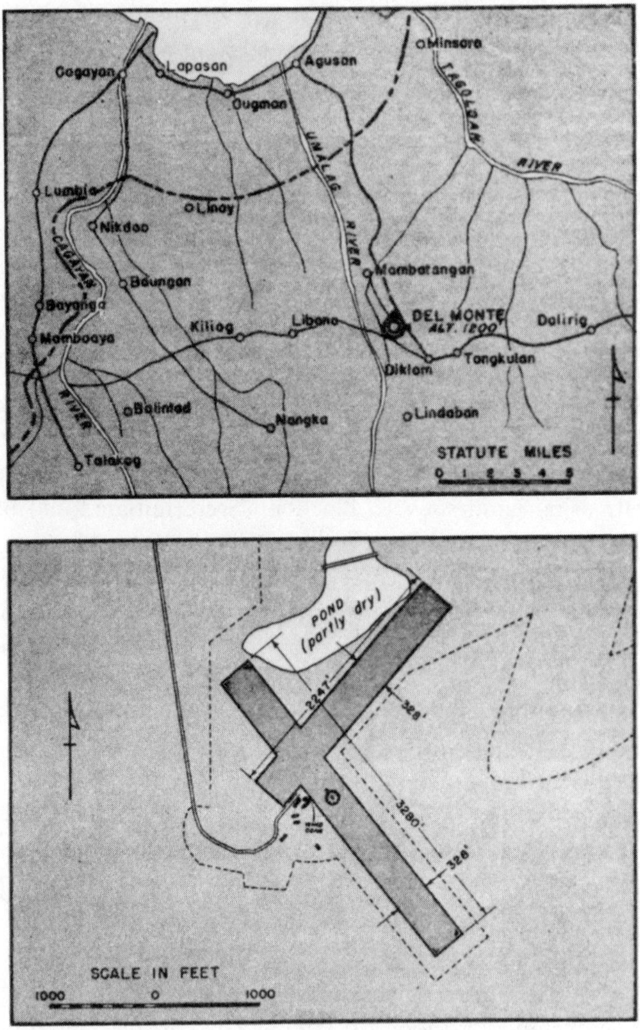

Del Monte airfield, 574 miles southeast of Clark Field, on the Philippine island of Mindanao, as depicted in the "U.S. Army Air Forces Air Route Guide." Designated by the guide as"one of the best in the Philippine Islands," it did not have a telephone but did have an aeronautical radio station.

personal equipment they had brought with their airplanes. There was, however, the always essential officers' mess and the Del Monte Company had a country club three miles from the field, complete with tennis courts, a swimming pool, and a golf course.[54] However, because of the lack of suitable washing facilities, the crews had to wash their clothes in a stream adjacent to the landing strip. In lieu of a washboard, they pounded the clothes with rocks as the natives did, using a soap made from fish oil. Hence they always smelled of fish when they perspired.[55]

There was no natural cover for the unpainted B-17s at Del Monte. Pilots 70 miles away reported seeing a glow in the sky over Del Monte from the sunlight reflected from the sixteen parked B-17s with their polished, natural finish as shiny as when they were delivered by Boeing. Brooms and brushes were used by the crews to apply the paint and one spray gun was used continuously in an attempt to camouflage the aircraft. The specified camouflage paint for the aircraft was not available, and the paint that was used turned out to have a glossy finish.[56] The men tried to tone it down and break out the lines of the aircraft without much success. According to one of the pilots, it was a sorry job; the paint failed to thoroughly cover the aluminum skin. In their new warpaint some aircraft looked green, others a shade of brown, but they all still reflected sunlight. The dispersed aircraft were then covered with fish nets and coconut palm fronds. It took ten truckloads of fronds to cover one B-17.[57]

It was in this tense and primitive environment that the aircraft and crews of the 14th and 93rd squadrons spent their last few days of relative peace (see Appendix F for the crews of the 14th and 93rd squadrons). Soon the curtain would go up on America's involvement in World War II, a chapter of history that B-17D 40-3097 would experience from beginning to end.

Chapter 3

Combat Operations

Philippine Operations

On Sunday, December 7, 1941, at 7:55 A.M., Japanese sea- and carrier-based air forces attacked Hawaii. Because of time zones and the intervening International Date Line, it was 3:55 A.M. on December 8 in the Philippines. Someone who had been listening to the radio for the 6:30 morning news from Manila announced during breakfast to all within earshot that Pearl Harbor had been bombed. It was hard for some to believe that a stronghold such as Pearl would be attacked. Just a month before they had read an article titled "Impregnable Pearl Harbor" in the *Saturday Evening Post.* The author of that article outlined why Pearl Harbor could not be attacked.[1]

Major O'Donnell read a radiogram officially notifying him of the Pearl Harbor attack. Shortly thereafter, two B-17s from Del Monte were ordered to make reconnaissance flights around the island of Mindanao. One of the aircraft was B-17D 40-3097, now known to its crew as "Ole Betsy," piloted by Godman. (On this first U.S. flight mission of the war, the crew of Ole Betsy was the same that had flown the airplane from Hawaii to Clark Field in September.) The planes took off in opposite directions, encountering very bad weather off to the east but no enemy activity. Lieutenant Edward Teats, the pilot of the other airplane, has written that during this mission his radio operator intercepted a message regarding Clark Field being attacked.[2]

With the announcement of the bombing in Hawaii, all crews at Clark Field were ordered to stand by at their aircraft. At about 8:30 A.M., B-17s of the 28th Squadron took off to search for invading forces, heading west to the coast and then south down the Bataan peninsula. They landed at a strip called San Marcelino, about 30 miles from Clark, across the mountains near Subic Bay, which was a new landing strip that had been bulldozed clear of brush and trees for fighter aircraft.

B-17s had never before landed at San Marcelino. Upon landing, the aircraft were towed back under the trees out of sight. At about 10:30 A.M., they returned to Clark Field, where they were refueled and loaded with bombs for a planned mission to Formosa. According to General Brett, Lt. Gen. Lewis H. Brereton (commander of the Far East Air Force) had requested permission to bomb enemy ships and installations in Formosa, but did not get approval until later, at which time he recalled the B-17s to Clark. It has been reported that Gen. Douglas MacArthur was unsure that the bombing of Hawaii constituted an overt attack on the Philippines and decided to take only defensive precautions, which was given as the reason for the delayed permission to bomb.[3]

The rumored attack on Clark Field became a reality. At 10:45 A.M. that morning, Capt. Hideki Shingo had led forty-four Japanese fighter pilots off their landing fields on Formosa. Their destination was 500 miles away, and their mission to rendezvous with fifty-four medium bombers and destroy the Army Air Forces aircraft and facilities at Clark Field.

At about 12:25 P.M., Colonel Eubank was briefing the pilots of the B-17s on the upcoming mission to bomb Formosa.[4] Some of the crews stood by their aircraft and others ate their lunch. Fifty-three Japanese Mitsubishi G3M and G4M two-engine bombers flying in three triangles were observed approaching the field. The bombers made one pass at about 18,000 feet, dropped their bombs, and left, still flying in formation. Follow-up Japanese reconnaissance photographs showed that sixty U.S. aircraft had been damaged or destroyed, along with fuel dumps, one fuel truck, and one tanker truck. Of the B-17s at Clark, only seven survived.

Captain Shingo's fighter unit was supposed to fly cover for the bombers, but there was practically no need. Only thirteen P-40s were able to launch from Clark, nine confirmed kills and four probables for the Japanese. With the exception of one that crashed on takeoff from Formosa, the Japanese did not lose a single bomber and only five Zero fighters failed to return.

Immediately following the bomber attack, witnesses observed a large number of single-engine aircraft coming in low. They too dropped bombs and conducted repeated strafing attacks on the parked aircraft, hangars, barracks, gun emplacements, and other facilities. Clark Field erupted with small-arms return fire. In one instance, a B-17 gunner returned fire with .50-caliber guns as the plane sat burning on the ground. Nearly all the B-17s parked in the hangar area were burning. A Grumman twin-engine amphibian, the OA9, which had just carried Colonel Eubank back from Manila, was destroyed. Eubank survived the attack as did many others, in one of the slit trenches.

A B-17 bombardier on the ground who observed the attack stated that he believed that the Japanese were not attempting to destroy the landing area, only the U.S. air combat capability. He said that the bombs they used appeared to be contact fragmentation types, which exploded without creating large craters. Destruction on the ground was primarily from Japanese fighter machine-gun fire and bomb fragments.[5]

The operations of the 19th Bombardment Group and the 14th Squadron are clouded from the beginning of hostilities in the Philippines on December 8, 1941, until their evacuation to Australia, which began nine days later. Those days were filled with fury and confusion. The defenders were reeling from the surprise onslaught of superior invading forces on the land, sea, and in the air, shocked by the bombing and strafing of their primary airfield.

Contributing to the confusion was the lack of reliable and secure communications between the widespread elements of the 19th Bomb Group. What few communication lines that did exist were suspect because they were thought to have been penetrated by Japanese forces or their sympathizers. In fact, the fear of spurious orders given by radio or telephone delayed some tactics designed to counter the invasion. This paranoia was reinforced by suspected enemy action, such as the appearance of smoke near airfields, which were interpreted to be guides for incoming raids.

Pushed to exhaustion, the men of the 19th knew little of what was happening outside of their immediate area. Rumors and often inaccurate radio reports were their primary sources of information. Only their observations during their own missions told them the real story. The usual chroniclers of daily war reporting—news service correspondents—were almost nonexistent in that part of the world.

The men and machines of the 19th were often widely dispersed, making it impossible to maintain normal military recordkeeping. In addition, few records of the Group's operations were removed from the Philippines during subsequent evacuations. The "Narrative History of the 19th Bombardment Group," prepared by the XX Bomber Command, states that either the 19th left their records in the Southwest Pacific or they were lost in transit. Only a passing reference was made concerning the 14th Squadron in that document.

Operations records specific to the 14th Squadron were even more sparse. O'Donnell's men and aircraft had been organized as a provisional squadron before they had left Hawaii and, while records indicate that the squadron was assigned to the 19th Bomb Group on November 14, 1941, in fact they had not been fully integrated into the Group prior to the outbreak of hostilities. In spite of the 14th's evacuation from the Philippines in December 1941, the records continued to place the unit's headquarters there as late as 1943.[6]

Edward Teats wrote that no man could keep track of the missions flown. He recounted that the attempts to recall and document the events of the time did not occur until after the evacuation from Java in March 1942. Following their return to Australia, Teats and three others attempted to reconstruct their Philippine experiences.[7] The result of that effort was the "19th Group Journal," apparently used later by others to reconstruct the events of the 1941 air war in the Philippines.

In what they would consider to be a final report to the American public on the activities of the Army Air Forces in World War II, Wesley Frank Craven and James Lea Cate edited a series of seven volumes for the Office of Air Force History.[8] In the first volume, Craven and Cate make a significant observation of the validity of documents used by many to elaborate on the events of the first ten days of the air war in the Philippines. While they agree that the daily summaries represent a record of events more accurate than any other documents known to exist, concrete evidence in many cases highlighted inconsistencies in reports.

Unfortunately, there are few survivors of those first days to fill in the blanks. Of the 19th Bomb Group's 210 officers and 1,300 enlisted men, only 140 officers and 240 enlisted men were evacuated from the Philippines, and fewer still have survived to this day. In using the survivors as a source of information, one must consider the fallible human memory in reconstructing fine, descriptive details of events that occurred half a century ago, although many of the survivors had personal diaries to help them in their recollections.

From December 8 to December 24, when Clark Field was completely evacuated, the base was subjected to daily air raids. The U.S. aircraft that remained in operation in the Philippines used Clark for staging to pick up ammunition and bombs. All other facilities at Clark Field were destroyed. The maintenance people made an outstanding effort to repair a small number of damaged aircraft by cannibalizing more extensively damaged aircraft.

Starting on the second day of the war, a nightly supply flight using the old B-18s was established between Del Monte and Clark Field. Flights into and out of Clark had to be made at dawn or at dusk to avoid the strafing attacks conducted several times each day by the Japanese. Those B-17 crews of the 19th Bombardment Group, left at Clark without airplanes, scraped through burned-out rubble for spare parts, which were then flown to Del Monte aboard the B-18s.

The various source documents fail to provide a logical sequence for many missions flown from Clark during those days. The records do not show that 40-3097 or its sister B-17s in the 14th Squadron flew any missions on December 9, 1941, which seems unlikely considering the fact that Japanese forces were landing troops on Philippine shores. According to the crew of 40-3097, however, they did fly a mission that day.

General Brereton has written that at about 4:00 P.M. on December 8, a message was received in Manila from O'Donnell at Del Monte containing a refusal to obey an order given that morning (both squadrons had been ordered to move to San Marcelino at dusk). The plan was to have O'Donnell's squadron fly to San Marcelino to prepare for operations out of Clark Field at daybreak on December 9. O'Donnell's refusal stemmed from the fact that the order had been sent in plain English and he feared that communication lines had been compromised and that the order was an enemy ploy. In response to O'Donnell's concerns, a coded message was sent. According to Brereton, the delay caused by encoding, transmitting, and decoding the message made it too late for O'Donnell to leave, considering the hazards of a night takeoff from Del Monte.

At 2:30 on the afternoon of December 9, Brereton wrote, "Seven B-17s led by Major O'Donnell took off from Del Monte and landed in San Marcelino after dark." This would place Colin Kelly en route to San Marcelino at the time he was reported to be on the mission that resulted in his death. General Brereton's diary was one of those providing questionable dates for the period December 8, 1941, through February 24, 1942.[9]

On the morning of December 9, 1941, three B-17s, loaded with bombs, took off from Del Monte to bomb Japanese naval forces. They were then to fly on to Clark Field. The three-plane formation was led by Capt. Colin P. Kelly. First Lieutenant Godman piloted B-17D 40-3097, with 2nd Lt. R. S. Clinkscales as his copilot; 1st Lt. G. E. Schaetzel was the pilot of the third B-17.

Following their bombing runs, the three planes headed for Clark Field as planned. Before dropping from 15,000 feet to begin the landing approach, Kelly radioed instructions to the other two aircraft to remain at 15,000 feet while he went down to assess field conditions at Clark. Soon after Kelly left formation, Godman heard a voice on the radio say, "Don't land here! Go someplace else, Godman." Godman recalled that he landed at an abandoned air strip at Marivales almost out of fuel. (John A. Wallach, the crew's bombardier, believes that they put down at San Marcelino.) From this short-field landing, the B-17 pilots of the 19th Bomb Group learned, contradictory to what some believed, that they could operate from any airstrip they could land on.

Upon landing, Godman found an abandoned fuel servicing truck and drums of aviation fuel that the crew was able to use to service their gasoline-starved airplane. Waiting until after dark, Godman lifted 40-3097 into the air once more for an uneventful flight to Del Monte. Schaetzel, in the third B-17, is reported to have landed at San Marcelino after Kelly's radioed admonition not to land at Clark.

Kelly's B-17 was attacked and shot down by Japanese fighter aircraft that were strafing Clark Field (records show that Clark Field was attacked early that afternoon). He became America's first hero of the air war. Much has been written about his tragic end. Most historians place the event on December 10, 1941, with the mission's destination Aparri in northern Luzon. If the operations history, written some time after the actual event, erred in arriving at the date, those who subsequently wrote of that event logically used the same date. But, in support of Godman and his crew, the official citation for the Distinguished Service Cross posthumously awarded to Kelly places the event on December 9, not December 10, 1941. The citation reads:

> For extraordinary heroism in action near Aparri, Cagayan, Philippine Islands, December 9, 1941. With his airplane a focal point of fire from strong hostile naval forces, Captain Kelly exhibited a high degree of valor and skill in placing three direct hits upon an enemy battleship, resulting in its destruction. En route to his home airfield upon completion of his mission, his airplane was set afire by the attack of two enemy fighters. This officer ordered his crew to bail out. Six men saved themselves thereby, but Captain Kelly, the last to leave his burning plane, was killed in the resulting crash.[10]

The military officials decided that the battleship attacked by Captain Kelly was the 21,000-ton *Haruna*. It has been determined, however, that the Japanese did not use any battleships during the Aparri landing; the report of the sinking was apparently erroneous. Lieutenant General Brereton said he was never able to ascertain the source of this misinformation.[11] The official reason given for Kelly carrying only three bombs when five more could have been carried was that an air raid alert sounded as he was ordered to take off. Other unlikely scenarios found their way into the official description of Kelly's death, including that of finding a big ship all alone, which sent up no antiaircraft fire, took no evasive action, and permitted the bombardier to make a 10-minute run.[12]

Meyer Levin, Kelly's bombardier, related bits and pieces of the attack on their airplane to the crew of 40-3097 when they met in Melbourne in May 1942. Levin's story of Kelly's death differed from that reported to the public.[13] Levin was killed during a bombing mission off the east coast of New Guinea in late 1942, when the U.S. Army Air Force confronted the Japanese as they were trying to establish a beachhead on Gasmota, north of Milne Bay, and therefore his story cannot be verified.

The official history of the Air Force records that not three but five B-17s of the 14th Bomb Squadron were involved on December 10, the supposed day that Captain Kelly was killed. Three took off initially, piloted by O'Donnell, Parsel, and Montgomery. The two remaining B-17s, one piloted by Kelly, took off later.

According to Levin, Kelly's entire crew was at their gun positions on the return flight to Clark, with the exception of the radio operator, who had left his gun position to receive landing instructions from the tower at Clark Field. Levin recounted that as Kelly's aircraft approached

Clark Field, it was suddenly attacked by two enemy planes. The plane was thoroughly riddled and the empty bomb bay engulfed by flames from the damaged fuel tank in that compartment. Kelly ordered the crew to bail out. Kelly and his copilot prepared to follow the crew out when a violent explosion blew the copilot out of the plane, whereupon he was fortunate enough to be able to pull his ripcord. All of the crew who bailed out survived. Kelly's body was found near the wreckage of his aircraft.

Assuming that the date given in the posthumous citation is correct, all of the events reported in the 19th Bomb Group reports mentioning the activities of Colin Kelly on December 10, 1941, come under speculation if he was indeed killed on the previous day.

On December 10, 1941, two missions were apparently flown by Godman in 40-3097. These missions do not agree with events as reported in the 19th Bomb Group historical documents. According to crew members of 40-3097, the first mission that day departed Del Monte at seven in the morning when O'Donnell led two other B-17s on a mission to bomb enemy forces landing on Luzon. On O'Donnell's left wing, in the number 2 slot, was Lieutenant Schaetzel. Godman, in Ole Betsy, flew in the number 3 slot, with Lt. Richard T. Carlisle as the copilot.

O'Donnell and Schaetzel tried to bomb Japanese destroyers from 30,000 feet but missed, as the ships executed a hard turn shortly after the bombs left the bomb bays. It seemed to Godman that ships that were traveling around 30 knots must have had officers with binoculars trained on the bombers who must have ordered the turns as soon as the falling bombs were sighted. The Norden bombsight in the B-17s could only predict where a target ship would be if it stayed on a straight course. Realizing that it was not possible to hit the moving targets at that altitude, Godman turned back to the Vigan beach where a troop transport was unloading men and supplies. He dropped his bombs from a lower altitude and hit the stationary target.

Carlisle reported that he had seen enemy fighters taking off from the beach to the east. Although Godman couldn't see them, he pushed the throttles all the way forward. At high altitude, with superchargers turned to maximum and the aircraft being let down slightly at 200 to 300 feet per minute to gain extra speed, Godman estimated that his airplane was traveling at 300 miles per hour. Outrunning more than twenty attack fighters, Ole Betsy made the 770-mile return flight to Del Monte without seeing the other two B-17s.

Godman thought that this was the first real U.S. bombing mission of the war. The Air Force, however, attributes the first bombing mission to Maj. Cecil E. Combs. On December 10, Combs is reported to have led a flight of five B-17s to bomb shipping targets near Vigan. Combs's flight is reported to have taken off from Clark Field at 6:00 A.M.

Apparently, the second mission for 40-3097 on December 10 began that afternoon when Godman took off from Del Monte at 2:30 P.M. as part of a flight of B-17s headed to Clark Field for bombs and fuel. They landed at San Marcelino after being denied permission to land at Clark. Godman recalls that he remained at San Marcelino until 11:00 that night, when he departed for Del Monte, arriving about four hours later. Again, the 19th Bomb Group's records conflict with this account; the records show that O'Donnell and his B-17s arrived at San Marcelino on the night of December 9 and Godman departed at 11:00 the next night, after being denied permission to land at Clark Field earlier in the day.

According to the diary kept by John Wallach, at least one other mission the airplane participated in was not included in the official records. Both Godman and Wallach agree on the details. The mission, out of Del Monte, was to bomb in the vicinity of Vigan. It was one of the most exceptional missions flown by the 19th up until this time, since the mission took three days to complete.

At 7:30 A.M. on December 12, O'Donnell led a flight of five B-17s, including Godman in 40-3097, on a nonstop, round-trip bombing mission. However, after the planes turned back toward Del Monte after the raid, O'Donnell received a radio message in code from the Del Monte radio operator that led him to believe that the operator was transmitting under duress and was warning O'Donnell that the airfield was in enemy hands. On the day before, other pilots had received spurious reports of Del Monte's capture as they were returning to that base. On December 10, Combs and Lt. Walter R. Ford landed at San Jose, Lt. Elliot Vandevanter reportedly landed at Talcloben, and Schaetzel landed at Cebu, all because of similar false reports.[14]

Unable to land at Clark Field because of suspected enemy activity there, O'Donnell led his flight of B-17s to Marivales, the abandoned, partially completed landing strip on the southern tip of the Bataan peninsula. In the dimming afternoon light on December 12, the aircraft lined up in single file to make their landings without running lights. In the course of their landing approach, one of the B-17 propellers nicked the vertical stabilizer of the aircraft it was following. Apparently the damage to the stabilizer was minor, and although the damaged propeller caused some engine vibration, it was not bad enough to take the aircraft out of commission.

Only one option seemed available to the airmen on the ground at Marivales. They couldn't fly to Clark Field—it was under enemy attack. They couldn't return to Del Monte—supposedly it had been captured by the Japanese. They considered flying to Australia to escape their predicament, but they had inadequate fuel for such a long flight. Faced with this dilemma, the crews sat on the ground at Marivales. Recalling the time spent waiting, the crews were surprised that they had not been detected by Japanese aircraft as they overflew Marivales en route to bombing runs over the naval base at Cavite. Forty-seven years later, Wallach could still recall the peculiar sound of the unsynchronized propellers as the Japanese aircraft passed overhead.

Without an alternate source of food, O'Donnell and his men ate the emergency rations packed in the seat of their parachutes. Since the water at Marivales was of questionable purity, the men had nothing to drink. Without water, Wallach recalled, the hard chocolate in their emergency kits stuck in their mouths, making swallowing difficult.

On December 13, Guam fell and the next day the victorious Japanese flew their first reconnaissance flight over the airfield at Del Monte. Up to that time, the Japanese apparently did not know where this last bastion of the Flying Fortress was located. However, once they found it, they were determined to destroy it. With the elimination of the B-17s at Del Monte, the Japanese conquest of Luzon and the rest of the Philippines could proceed unimpeded by the surviving bombers of the 19th operating from that base.

O'Donnell and his force of B-17s sat on the ground at Marivales, without communication with the outside world and undetected by the Japanese, from December 12 to December 15. After hearing the reason for O'Donnell's concern regarding the status of Del Monte, Sgt. Norman P. Michelson, the radio operator on 40-3097, said that he was familiar with the Del Monte radio operator's sending technique and that he always made the same error in his transmissions that had given the original impression that he was operating under duress. O'Donnell then decided to chance a return flight to Del Monte. Once the aircraft were airborne and radio contact could be established with Del Monte, the explanation given by Sergeant Michelson was confirmed by a message from someone known to O'Donnell.[15] The six B-17s that took off on December 12 for a nonstop round-trip bombing mission landed safely at Del Monte in the fading light on December 15.

Retreat to Australia

General Lewis H. Brereton, commander of the Far East Air Force, obtained permission from MacArthur to move the surviving B-17s from Del Monte to Darwin in northwest Australia. General MacArthur concurred with the move so that the aircraft could be properly repaired. The maintenance facilities at their base in Australia, Batchelor Field, turned out to be not much better than those at Del Monte, but at least they would not be subjected to daily Japanese raids. At 2 A.M. on December 17, the surviving B-17s of the 19th Bombardment Group began leaving Del Monte on the nine-hour, 1,700-mile flight to Batchelor Field, 40 miles inland from Darwin, Australia. Some arrived with less than a 15-minute reserve of fuel.

Never intended for heavy bombers, Batchelor Field was a Royal Australian Air Force (RAAF) training base with two turf runways at almost right angles to each other in the middle of a clear space in the scrub-covered landscape. The only building was a frame shack among the gum trees. A tenting area for the crews was prepared under the trees facing the shack. The temperature often reached 118 degrees in the shade, and with constant rains it became a steambath. For the 19th Bombardment Group this was their new home, ending the first phase of their combat operations. While all missions were now to be flown out of Australia, the turf field at Del Monte would continue to be used for staging bombing missions against the enemy forces invading the Philippines.

Every airplane departing Del Monte for Australia carried a crew of eight, two maintenance men, and spare parts. Extra bomb-bay tanks were needed to supply the additional fuel necessary for the flight to Australia. Since all of them were at Clark, prior to the Group's departure from Del Monte two or three B-17s were flown to Clark each night to pick up spare parts and two bomb-bay tanks. Every tank not damaged by enemy attack was taken. Each aircraft also took empty oxygen bottles to Clark and flew out with full ones. All takeoffs from Clark on the return flight to Del Monte were overloaded far beyond the maximum allowable weight for the B-17.

Lieutenant Weldon H. Smith, who would later pilot 40-3097, flew another B-17 into Clark one night to obtain parts for the flight to Batchelor Field. In his diary, he wrote of his experiences:

> The place was a shambles to say the least. The leaves all off the trees. Bomb craters everywhere. The horrible stench of rotting flesh. One could see through the hangars in any direction. It was the most ghostly night I have ever seen.

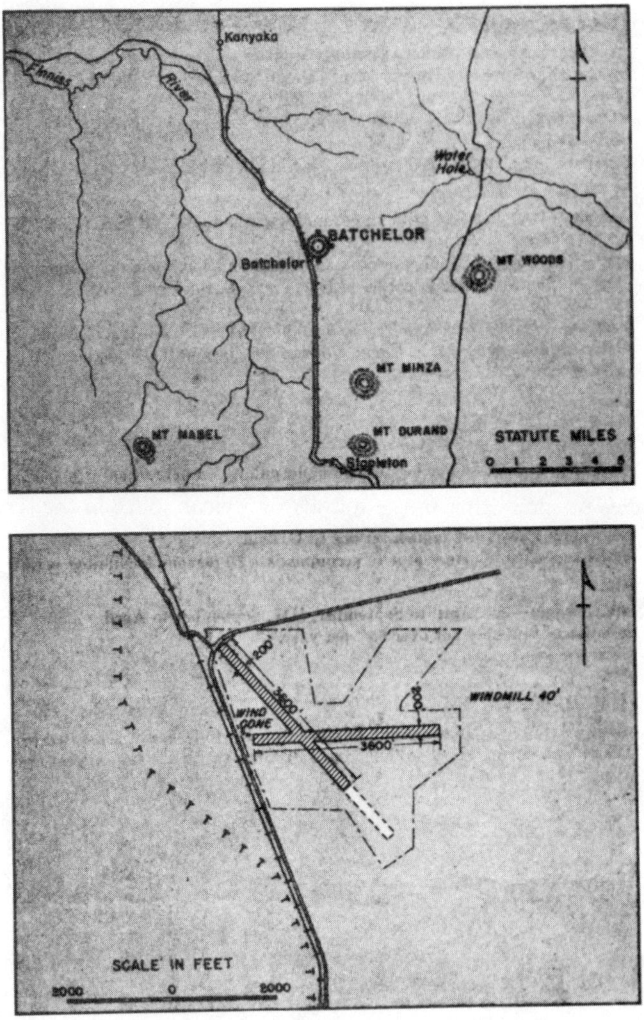

Batchelor Landing Ground in the northwest territories of Australia, as depicted in the "U.S. Army Air Forces Air Route Guide." On December 19, 1941, B-17D 40-3097 evacuated Del Monte and flew to this Royal Australian Air Force field.

> We salvaged a little that had not been destroyed. A bomb had hit the kitchen of our house—place was burned.

Clark Field was completely evacuated by U.S. forces on December 24, but the Japanese ground forces did not reach it until December 30.

On December 18, four more B-17s evacuated Del Monte at 2 A.M. for the flight to Batchelor Field (the last three left two days later) in what the crews hoped was only a temporary departure from the Philippines. B-17 40-3097, with Lt. Henry C. Godman as pilot, was one of four aircraft. His crew members on the flight to Australia were 2nd Lt. Morris N. Friedman, copilot; 2nd Lt. C. E. Epperson, navigator; S. Sgt. J. A. Wallach, bombardier; S. Sgt. C. L. James, engineer-gunner; Sergeant Jackson, assistant engineer-gunner; Sgt. H. E. Weist, crew chief; Sgt. N. P. Michelson, radio operator; Pfc. S. G. Brooks, assistant radio operator; Light and Conrad Marvel, maintenance technicians. Lieutenant Frank Kurtz, who later would become closely associated with the Swoose, also left Del Monte on the eighteenth, as the pilot of B-17-2072. On the way to Batchelor, Godman bombed the docks at Davao, where the Japanese were landing.[16]

On December 19, the Japanese strafed Del Monte for the first time. They missed the remaining three operational B-17s, but destroyed three B-18s parked on the field. Lieutenant Weldon Smith left Del Monte after the air raid on the nineteenth in his B-17, the "Gazelle." He described conditions at Del Monte during the days following his evacuation:

> We worked on our ships today [December 21]. Nine ships left for Del Monte to bomb Japanese forces and reported 80 ships off Lingayen Gulf. Japanese bomb Del Monte every day now. The personnel are living in the hills and working at night.[17]

As the crews were evacuating their base in the Philippines, the Pacific war continued unabated in the air and on the ground. On December 18, while flying a P-40, Lt. Boyd "Buzz" Wagner, who commanded the 17th Pursuit Squadron based at Nichols Field, shot down his fifth Japanese aircraft to become the first American ace of World War II. (Buzz would be a passenger in 40-3097 on a flight from Port Moresby to Australia in 1942.) On December 23, 1941, Wake Island fell to the invading enemy forces, closing the air route to the Philippines pioneered earlier by the 14th Squadron.

At their new home, the crew of B-17D 40-3097 and the others performed long-needed maintenance and repair using the meager supplies they had brought down from Del Monte. It was not until they arrived in Australia that the crews were issued clothing to replace what had been left at Clark Field. Instead of trousers, however, they were issued shorts, knee-length stockings, black shoes, short-sleeve shirts, and Australian "Digger" hats. The Australian Comfort Fund (their version of the American Red Cross) issued the men toilet articles in ditty bags.[18]

As noted earlier, one of the combat weaknesses in the early B-17s was armament for defensive purposes. The most significant of these shortcomings was the lack of firepower to defend against rear enemy attacks. Rear-firing guns in the belly were of little use to ward off attackers approaching directly aft of the airplane. To correct for this deficiency, tail guns were installed for the first time in the model E series. The C and D models had no provisions for such installations and were therefore clearly vulnerable to attacks from the rear.

It was during the first few days at Batchelor Field that B-17D 40-3097 was fitted with a makeshift tail stinger. Sergeants Michelson and Weist and Lieutenant Wallach installed a .30-caliber gun in the tail by first cutting off a portion of the tail cone, just enough to let the gun project through the cone.[19] The remaining portion of the plastic tail cone shattered when the loosely installed gun was tested. The loosely mounted gun was activated by pulling a cable that ran to the two waist-gunner positions. A wood and wire grip from a small bucket was attached to the cable so that one of the gunners could fire the new tail gun at an appropriate time to discourage the popular Japanese tail-end attacks.

The crews did more than work on their planes after arriving in Australia. From Batchelor Field, Godman flew two more missions to bomb Davao. With Godman as pilot, Clinkscales as copilot, and the crew from Del Monte, Ole Betsy departed Batchelor at 10:40 A.M. on December 22 as part of a flight of nine B-17s to bomb seven transports in the harbor at Davao.[20] Davao was in the southern part of Mindanao, 600 miles from Manila and 1,360 miles from Batchelor. This first U.S. bombing mission to be flown from Australia was led by Maj. Cecil E. Combs. The mission's final destination was Del Monte.

Each B-17 had nonself-sealing bomb-bay tanks to carry the extra fuel needed for the long flight. Consequently, as with many of the earlier missions flown in the Philippines, only half of the bomb bay could be used for bombs, so only four 500-pound bombs were carried.

Never having had fighter support, and operating singly or in small formations, the men of the 19th were always compelled to use the element of surprise while flying their missions. They always tried to plan their missions so as to arrive over the target at sunset or sunrise. The aircraft en route from Australia to Del Monte bombed the harbor at Davao at sunset, sinking a 10,000-ton tanker. All but one of the B-17s dropped its bomb load; that one had three of its four bombs hung up in the bomb bay. Because of the bad weather, the nine aircraft became separated, but one by one they found their way to Del Monte, where they landed after dark, 10 hours and 25 minutes after they took off from Australia. The field had been badly plowed as a result of enemy air raids and only a few aircraft could be serviced at one time. In the darkness the airplanes were refueled and loaded with small bombs.[21]

By 3 A.M. on December 23 (the day the Japanese occupied Wake Island, cutting the air route out to the Philippines) the first four B-17s were ready for takeoff from Del Monte to bomb eighty Japanese transports in the Lingayen Gulf, 800 miles north. Following completion of the mission, they planned to fly back to San Marcelino and land, if feasible; if not, they would return to Australia.

Godman in 40-3097 and two other B-17s took off at 30-minute intervals beginning at 4:30 P.M. Because servicing was slow and word had been received that an air raid was coming, two of the planes carried seven 300-pound bombs, and the other had a load of 100-pounders. Shortly after takeoff, 40-3097 developed engine trouble and Godman had to shut down and "feather" the bad engine. Instead of aborting the mission and returning to Del Monte, Godman elected to drop out of the formation and head for Davao, an alternate target.[22]

It was dark when Godman's crew arrived over the target area, but lights and movement could still be seen in the harbor. Godman set a course using these lights and turned the airplane over to his bombardier, John Wallach, who synchronized on the lights and released the bomb load. After the bombs hit, Wallach could still see the lights, now scattered about. This appears to have been the first night bombing made by the United States in the war. Limping home on three engines, Godman flew the airplane back to Del Monte, where all the crew members pitched in to help the flight engineer, Sergeant Weist, repair the disabled engine. They then boarded the aircraft and returned to Australia, landing at Batchelor Field after flying more than 20 hours without sleep.[23]

The day after their return to Batchelor from Del Monte, the crews went to work servicing and repairing their aircraft for imminent transfer. They worked all Christmas Day at these tasks. The nine B-17s that took part in the missions on December 22 and 23, plus one on the ground at Batchelor for repairs, constituted the entire total bomber strength of the U.S. Far East Air Force.

Godman recalled that he and his crew in 40-3097 flew other missions to the north out of Batchelor Field during the remainder of December, although these were never documented in the synthesized records. Lieutenant Weldon Smith flew a mission from Batchelor to Del Monte on Christmas Day, in B-17 40-3079. Preparing for the return trip, as he was taxiing out for takeoff, a tire blew out. Since there were no facilities at Del Monte, the crew blocked up a wing and dug a pit under the tire, repaired the damaged tire, remounted the wheel, filled the hole, and knocked out the wing blocks. Smith took off during a strafing attack.[24]

Although Army Air Force records do not indicate it, according to John Wallach's diary, on December 29, 1941, Ole Betsy was flown by Godman and his crew from Batchelor Field to Darwin and returned the next day. The pilot of one of the other B-17s at Batchelor wrote that he flew all day that same day to keep his plane out of bombing range; they had heard there might be a Japanese air attack and radio communications with Darwin had been jammed all night.[25]

Following their return to Batchelor Field on December 30, the long partnership between Godman's crew and Ole Betsy came to a close. The crew and their airplane had flown together since the early days in Hawaii, before the war began. Godman's crew was reassigned to B-17D 40-3062 and ordered to change all four engines. That airplane had been flown to Batchelor Field from Del Monte by Major Combs.

Godman's return to combat with the 19th was delayed for more than a month. Following the replacement of the four engines, the crew and their new airplane were pressed into service in another role. They flew men and material to and from various locations in Australia. They were next reported in the records of the 19th on February 14, 1942, when they landed at Malang, Java, with a load of spare parts for the Curtiss P-40s and the single-engine attack bomber Douglas A-24 that were operating in the Netherlands East Indies. Prior to their arrival in Malang, they had landed the previous evening at Koepang on Timor Island. Upon awakening the next morning, they found the landing gear had settled into the mud and the airplane was firmly trapped. With the aid of natives, they were able to lift a wing and place rocks under the wheels until the airplane was free to taxi.[26]

Five days after the arrival at Malang, Godman and his crew were back in aerial combat as they set out to attack an enemy convoy at Bali in a recently acquired B-17E. Ferried from the United States by way of the South Atlantic and across Africa, B-17E 41-2478 had arrived in Java on January 28.[27] Equipped with thirteen machine guns, the E model was a far cry from the armament in the B-17D models they had been flying. With power turrets on top of the airplane above the pilot's compartment, a ball turret on the underside of the fuselage near the trailing edge of the wing, and a gunner's compartment in the tail, the new airplane was truly a Fortress.

Before continuing with the saga of 40-3097, we can gain some insight into the hazards of air operations in the early days of 1942 by recounting the events of a mission flow by Henry Godman after his stint as pilot of 40-3097.

One of the most harrowing missions Godman flew in the Southwest Pacific began in Australia on March 11, 1942, when he piloted one of four B-17s that took off from Melbourne for Daly Waters on a special mission. Since two of the aircraft made forced landings en route to their port of embarkation at Darwin, only Godman, and Lt. Harl Pease Jr. in another B-17E, actually departed on the special mission.[28]

The eight- or nine-hour mission was a 1,500-mile flight from Darwin to Del Monte to resupply and rescue trapped personnel. No bombs were carried, however; one-half of the bomb bay carried an auxiliary fuel tank, and the other half was filled with mortars, machine guns, and ammunition to be delivered to the forces defending the Philippines.[29]

Shortly after their departure from Darwin, the two aircraft became separated. Godman climbed to 10,000 feet, set the engine for long-range cruise, and enjoyed the beautiful day, the sky covered with cumulus clouds and visibility about 30 miles. They passed the island of Timor and on through the islands of Buru and Ceram without making any contact with the enemy. Although it was a boring flight, the guns were ready for action since the men didn't know what islands the Japanese had occupied.[30]

At the "point of no return"—when there was just enough fuel in the wing tanks for a safe return to Australia—fuel consumption was as expected and the estimated time of arrival over Mindanao was confirmed in their calculations. It was now necessary to transfer fuel from the auxiliary tank in the bomb bay into the main feeder tanks in the wings.

About five minutes after Godman ordered the crew chief to start the fuel transfer, he noticed that the main fuel tank levels appeared to be falling instead of filling. He knew immediately what had happened. The fuel transfer motor switch had been thrown in the wrong direction and fuel was being pumped from the wing tanks into the full bomb-bay tank, which was now overflowing into the bomb bay. Although the pump action was quickly corrected, many gallons of fuel had been lost overboard.

Since there was no longer any turning back, the engine power settings were adjusted to maximum economical cruise to stretch the available fuel as they pressed on toward their destination at Del Monte. The navigator, Carl Epperson, estimated they might have just enough fuel to reach Mindanao under the new power settings, but their estimated time of arrival was extended from eight or nine to ten or more hours because of the slower air speed. At that rate, they would be over the northern shore of Mindanao at about 11:30 P.M.

As the day wore on, Godman kept reducing the power to maintain a constant air speed as the fuel consumption decreased the aircraft's weight. As they approached Mindanao, Godman started his descent. Since the moon was obscured by clouds, it was pitch black and no visual sightings were possible. Godman wanted to get as low as possible to avoid radar detection from Japanese forces on Davao and Mindanao. Before they had encountered the overcast, Epperson had gotten a star fix. From then on, the flight course would be by dead-reckoning.

Lieutenant Epperson announced when he calculated they were 60 or 70 miles from Mindanao, at which time the fuel gauges showed about 30 gallons per engine, or about an hour of flight at maximum range–condition power settings. The crew remained calm as the fuel gauges approached the empty mark. Lieutenant Richard T. Carlisle, the copilot, exchanged silent glances with Godman. They were over Illigan Bay, looking for Cagayan Bay, where they could turn inland. Godman thought about signaling with flares, but he knew the people on the ground wouldn't turn the lights on since there were no codes and the B-17 wasn't expected. It was almost midnight on March 12, 1942, when the aircraft flew a circular pattern over the bay and headed toward shore, only two to three miles away.

In the shallow bank just before leveling out to start a descent, and with the altimeter still reading 1,200 feet, the B-17 hit the dark waters of the bay at 170 miles per hour. Actually, the airplane hit the water twice. At the first impact, when the propellers hit, Godman threw both arms around the control wheel and pulled back. The airplane apparently climbed up slightly before hitting a second time. That impact killed two of the crew and injured all the rest.

Godman was thrown forward in the airplane and momentarily knocked unconscious. When he came to, realizing that he was still alive, he opened the sliding window on the pilot's side of the fuselage, climbed out on the wing, and inflated his "Mae West" life vest before jumping into the water. He climbed back on the wing just as Epperson stuck his head out of the window. He then dragged Epperson out onto the wing and into the water. They turned to see the airplane slowly nosing down until it was perpendicular to the water with the tail slowly disappearing beneath it. As the airplane disappeared from view, they saw six bobbing heads in the water.

Epperson was partially paralyzed and bleeding from his back and hand. Godman told Epperson to suck the cut on his palm since he feared the blood might attract sharks. Encouraging the men to swim the estimated mile to shore, Godman led the men while towing Epperson. After hours of swimming, Godman saw what appeared to be masts of boats coming toward them. He thought the Japanese were coming to take them prisoner, but he soon realized he was seeing native fishing traps on shore.

The men dragged themselves up on the beach and lay motionless. It had taken the eight survivors four hours to swim the relatively short distance from the crash site to the shore. Shortly after reaching land, the men heard the engine of a motor vehicle in the distance. They decided that since they all needed medical attention, they would make themselves known to whomever was driving the vehicle, friend or foe.

Godman stood up, ready to shoot with his wet but still functional .45-caliber pistol, when he realized that the approaching men were Filipinos in a jeep, in search of crash survivors. The crew members were taken to a native house until daylight, when they were driven to the field at Del Monte.[31]

The commander at Del Monte was surprised when Godman told him of his mission to evacuate military personnel. Since Godman knew that Gen. Douglas MacArthur's arrival at Del Monte was imminent, he correctly assumed that the general was to be among his passengers flown out on the evacuation flight to Australia. Godman convinced General MacArthur himself to let him accompany his party in the replacement B-17 being sent to evacuate the general. General MacArthur's chief of staff, Maj. Gen. Richard K. Sutherland, concerned that the B-17 would be overloaded, denied permission for Godman's copilot, Lieutenant Carlisle, and others to accompany the group to Australia. Approximately 15 minutes before takeoff Godman, knowing that the plane was far from overloaded, ordered Carlisle to crawl into the tail gunner's position and close the door behind him. (Normally that position was not occupied during takeoff, because of the risks involved in case of an accident.) Just before takeoff, Godman explained the unusual seat assignment to the pilot, Lt. Frank Bostrom.

As a result of this encounter, Godman became MacArthur's liaison officer and aide in Australia. Later he became his personal pilot, flying a KLM Airline DC-3 allocated to MacArthur, and then a B-17E named "Bataan." Godman flew the Bataan from the United States to Australia in 38 hours when he delivered it to MacArthur.[32]

After 19 months with General MacArthur, before returning to the United States in October 1944, Godman flew a number of combat missions in the Southwest Pacific in a B-24 Liberator as part of the "Jolly Rogers" 90th Bomb Group. He subsequently retired from the Air Force after 29 years of service.

Australia to Netherlands East Indies

In the last days of December 1941, as Godman and his crew prepared to leave Ole Betsy, the Japanese landed in Borneo and occupied the oilfields near its southern end. Balikpapan on the northeast coast was in range of land-based Japanese air forces. Because Balikpapan could then be used by the Japanese as a base for further advances south toward Australia, it became evident that air strikes were necessary to delay the Japanese movement.

The B-17s of the 19th Bombardment Group flew only two bombing missions from Batchelor Field to the Philippines, proving in the process that the distances involved were too great for effective bombing.[33] By this time, the 19th had been at war for about three weeks and had lost two-thirds of its original aircraft. In an attempt to delay the Japanese approach to Australia, the surviving B-17s of the 19th at Batchelor Field in Australia were ordered to move to Malang, Java, about 80 miles south of Surabaya. A new airfield at Singosari had been built six miles from Malang and was considered to be the best field in Java for the heavy B-17.

Nine of the B-17s, including 40-3097, were ready to move by December 29. The 19th Bomb Group Diary of Operations records that at 8 A.M. on December 30, 1941, Maj. Cecil Combs, in command of the nineteen surviving aircraft, took off in 40-3097 to lead a flight of seven B-17s from Batchelor Field in Australia 1,300 miles to Singosari, landing there at 4 P.M. The other B-17s involved in this operation and their pilots were: 40-3061 (Maj. Birrell Walsh), 40-3064 (Lt. William J. Bohnaker), 40-3074 (Lt. Elmer L. Parsel), 40-3067 (Lt. Frank A. Kurtz), 40-3079 (Lt. Weldon Smith), and 40-2062 (Lt. James T. Connally).[34]

Major Combs, a native of Texas, was a graduate of the U.S. Military Academy. Before the outbreak of war, Major Combs commanded the 93rd Bomb Squadron of the 19th Bombardment Group. Once in Java, he commanded the Group itself.

The crew members of 40-3097 who arrived at Singosari with Major Combs on December 30, 1941, were 2nd Lt. Vincent L. Snyder, copilot; 2nd Lt. Anthony E. Oliver, navigator; 2nd Lt. Maxwell D. Stone, bombardier; T. Sgt. James Hanna, engineer; Pvt. Henry Sanders, assistant engineer; Pfc. Jack W. Douglas, radio operator; and Cpl. Jean A. Byers, assistant radio operator. Three maintenance technicians accompanied the crew: M. Sgt. R. Olsen, T. Sgt. F. C. Secrest, and Sgt. W. H. Quinzel.[35] As the commander's airplane, the craft that would later be christened "The Swoose" became the lead aircraft in many of the subsequent bombing missions flown by the 19th.

Singosari had a single 4,000-foot turf runway. The advance bases they were to use were camouflaged Dutch fields at Kendari, Celebes, and at Samarinda, 30 miles inland from Macassar Strait, on Borneo, 120 miles north of the Balikpapan oilfields.

On January 2, 1942, Manila and Cavite in the Philippines were captured by Japanese forces. United States and Philippine forces fortified their positions on the Bataan peninsula, where they held out until April 9. The island fortress at the entrance to Manila Bay known as Corregidor did not fall until May 6, 1942.

In that part of the world, equatorial fronts hang in a line from the northwest to the southeast, shifting back and forth as the weather changes. Throughout the seasons, the weather can be clear one moment and a solid sheet of rain the next. Provided with inadequate weather forecasts, the pilots and their crews often had to force their way through this weather while going to and returning from their targets. The buffeting took a lot out of both the crews and their airplanes and caused many aborted missions. As thunderstorms sometimes extended from sea level to 30,000 feet, trying to fly over the weather resulted in carburetor and wing icing, adding to the hazards.

The weather in the tropics produce more thunderstorms than in any other place in the world; Java alone has 223 storm days each year.[36] Navigators had the difficult job of flying over sea and jungle, often without landmarks, adequate maps, navigational aids, or radio directional facilities. Because of the heavy cloud formations, they were often unable to use celestial navigation to guide them to the target or the return to a friendly air base.

On January 2, 1942, Major Combs in 40-3097, leading a flight of nine B-17s, took off from Singosari at 8:30 A.M., for Samarinda, Borneo, to load bombs. The weather two hours over the Java Sea forced the planes to turn back to Malang. When they tried again on January 3, the weather was still bad; however, the flight was made in a little over four hours.

Samarinda was simply an airstrip, nothing more, where Dutch bombs were to be loaded. Crews found the food inedible so they limited themselves to bread. It was difficult to get the fuses for the Dutch bombs properly aligned, but by 8 P.M. all the aircraft were refueled and loaded with bombs. At 5 A.M., January 4, Major Combs took off from Samarinda, leading the flight of nine B-17s, to attack huge formations of Japanese transports near Davao, a 730-mile flight. The crew of 40-3097 also included 2nd Lt. Vincent L. Snyder, 2nd Lt. Anthony E. Oliver, 2nd Lt. Maxwell D. Stone, Sgt. James Hanna, Sgt. H. Sanders, Sgt. J. W. Douglas, Pfc. Jean A. Byers, Kattary, M. Sgt. Richard Olsen, and Capt. Edward Broadhurst, the Group's executive officer.[37]

Arriving over Davao Bay at 25,000 feet, they found a perfect target. It seemed as though half of the Japanese fleet was there—cruisers, one battleship, twelve transports, six destroyers, twelve submarines, and many smaller craft were sighted. The nine B-17s dropped thirty-two 600-pound bombs (almost 10 tons of bombs), sinking one destroyer, making three hits on a cruiser, and causing damage to other vessels.[38]

Antiaircraft fire reached 25,000 feet, but was not heavy enough to interfere with the bomb run. As the nine planes pulled away, five attacking Zeros were spotted at about 10,000 feet. Since the B-17s were flying at better than 300 MPH, the Zeros were unable to overtake them.[39] At 2:30 P.M. on January 4, 40-3097 and the other eight B-17s returned to Samarinda without a casualty, having conducted the most successful U.S. bombing mission of the war to that time.

Weldon Smith, piloting B-17 40-3079 during this mission, described the events as follows:

Headed for P.I. [Philippine Islands] today. Schaetzel's ship [3070] broke down so Teats and I were on Parcell's wings in B Flight. At Davao we hit a battleship with four 500 pounders and really made it jump. The other flights got a cruiser and a transport. No enemy planes could catch us. Saw some pursuit. The AA [antiaircraft fire] was bursting behind us and very close, but of course one does not know until afterwards.[40]

The attack on Davao Bay was recognized in Washington as a significant accomplishment. On January 6, General Arnold sent the following cables to General Brereton: "Great admiration and acclaim here for feat of Air Force of your command at Davao against the Japanese fleet. Hearty congratulations to you and your personnel."

No further bombing missions could be staged from Samarinda; no 100-octane fuel remained after each of the B-17s had been serviced. Only two other B-17s would ever again land at this field. B-17 40-3097 and the other seven B-17s returned to Malang from Samarinda on January 5, 1942.

Three days later, on January 8, Major Combs in 40-3097 again led the nine B-17s out from Singosari. This time the staging was Kendari on the southeast corner of Celebes, the best camouflaged and one of the best of all Dutch bomber fields. At Singosari, combat crews, both officers and enlisted men, worked under the direction of ground maintenance men to get the airplanes ready for the combat mission in such a short time. The objective was to load bombs at Kendari and once again attack the enemy ships in the Davao Gulf.[41]

The formation took off from Kendari on January 9, 1942, at 12:30 A.M., with a solid overcast at 2,000 feet. Eight of the aircraft rendezvoused with Combs in 40-3097. They flew in formation all the way to Mindanao. Much of the time visibility was so bad that the pilots could not see each other's pale blue formation lights. The planes were tossed about with a violence none of the pilots had ever before encountered. They came out of the weather south of Mindanao with only five of the aircraft still in the formation. Two had turned back with engine trouble, and two lost formation because of the violent weather and the darkness.[42]

Weldon Smith described the events of January 8 and 9:

January 8. Took-off for Kendari—Celebes—the island looks very much like Hawaii. On the way the native villages on small coral reefs were most interesting. The reefs are covered with palms, with green and palm growth all over. Kendari is a beautiful field and quite hard to find. We loaded and gassed.

January 9. Headed for Mindanao at midnight in formation. About half-way there, we had tracer bullets flashing all around us and, when we called up to tell the lead flight to quit clearing their guns, they were quite surprised as they had not touched them. The Nips did not hit anyone but it sure was fun to watch. Only 5 ships got to the target. We had to turn back and on the way ran into Jap ships, but avoided them in the clouds.[43]

The remaining aircraft made landfall early and, since it was still dark, Major Combs led the flight inland over Mindanao to kill time. Here in the darkness they encountered another weather front and two more aircraft dropped out of the formation.

Combs, with the remaining two aircraft in formation, bombed ships in Davao Gulf as planned. They made a direct hit on the cruiser hit in the previous raid and a waterline hit on a battleship which set it on fire. Another bomb hit an antiaircraft battery on shore. The two aircraft that had dropped out of formation earlier came into the target area separately, at dawn, and dropped their bombs on a transport.[44]

Low on fuel and unable to get back to Kendari, the flight put into L'Honga, a Dutch auxiliary field on the extreme tip of Sumatra. It was not much of an airfield but it had gas. Major Combs discovered on landing that the tail wheel tire on 40-3097 was flat. He knew that if it couldn't be fixed, he would have to take off with the flat tire. The crew managed to wrestle the airplane's tail over a barrel. Combs took a heavy duty inner tube from a Dutch truck. They then wrapped the inner tube over the tail wheel hub twice, cut a hole in the tire side wall for the valve, inflated it to 35 pounds, and left it overnight. The next morning, the tire and tube were still inflated and Combs took off without incident.

Combs landed at Singosari at noon. The crew worked all that day to get the airplane ready for still another high-altitude mission the next day.[45] As a result of the attack on Davao, Combs (and the pilots of the other two B-17s) was given a citation, which read:

For attack on enemy shipping at Davao, Mindanao, PI, on January 9, 1942, which resulted in direct hit on an enemy battleship and the destruction of enemy supplies and several gun positions on shore. During the flight the weather conditions were extremely dangerous. Extreme carburetor icing and turbulence of an equatorial front made formation flying almost impossible and threatened success of the mission. It was only by exceptional skill and determination to reach the objective, inspired by the urgency of the mission, that Major Combs led his flight to the objective, and that his two wingmen [Patrick W. McIntyre and Donald M. Keiser] were able to follow him through.

At long last, the first replacement aircraft and crews began arriving in Sumatra on January 10. The aircraft were the longer B-17Es, with their large dorsal fin, under which was a tail-gunner position with twin .50-caliber tail guns and power turrets on the top and bottom of the fuselage.

All the replacement Es had been sent from Hamilton Field, California, east over the Atlantic, Africa, and India, instead of the central Pacific route established by the 19th Bomb Group the previous September. The Pacific route had been cut by the Japanese landing at Wake Island. Later, reinforcement B-17s, B-25s, and B-26s would fly a new southern Pacific ferry route to Australia from Hawaii. This new route to Australia and Java, via a string of Pacific atolls, was inaugurated a few days later, on January 14, 1942, by three B-17s from Hickam Field.[46]

The last combat mission flown in Java by B-17D 40-3097 took place on January 11, 1942. The events involving the airplane on that mission are the subject of some disagreement. Official records specify that the airplane was flown by the flight leader, Major Combs, who had flown the same airplane in all his combat missions since December 29, 1941, when he took the airplane from Henry C. Godman. The same records identify the B-17 flown by Frank Kurtz on that mission as 40-3067. Kurtz believes that the record is in error, since his diary records the airplane he flew as 40-3097.[47] At the time, the use of serial numbers painted on the vertical stabilizer had not yet been adopted in the Pacific war zone for B-17Cs and Ds and one could not readily identify the number.

According to the 19th Bombardment Group records, Major Combs took off in 40-3097 at 5:55 A.M., leading a flight of seven B-17s to bomb ships of the Japanese invasion force on the eastern coast of Borneo, in the Tarakan area. One hour out, a severe weather front forced the pilots to spread out the formation before penetrating the front.[48]

Four of the aircraft turned back inside the front because they lost radio contact. Only 40-3097 and two other aircraft continued the mission; the pilots of the other aircraft were Kurtz and Connally. Combs came out of the front first and circled, waiting for the others. Since the target area was only 50 miles north, he decided to go on and attack alone. Climbing to 23,000 feet as they approached the target, at 11:30 A.M. they spotted a Japanese convoy. Sergeant Stone, the bombardier, took over on a 10-minute bomb run.

During that bomb run, three Zeros were spotted. The threat of the approaching enemy aircraft forced Combs to teil Stone to pick the nearest target, not the biggest ships, and drop the bombs. The three enemy aircraft pressed their attack on 40-3097 for 35 minutes. Combs, in an effort to shake the Zeros, headed for the biggest, blackest cloud coming from burning Dutch oilfields, but the pursuing enemy aircraft subjected Ole Betsy to fire from 11:30 A.M. to 12:05 P.M., by which time the crew had shot down two of them.[49] Fifteen minutes after 40-3097 attacked, Kurtz and Connally in the other two B-17s came over the target without meeting any opposition.

At 4:35 that afternoon, Major Combs landed 40-3097 at Malang, while the other two B-17s landed elsewhere.[50] The rest of Ole Betsy's crew included Snyder, copilot; Oliver, navigator; Stone, bombardier; Hanna, engineer; Sanders, assistant engineer; Douglas, radioman; and Byers, assistant radioman.[51]

On July 9, 1941, Lt. Gen. George H. Brett presented Capt. Frank A. Kurtz with the Distinguished Flying Cross for his participation in the mission flown on January 11, 1942. The award was given in recognition for completing "the longest bombing mission ever undertaken from Java, an attack on Tarakan, Borneo, involving a round trip of more than 1,500 miles. Attacking successfully with a B-17, he returned to his base on three engines."[52]

Dutch maintenance facilities in Java were inadequate for the B-17s. In spite of the efforts of the overworked young men to patch the aircraft and get ready for repeated combat missions, the lack of proper maintenance resulted in a falloff in engine performance, causing the four-engine airplanes to lose speed or fail to attain operationally safe altitudes. This was often the reason for failure to reach designated targets. In spite of everything, the combat-weary men flying their marginally performing airplanes without fighter aircraft protection, often with only one waist gun fit to fire, destroyed six enemy aircraft for every B-17 lost in Java.

As had been the case in the Philippines, aircraft losses in Java were mainly caused by enemy attacks as the heavy bombers sat on the ground. During operations in Java, the United States lost fifty-three four-engine bombers. Only five of the airplanes were actually shot down. Many of the remainder were destroyed on the ground by Japanese strafing using explosive incendiary bullets.

While the B-17 proved to be a difficult airplane to shoot down, it was subjected to considerable damage from attacking fighters. Whenever possible, the most serviceable aircraft were kept in operation by cannibalizing parts from those that were more heavily damaged.

The reduced performance, coupled with deterioration of the Dutch airfield surfaces, made every takeoff extremely hazardous. With the heavy rains that came in mid-January, a dip developed midway down the length of the 4,000-foot turf runway at Singosari. By the end of January, that section became a sea of mud and water and half of one side of the runway had to be closed off while native workers filled the mud hole with rock, leaving just enough room for taking off. The heavy B-17s cut foot-deep grooves in the rest of the field.

Pilots taxiing their airplanes with a full load of gasoline and bombs described the experience as similar to maneuvering a boat. Even slight pressure on the brakes would cause the wheels to slide. Mud would pile up in front of them, making it necessary to taxi at higher than normal speeds to prevent bogging down. Takeoff from Singosari was treacherous. It was necessary to roll as fast as possible before the low spot in hopes of picking up enough of the speed lost going through the mud to gain takeoff speed on the other side.

The mission over Borneo on January 11, carried out during the first full month of war in the Pacific, was to be the last combat mission for B-17D 40-3097. Damage to Ole Betsy from the battle with the three Zeros and general deterioration of its engines rendered it unfit for combat operations. The airplane was grounded at Malang on January 13, pending needed repairs to make it airworthy for a flight to Australia for more extensive depot repairs.[53]

Retreat from Java

When one of the B-17s being used by the 19th Bombardment Group in Java required repairs that could not be performed by maintenance crews in the field, the aircraft was flown at first opportunity to the repair depot near Melbourne, Australia.[54] Such would be the path of Ole Betsy.

Local work to make temporary repairs to the battle damage suffered by Ole Betsy was completed and, at 9:13 in the morning of January 27, it took off from Singosari for the 3,000-mile flight to the RAAF base at Laverton, outside of Melbourne, Australia. The route to Melbourne included a stop at Darwin. The pilot was Donald M. Keiser, with Elliott Vandevanter as copilot. B. R. Work was the navigator and T. Sgt. James Hanna and Cpl. Jean. Byers made up the rest of the crew.

Fifteen minutes after Keiser departed in 40-3097, a second B-17D (40-3067) also departed for Laverton with Lt. Edward Teats as its pilot.

Teats described the airplane he was to fly as a "battered wreck." Its hydraulic system had been damaged; three of its engines were running rough and the fourth had been hit by a 37mm antiaircraft shell that had also weakened one of the wings. Teats said that it had to be flown with one wing about 10 degrees below the other so that it could be crabbed along at low altitude and low speed.[55]

The flight to Darwin took seven hours, with the last two and one-half hours flown on three engines. The next day, as Teats took off from Darwin, an engine failed and the aircraft crashed and was destroyed. (Teats would later be the copilot of the B-17 that evacuated General MacArthur and Henry Godman from Del Monte.)

Laverton, an RAAF installation, was used as an overhaul base and base of operations for B-17 antisubmarine patrols. At the time of its arrival in Laverton, B-17D 40-3097 was one of only two of the original force of B-17s stationed in the Philippines on December 7, 1941, to be operational having survived to reach Australia. The other, a B-17C, was by then being used as a transport.

No detailed record exists today of the work performed on Ole Betsy while at Laverton, other than its tail having been partially replaced with one taken from another damaged B-17 (40-3091). As was the custom of the time, since there were no new spare parts, all materials used to repair the aircraft were obtained from other battle-damaged, war-weary B-17s. The engines of 40-3097 were probably replaced. Replacement engines, however, were often in worse shape than those that had been removed since they had been overhauled by civilian contractors, working outdoors in the sand and dust of summer in Australia.

B-17D 40-3091, whose tail was transplanted onto Ole Betsy, had been flown out of Del Monte in the evacuation to Batchelor Field on December 20, 1941. Its pilot was 1st Lt. George Schaetzel. On January 13, 1942, the airplane was reported out of commission at Darwin for depot repair. Lieutenant Schaetzel had participated in a bombing mission in that airplane on December 10, 1941, when he was attacked by enemy aircraft. Considerable damage was inflicted on 3091, but there were no casualties and the airplane returned to Del Monte safely after an emergency landing where an aileron control cable was repaired.

It is presumed that the damage inflicted on Schaetzel's airplane during the mission on December 10 contributed to its being out of commission after it was evacuated to Batchelor Field. The tail assembly on 3097 did show battle damage when patches were replaced years later. Schaetzel's airplane must have had temporary repairs made at Darwin and was then flown to Laverton between January 13, 1942, and the latter part of January, when 40-3097 arrived there for its well-deserved overhaul.

"Ole Betsy" Becomes "The Swoose"

In late February 1942, Capt. Weldon Smith wrote that he went to nearby Melbourne, where he purchased champagne to christen the airplane "Swoose," and to celebrate "the completion of the assembly job that would once more put us [his crew] into the war."[56] Smith said they "uncorked the bottle in the approved manner, squirted the first burst of bubbles [on the aircraft] and then filled their cups with the balance to drink a toast to 'The Swoose.'"[57]

The name "Swoose" came from a song made popular by Kay Kyser on his radio program, "The Kollege of Musical Knowledge." Copyrighted in 1941, the song "Alexander the Swoose (Half Swan—Half Goose)" was written by Ben Forrest, Leonard Keller, Glenn Barrs, and Frank Furlett. The song concerns a gander whose appearance is different from the other geese. He is tormented by his contemporaries with the words, "Here comes little Alexander, what a funny looking gander. He's half swan and he's half goose, ha ha ha, he's just a swoose." According to Smith, the plane's name was prompted by the fact that the airplane, now having parts from other aircraft, had become a hybrid, analogous to the Swoose.

Present at the christening ceremony were the other members of the crew, Lt. Morris N. Friedman, Lt. Addie W. Hayman, Lt. Ernest C. Wade, Sgt. Glover J. Bourke, Sgt. George Brandes, Sgt. J. Diehl, and Kenneth B. Park. Lieutenant Friedman was an old friend of 40-3097, as he had previously served as Godman's copilot when the airplane was known as "Ole Betsy."[58]

The aircraft's name was conceived by Smith while they were at Newcastle in New South Wales, Australia.[59] He designed and painted the logo, which depicted the fictional bird. Beneath the words "It Flys?," he added, "Sometimes!" Later, according to Captain Smith, a British flyer who had occasion to take a trip with the Swoose obliterated the word "Sometimes!," and lettered in its place "You bet your life it flies." That in time was erased too, but "The Swoose, It Flys!" marked the aircraft when it later became Gen. George Brett's plane.[60]

The Pacific war continued unabated during this milestone in the life of 40-3097. On Sunday, February 15, 1942, the great British naval base at Singapore fell to the Japanese. This was to be the prelude to the darkest period in the Allied campaign in the Southwest Pacific. The Japanese had swept down through the Philippines, Malaya, and Burma. The loss of Singapore was called by Winston Churchill "the worst disaster in British history." The fall of that fortress led to the subsequent Japanese conquest of the islands to the south, leading toward Australia and New Zealand.

With the new threat of Japanese penetration to the south following their invasion of Java, the evacuation of U.S. air forces from the Dutch East Indies was begun. The 19th Bomb Group was reorganized at Laverton, Australia, following their evacuation from Java.

On February 19, 1942, the Japanese bombed Darwin and on March 4, Broome, Australia, was attacked while jammed with aircraft and evacuees from Java. Broome was being used as a refueling stop on the escape route from Java. There was great fear that in their southward march Japanese forces would embark on an invasion of northern Australia. Great efforts were being made to deploy a force of fighter aircraft in the north to bolster Australian defenses. These fighters, mainly Curtiss P-40s, were shipped by sea transport in crates from the United States. The ships were unloaded at eastern Australian ports and the aircraft were assembled at nearby airfields.

Since there were few air navigation facilities in Australia, the fighters were usually led north over the desolate interior of Australia by larger aircraft such as the B-17. Earlier in January 1942, Australian aircraft accompanied P-40s from Brisbane to Darwin on their way to Java by way of Rockhampton, Townsville, Cloncurry, and Daly Waters. Flying Fortresses of the 19th Group took over this operation and also flew antisubmarine reconnaissance patrols from Laverton as well as combat missions to the Philippines by way of intermediate landing fields.

While documents indicate that the Swoose flew 38.5 hours in February 1942, the first recorded mission of the newly named plane took place on March 6, 1942, when Weldon Smith flew the airplane north over Australia, guiding a group of pursuit aircraft.[61]

On March 17, the day General MacArthur assumed command of the combined Allied forces in the Southwest Pacific, Captain Arthur A. Fletcher of the 19th Bomb Group's 28th squadron returned to Laverton from Batchelor in 40-3097 at 1:50 P.M. The engines were in poor shape and it was placed in the depot for work.

Weldon Halliwell Smith, pilot of 40-3097 during its metamorphosis from Ole Betsy to the Swoose, was born in Carson City, Nevada, and graduated in 1937 from the University of California. As captain of the swimming team at Berkeley, he entered graduate school there, but elected to cut short that endeavor to enter the Army Flying School at Randolph Field, Texas, in October 1937. He graduated as a second lieutenant in 1939, and was assigned to the Hawaiian Department of the U.S. Army. In Hawaii, he was to pilot the Army Curtiss A-12 Shrike in the 26th Attack Squadron of the 18th Pursuit Group stationed at Wheeler Field. Smith had been one of the original 14th Squadron pilots assigned to fly the first B-17s to arrive in Hawaii on May 13, 1941. He was also the pilot of one of the aircraft to pioneer the central Pacific ferry route to Clark Field in the Philippines as part of the 14th Bomb Squadron.

Captain Smith's last combat flight of the war would be in a B-17E on a mission to bomb Kendari in June 1942. It was the longest combat mission ever flown by the 19th with a return to the same airfield. Earlier reconnaissance flights over the main Japanese bases and positions northwest of Darwin showed that Kendari, on the southeastern coast of Celebes, was being used as a staging center for Japanese aircraft. Over 100 Zeros and more than 50 bombers were massed on the field almost 1,000 miles from Darwin.

Five B-17Es, led by Capt. Edward C. Teats, took off from Darwin at two in the afternoon on June 30. Their plan was to surprise the enemy by arriving over the target just before sunset. As recounted by Teats, as they approached the Japanese base, they found three separate layers of clouds that they used to conceal their approach from ground observers.[62]

Coming down to low altitude under the clouds through a haze, the aircraft made a straight run for the target area and dropped their bombs. One made a direct hit on three bombers; another hit one of the largest buildings on the field. It was estimated that the attack also seriously damaged forty aircraft. As they passed over the target, crews also threw bundles of incendiary-like material out of the side gun ports.

Only one Zero came up to intercept from one of the satellite airfields about 20 miles south of Kendari. He attacked Lieutenant Smith's aircraft, which was leading the second flight of two airplanes. The Zero made six passes, the last one passing only 20 or 30 feet above the B-17. Smith's airplane took all the hits; none of the other aircraft was struck. Both aircraft of the second flight trained all guns on the Zero as it made one of its passes and shot him down. The Zero continued in a shallow dive, all guns firing, until he passed out of sight in the clouds.

On this last pass, the Zero's guns hit one of Lieutenant Smith's engines. When he took off for Kendari, Smith knew that one of the engines was burning too much oil and he planned to feather that engine and come back on the other three after dropping his bombs since he would have darkness as a cover. About 30 miles north of Darwin, after limping along on three engines for 600 miles, one of the three remaining engines suddenly stopped. Unfortunately, it was on the same side as the bad engine whose propeller had been feathered. As he was trying to get the feathered engine started, the controls that had been badly damaged during the attack gave way and the B-17 spun into the ground.

Three of Lieutenant Smith's crew died in the crash; all the others were injured. Killed were Sergeant Bourke of Topeka, Kansas, who had been a crew member of the Swoose, Cpl. Robert A. French of Brownwood, Texas, and Cpl. Brysen C. West of Oaklawah, Florida.

Chapter 4

Command Airplane in Australia

In March 1942 the Swoose, in need of repairs, sat on the ground at Laverton, Australia, outside of Melbourne. Although destined to become a historical museum artifact and a memorial to the heroic members of the Army Air Corps who fought valiantly to stem Japanese aggression following their attacks on Hawaii, the Philippine Islands, and the Netherlands East Indies, its combat life was over. Those accomplishments in the Pacific had not been unique, but while its contemporaries had been destroyed on the ground and in the air, this particular airplane had survived.

The crews of the 19th Bombardment Group and their reinforcements were preoccupied with the fight against the advancing Japanese who now threatened Australia. Anything that could fly was being used, and disabled aircraft such as the Swoose were shunted aside in favor of those that could be returned to service in the shortest time, especially the newer and more heavily armed B-17Es, which were then arriving in small numbers from the United States.

The Swoose may have been destined for cannibalization and the scrap yard or relegated to cargo-hauling duties if circumstances regarding a Consolidated B-24A Liberator had been different. That B-24A was Gen. George H. Brett's staff aircraft, which had recently brought the general to Australia from his former headquarters in Java. General Brett, now commander of the U.S. Army in Australia, would become the vehicle by which the Swoose would gain still more fame. The two would be partners until they both retired some three and one-half years later.

George H. Brett was born in Cleveland, Ohio, in 1886. A graduate of the Virginia Military Institute, he was commissioned a second lieutenant in the Philippine Scouts and subsequently assigned to Fort Ethan Allen in Vermont. He initially tried to enter the Coast Artillery, but was not accepted because he was colorblind. The first military air force in history to fly airplanes, the Aviation Section of the U.S. Army's Signal Corps maintained a flying school at North Island in San Diego. In 1914 Brett wanted to transfer to the new air service but there was concern that his colorblindness would affect his performance. However, the Army, hungry for volunteers to attend its new flying school, decided to send the colorblind candidate as an experiment.[1]

Brett and his five classmates were taught how to fly by two civilian instructors, "Doc" Williams and Oscar Brindley. Due to his colorblindness, Brett had to go through an extra test to get his wings. Lieutenant William C. Ocker, who would become a pioneer of the technique known as "blind flying," took Brett up to test his skills. Ocker throttled back the engine, pointed to a field and yelled, "What's that?" Brett shouted, "Mesquite!" They landed and George Brett became a pilot, probably the only genuinely colorblind military pilot.[2] Brett was 30 years old when he made his first solo flight. Candidates for the flying school had to serve a period with the ground forces before they were eligible to make application for the school. Most others at the school were about 25 years old.[3]

Following his designation as a Junior Military Aviator (three years later he received his rating as Military Aviator), Brett began a series of assignments that would give him a broad range of training and experience. Colonel Brett was assigned as the aviation representative in the Office of the Chief Signal Officer in Washington, D.C., in September 1916. One year later he was ordered overseas and became responsible for logistic support for the Air Service in France, and later chief of the Material Division for the Air Service in the American Expeditionary Force (AEF). He returned to the United States in December 1918 to take command of the Aviation General Supply Depot at San Antonio.

Starting in 1919, for the next two years Colonel Brett was assigned to a succession of duties at Kelly Field, Texas, Fort Sam Houston, Texas, Morrison, Virginia, and finally Washington, D.C.

In October 1921 he was assigned the command of the Presidio of San Francisco. While in command of this post, he also commanded the 91st Observation Squadron based at Crissy Field located at the Presidio. Beginning in March 1924, he was chief of the Field Service Section of the Air Corps at Fairfield, Ohio, for three and one-half years. In August 1927 he was detailed as a student at the Air Corps Tactical School at Langley Field, Virginia. Upon graduation the following year, he became a student at the Command and General Staff School at Fort Leavenworth, Kansas, where he completed the two-year course in June 1930. He returned to the school for two years as an instructor following a three-year assignment as the commander of the First Pursuit Group at Selfridge Field, Michigan. In 1936 Brigadier General Brett graduated from the Army War College in Washington, D.C., and took command of the 19th Composite Wing in the Panama Canal Zone. He became chief of staff of the General Headquarters of the Air Corps at Langley Field, Virginia, in September 1938. The following year, in March 1939, he was appointed assistant chief of the Air Corps and became commandant of the Engineering School at Wright Field and chief of the Materiel Division.

In October 1940 Major General Brett was made acting chief of the Air Corps. He was then appointed chief of the Air Corps, which title he held in the creation of the Air Force. On June 20, 1941, the U.S. Army Air Forces was created under a single commander, Gen. Henry H. "Hap" Arnold. Major General George H. Brett succeeded General Arnold as chief of the subordinate Army Air Corps and was chiefly responsible for directing procurement of aircraft and training.[4]

That same year, General Brett received the premier award in aviation, the coveted Collier Trophy, established in 1911 and presented annually by the president in recognition of the greatest achievement in U.S. aviation. Brett was the joint recipient of the trophy with Dr. Sanford A. Moss, in recognition of their development of the turbo supercharger that enabled aircraft to fly and fight in the stratosphere. President Roosevelt was to present the trophy on Kitty Hawk Day, December 17, but Brett had more pressing matters to deal with when the time came.

Beginning on August 31, 1941, with Lt. Col. Caleb V. Haynes as pilot and Maj. Curtis E. LeMay as copilot, General Brett was flown in a B-24A from Bolling Field outside of Washington, D.C., to Basra in the Persian Gulf. Under orders from President Roosevelt, Brett was to collect information on the performance of U.S. equipment being supplied to the Royal Air Force (RAF) and seek ways to provide assistance to the British forces in the repair and maintenance of their U.S.-built aircraft.[5] Little did he know that this flight would eventually lead him to the Swoose.

While regular U.S. military air service from the United States flew over the North Atlantic to England (beginning in July 1941), General Brett's trip was the first flight over the South Atlantic route from the United States to the Middle East. This flight pioneered the shuttle air route from Florida to Natal, Brazil, across the South Atlantic to Freetown, up the west coast of Africa via Bathurst, Tokaradi, then east across the desert to Khartoum and into Cairo. This route was destined to expedite the flow of aircraft and equipment to the British fighting forces in the Middle East and England, and later to the Soviet Union.[6]

The modified B-24s used by the Ferry Command at Bolling Field had most of the armament removed and the bomb bays altered to accommodate passengers and freight. These aircraft, which could be flown with relatively large overloads, were roomy and had easy loading characteristics. Designed to carry loads of 50,000 pounds, they were used later in the South Pacific combat zone with takeoff weights over 70,000 pounds.

The early B-24s had a greater range than the B-17, had two bomb bays (each twice the size of the B-17's), and could carry an 8,000-pound bomb load versus the 6,000-pound load for the B-17. However, the B-24 required better landing fields and its performance at high altitude was inferior to the B-17.

Later models of the B-24 used in the European Theater lost their overall advantage over the B-17 as a result of modifications necessary to improve protective armament and armor. In October 1942, the Air Forces prepared to replace the 19th Bombardment Group with the 90th, who were equipped with B-24s. The lack of lower turrets in the B-24s brought considerable concern to the flight crews, who felt that the B-24s were inadequate replacements for the B-17Es with lower gun turrets.[7] By November 1942, the B-24 outnumbered the B-17 in combat operations against the Japanese in the Southwest Pacific. By October 1943, there were only three first-line B-17s in the entire Pacific Theater while the B-24 strength stood at 612.

On September 10, 1941, Major General Brett and his group of Army Air Force officers arrived in Cairo to start their tour of British bases in Africa, the Middle East, the Mediterranean, and England. After flying

19,000 miles inspecting British operations in the western desert and Palestine, and a week's stay in Malta, Brett flew on to London on October 15. He remained in London until November 23, 1941, when he departed onboard an RAF aircraft for the flight back to Cairo, from where he was to begin his return trip to Washington by way of the Middle East and the Pacific. General Brett was accompanied on this leg of the trip by his aide, Maj. John Gowen.[8]

Once in Cairo, General Brett obtained a B-24, Serial Number 40-2374, for his future travels. This same airplane had been one of two to carry part of the joint U.S.-British delegation to Moscow in September 1941. After it had been removed from the North Atlantic shuttle service flying from Washington to Great Britain in October 1941, it most likely was assigned to the new South Atlantic route to Cairo.[9]

On December 4, 1941, General Brett was still in the Middle East at British headquarters in the western desert (Sahara) of North Africa. At a farewell party being given for him in Cairo, General Brett received a cable from Washington directing him to Chungking, China, to attend a Chinese-British-American conference. From Chungking, Brett was to proceed home by way of the (soon to be attacked) Philippine Islands.

Before Brett's departure from Cairo, his B-24 was christened the "Arabian Knight." Piloted by Capt. Paul Davis, the Arabian Knight's copilot was Lt. Jack Wilson Berry and Lt. Carroll Cain the navigator. Five enlisted men filled out the flight crew. Brett's party also included Major Gowen, Lt. Col. Edwin Perrin, Maj. Edward Alexander, and Lt. James Crain, a physician.[10]

With a takeoff weight of 55,000 pounds, the Arabian Knight left Cairo on December 7, 1941, with what was believed to be the heaviest load a B-24 had ever carried for a takeoff. The destination was Rangoon, Burma. Two days later, the plane was on the ground in Teheran with engine trouble.[11]

The trip east was divided into three hops. Excluding the delay in Teheran, the flight from Cairo to Shaibah, Iraq, took 5 hours and 20 minutes. The second leg, from Shaibah to Karachi, India, was flown in 6 hours and 10 minutes. The final leg into Rangoon was flown in 9 hours and 40 minutes. Arriving in Burma after blazing the new air supply route from Cairo to India, the officers and enlisted men were welcomed by British and Burmese officials.

On December 22, General Brett departed Burma for Chungking with Gen. Sir Archibald Wavell in a China National Aviation Corporation (CNAC) DC-2, while Brett's B-24 remained in Rangoon. While attending the meeting in Chungking, Brett was ordered to proceed to Melbourne, Australia, where he was to take command of the U.S. Army Air Forces in Australia (USAAFIA), charged with supporting the troops then defending the Philippines.[12]

On the return flight to Rangoon with General Wavell, Brett's party encountered a flight of seventeen Japanese aircraft. After landing safely at Mingaloden in Burma, they dove into a trench to escape the bombs and machine-gun fire from the attacking Japanese.

En route to his new duty station in Melbourne, General Brett made a stop in Java to confer with Dutch officials. It was also reported that Brett visited the Philippines on his way to the Dutch East Indies.[13] On January 1, 1942, Brett left Townsville, Australia, for Brisbane with Gen. Lewis H. Brereton, who had flown out of the Philippines. The two of them would have to maintain a very close relationship since Brett, as commanding general of the U.S. Army Air Forces in Australia, was charged with organizing air bases in Australia while Brereton, as commander of the Far East Air Force, was supposed to establish advance operation bases and direct the air force in maintaining the lines of communication with MacArthur's forces and support the defense of the Philippines. Arrangements for the use of Australian facilities and communications would require considerable cooperation from the Australians, which was of vital concern to both men.[14]

Exhausted by his travels, Brett would get little chance for any rest. His attempts to develop a method to deliver badly needed supplies to the Philippine defenders futile, on January 2 in Brisbane, Brett received yet another directive that would take him in a new direction.[15]

At the meeting on December 22 of the British and U.S. military staffs in Washington, D.C., Chief of Staff Gen. George C. Marshall had proposed that a single commander be named for all ground, sea, and air forces for the area from the Bay of Bengal to Australia to be known as ABDA (American-British-Dutch-Australian). The U.S. Navy was given responsibility for all of the northern and central Pacific, which constituted all of the Pacific east of the Philippine Islands and Australia, including U.S. approaches to Australia.

Roosevelt proposed that General Wavell of Britain, then in India, become supreme commander for the unified ABDA forces. General Brett was named deputy supreme commander. It was hoped that the Japanese southerly conquest could be delayed at Singapore by ABDA to give the United States time to recover in the Pacific and provide military support to the defense of Australia. On January 3, 1942, the new command structure was announced to the public.[16] Headquarters for ABDA was established in Surabaya, Java.

Having been in Australia only eight days, Brett was given a promotion to lieutenant general, along with orders to take this new command. Accompanied by General Brereton and Sir Charles Burnett, Australian Chief of Air Staff, Brett flew in the Arabian Knight, arriving at the ABDA headquarters in Surabaya, Java, on January 9. That same day, Brett flew on to Batavia in order to meet his new commander, General Wavell, upon his arrival the following day.[17] With the fall of Singapore and Burma, however, the swift advance of Japanese forces gave Wavell and Brett no opportunity to organize their new command before they were forced to abandon the ABDA plan and retreat.

General Brett's B-24 was one of three former Ferry Command B-24s used in the Southwest Pacific whenever and wherever they were needed, shuttling among Australia, the Dutch East Indies, and Burma. Following the disintegration of the Allied effort to defend the Dutch East Indies, General Brett left Java for the final time early on the morning of February 23 and flew to Melbourne for what was intended to be a short visit before proceeding to India to establish a command there.[18]

During his planned stopover in Australia, General Brett finally received orders to stay put—as the commander of the U.S. Army Forces in Australia. The United States planned to develop Australia as a major base since they now took responsibility for its defense and it was Brett's responsibility to organize and take command of all U.S. forces there.

Starting on February 25, all available long-range aircraft were pressed into service for the evacuation of military personnel from the Dutch East Indies to Australia. The little town of Broome on the northwestern corner of Australia was established as the evacuation base for all flights from Java. Temporary facilities had been established there on February 24 by Lt. Col. Edwin S. Perrin, who selected members of the 19th Bombardment Group to service the evacuation force on their way south to Melbourne.[19]

By March 1, Jogjakarta was the sole airfield in Java remaining in Allied hands. On the following night, 260 officers and enlisted men still awaited evacuation and only five B-17s and three B-24s were available. Each B-24 took off with thirty-five passengers and each B-17 with thirty-one, some of whom had to stand all the way on the long journey to safety. As the last airplane took off, the Japanese were but 18 miles away.[20]

The eight bombers and their human cargo reached Broome on the morning of March 3. During the night, a Japanese reconnaissance airplane had been seen, and plans were made to expedite the departure of evacuees from Broome by 10 that morning to avoid the expected air attack. At that hour, a dozen Japanese fighters pounced on the airfield and the harbor at Broome, destroying twelve flying boats, two B-17s, two Lockheed Hudsons, and two B-24s, one of which was General Brett's Arabian Knight, which had been participating in the evacuation. On March 11, 1943, the battle-weary men of the 19th Bomb Group were ordered to leave (see Appendix G).

Captain Paul Davis, pilot of the Arabian Knight, along with Capt. Jack W. Berry, copilot, watched the well-traveled aircraft burn from under a low bush.[21] The second B-24 had just taken off when Zekes (the Allied Air Forces's code for the Japanese navy's Type-Zero fighter, the Mitsubishi A6M) appeared, shooting down the B-24 and killing all but one of its crew and passengers.

On April 20, 1942, General Brett became the commander of all Allied air forces in Australia, two days after Gen. Douglas MacArthur assumed command of the Southwest Pacific area.[22] General Brett laid down this rule for Air Corps in Australia: "Our first principle must be: no more uncrippled airplanes destroyed on the ground. If destroyed in the air, fighting, attacking or on the ground while unflyable, that's okay—that's part of the fortunes of war."

The General Takes the Swoose

Japanese bombers had bombed and strafed Darwin in northern Australia. On February 19, 1942, with the subsequent attack on Broome, the Japanese demonstrated their ability to reach out to the island continent. Fearing for their safety, many Australians were planning to evacuate their families into the interior.[23]

The continent of Australia is a land of great distances. The interior is a vast, sometimes barren desert. In 1942, surface transportation was inadequate to support the movement of men and materials to aid the war effort. Railways in different parts of the country had tracks of varying gauges so rail cars on one line could not be used on another. Airplanes became the only effective means of transportation. Every airplane that went north from Melbourne was loaded to capacity with supplies for the forces that were striking at the enemy in their drive toward Australia.[24]

Working 16 to 18 hours a day, General Brett and his deputy, Brig.

Gen. Ralph Royce, had to supervise the reinforcement of northern Australia and the disposition of the evacuated U.S. forces, as well as arrange for bases to house the influx of troops and equipment that would be flowing in from the United States to defend Australia. A search was begun for a suitable replacement for the Arabian Knight. (A third B-24, which had reached Melbourne before the Japanese raid on Broome, was lost as a result of a forced landing in early March 1942.[25])

Enter the Swoose. Since its last flight on March 17, 1942, the Swoose sat parked on the field at the Laverton Depot awaiting disposition. One of the last B-17Ds in Australia, the bomber was now a war-weary relic. A number of the newer, larger B-17Es with tail guns and upper and lower electrically activated gun turrets were arriving in greater numbers and were in great demand for strikes against the southward moving enemy.[26] Accordingly, these newer aircraft were given priority over the Swoose as they limped into Laverton from Java for the depot repairs that would return them to battle.

In all probability, the Swoose would have eventually been abandoned and cannibalized for spare parts had it not been chosen by Frank Kurtz and his crew as the best available airplane for the general's use from among those that could not otherwise be used in combat. Using General Brett's authority, the Swoose was ordered repaired and returned to flying status.[27] Thus began a wartime partnership between General Brett and the Swoose which would continue until December 1945 when, following the total victory over the Axis powers, they would simultaneously retire from military service.

The Swoose Crew

Selected as General Brett's new pilot, Capt. Frank Kurtz would remain in that capacity for the next 10 months. As it turned out, Kurtz's name would be closely linked to the Swoose from this point on. Years later, he would play a prominent role in saving the airplane from ignominious destruction and, still later, from abandonment.

On June 17, 1930, as a seventeen-year-old pilot, Frances Allen Kurtz flew in an open cockpit Waco Taper-Wing biplane at a speed of 124.852 miles per hour over a three-kilometer course in Orange County, California. Kurtz, with 50 hours of solo flying, had thus established the first junior air speed record, recognized by the National Aeronautics Association and Fédération Aéronautique Internationale.[28]

On May 8, 1935, Amelia Earhart became the first person to fly non-stop from Mexico City to Newark Airport (which was then the New York City metropolitan airport). Her flying time was 14 hours and 9 minutes.[29] Six months later, as a twenty-year-old student at the University of Southern California, Kurtz set out to almost duplicate Earhart's feat and establish a junior solo speed for a flight from Mexico City to Washington, D.C. He carried a goodwill letter from the president of Mexico to Pres. Franklin D. Roosevelt.

Unfortunately, Kurtz's flight was plagued with misfortune. He had to make four stops before landing at Floyd Bennett Field in New York City, without making his planned stop in Washington.[30] Leaving Corpus Christi, Texas, following a refueling, Kurtz ran into a storm over the Gulf of Mexico. Unable to determine his position, he battled the storm for four hours. As he was making preparations to abandon the airplane, Kurtz saw the lights of New Orleans and landed safely.

At his next stop in Atlanta, Kurtz was detained by customs agents, who were uncertain that he had properly cleared customs upon entering the United States from Mexico at Corpus Christi. He was cleared by Lawrence W. Robert Jr., assistant secretary of the treasury.[31] Although physically exhausted, Kurtz remained at Floyd Bennett Field only long enough to make temporary repairs on an engine exhaust valve before taking off for Newark Airport on his flight westward. The Newark Chamber of Commerce subsequently recognized his "record flight from Mexico City to Newark" by presenting him with a trophy.[32]

Kurtz had been a member of the U.S. Olympic diving team in the 1932 Olympics in Los Angeles, and was again in the 1936 Berlin Olympic Games. He became the first man to earn a place on three American Olympic teams when he was selected to go to the 1940 games in Finland that were subsequently canceled by the war.[33]

Following graduation from the University of California in 1937, Kurtz entered the Air Corps at Randolph Field, Texas. While a cadet, he was engaged in a public relations effort to stimulate recruitment. In the 1940 Army maneuvers, Kurtz served as an aide to nine generals. Assigned to the 19th Bombardment Group, Kurtz was a copilot on one of the twenty-one B-17s secretly flown by the 19th from the U.S. mainland to Hawaii on May 13–14, 1941. Captain Harry Schreiber of Galveston, Texas, who was to become the navigator on the Swoose, was a navigator on the same flight of B-17s that included the future Swoose. During the December 8, 1941, Japanese bombing and strafing attack on Clark Field, Kurtz and his navigator, Anthony E. Oliver, lost all of their crewmates and "Ole 99" (B-17D 40-3099), the airplane he commanded, when they were caught on the ground during the attack.[34]

Following combat service in the Dutch East Indies, Kurtz eventually returned to Australia, after leading seventy-six Americans to safety so they could board the last B-17s to leave Java. His next assignment would have a lasting impact on his future, as well as the survival of the Swoose. Kurtz was appointed by Col. Eugene Eubank to be General Brett's personal pilot and senior aide. Kurtz subsequently selected the crew that would serve under him.[35]

Kurtz directed his new crew chief, Sgt. Harold Varner, and his new engineer, Sgt. Roland A. Boone, to inspect the available B-17s at Laverton and identify those that might be suitable as General Brett's flagship. Following receipt of their report, Kurtz climbed through several of the B-17s to assess their condition. In addition to a visual inspection of the candidate aircraft, Kurtz reviewed the Form 1s and Form 40s for each of the aircraft to evaluate the deficiencies that had been reported by previous flight crews. On the basis of this survey, Kurtz selected B-17D 40-3097, now know as the Swoose.

The Swoose had fewer reported deficiencies than the other war-weary, scarred B-17s at Laverton. Additionally, the Swoose had not yet been cannibalized to the degree the others had; their installed equipment and parts had been used to keep the newer E models as close to combat-ready as possible. (Some of the machine guns had been used so much that the rifling in their barrels was worn smooth.) Most important, the Swoose alone still had its radio equipment and guns installed.[36]

Since the airplane would have to carry Brett and his staff into combat areas, its original armament was retained. Modifications were made to the radio compartment to provide a bench for sleeping and similar benches on each side of the fuselage in the waist-gunner compartment. Later, one side of the bomb bay was provided with a floor for carrying cargo. The other side of the bomb bay was occupied by the auxiliary fuel tank.[37]

The other members of Kurtz's hand-picked crew of the Swoose selected to serve General Brett included Lt. Marvin L. McAdams, the copilot, from Frederick, Maryland. The navigator was Lt. Harry J. Schreiber from Galveston, Texas. The engineer was Sgt. Roland A. Boone of Hemet, California, and Sgt. Charles Reeves of Bakersfield, California, who had been a bombardier, served as a gunner. Corporal Aubrey Fox of Dayton, Ohio, was the radio operator, and Sgt. Harold Varner of San Rafael, California, was crew chief. Since they traveled without escort fighters, the crew members were called upon to man the Swoose's guns on numerous occasions. The crew stayed with General Brett and the Swoose until November 1942, when the enlisted men were reassigned.

Much of the time during their Australian assignment, the crew was forced to live in the Swoose during overnight stays at advanced landing strips where General Brett made frequent visits. Sergeant Varner acted as housekeeper, making the morning coffee and rousing the crew and passengers from their makeshift sleeping quarters in the airplane.

Air Operations in Australia

From the time of its return to flying status in April 1942, until August 1, 1942, when both Kurtz and the plane left Australia, Kurtz estimated that the Swoose was flown 150 hours a month. The Swoose made many trips to advanced outposts in the Southwest Pacific and across the barren stretches of the interior of the Australian continent. Weekly trips were made to northern Australia and Port Moresby in the combat zone.[38]

Most trips carrying General Brett across the sea barrier to Port Moresby were planned so that the Swoose would arrive at nightfall. To protect the aircraft from the daily Japanese air attacks, the general's party would leave early the next morning.

On those occasions when the general planned to spend more than one day in Port Moresby, Kurtz would take off the next morning for Townsville, where he would wait. He would return at dusk for a takeoff with the general early the following morning. If the general's departure was delayed, Kurtz would take off and head out over the water for 30 or 40 minutes before coming back to recover the general and head back to Australia.

On occasion, the Swoose would clear the field at Port Moresby just as the air-raid alarm sounded. To avoid detection by the enemy, Kurtz would fly low over the water for the first 30 or 40 minutes en route to Australia. On one occasion, the Swoose was attacked by twelve Zeros as it departed Port Moresby. Because of this need to protect the Swoose, General Brett might get 60 hours per month in the airplane, 30 of them in a combat zone, while the Swoose and its crew logged 150 flying hours.[39]

Australia, almost as big as the United States, had most of its population in large cities—such as Sydney, Brisbane, Melbourne, and Adelaide—in a crescent running along its eastern and southern coasts. Similarly, most of the industry was grouped around the metropolitan area of these cities. West of the eastern crescent of these cities is a large semi-arid area that the Australians call the "outback." Beyond the outback is the western desert.

Each of the political subdivisions on the eastern coast had developed its own transportation system, including the railroads of varying gauges. Equipment loaded at Adelaide in the south would have to be loaded and unloaded several times before it arrived at its destination at Townsville, 2,500 miles away, where most of the 19th Bombardment Group was stationed.

In order to move equipment from Adelaide more than 2,000 miles north to Darwin, all cargo had to be transported first to Alice Springs, in the center of the continent, on a slow narrow-gauged railroad (there was no usable highway from Adelaide). A 600-mile highway had been constructed from Alice Springs to a railhead 200 miles south of Darwin, where cargo had to be loaded on another small-gauge railroad for transshipment into Darwin.[40]

These inefficient travel conditions made air transportation vital to the war effort. While Australia had developed a system of air ambulances in order to care for people who lived in its interior, because of the rocky nature of the land the airports could not easily be expanded for military operations without the use of heavy, earth-moving equipment.

When construction of operational strips large enough to accommodate heavy bombers began, the topsoil was moved and dust became a problem in aircraft engines, wheels, machine guns, and support equipment. Since blacktop was not available to cover the landing strips, the Australians used a trick discovered in the Philippines—they coated the landing strips with surplus molasses to hold the dust.

Most of the air operations took place in the northeastern and northwestern parts of Australia. For operations out of New Guinea, the bombers had to fly 1,000 miles from their bases on the northeast side of the mainland of Australia before reaching Port Moresby, their departure point for the raid. If Rabaul was the target, the pilots had to avoid the 14,000-foot Owen Stanley mountain range, which loomed within 60 miles of takeoff. They would first fly to Port Moresby, refuel, and then head for Rabaul, 550 miles away. This meant a total of 3,200 miles to make a single raid, or about 18 flying hours.

In February 1942, when General Brett took over as commander of the American forces, there was no large U.S. Army and Air Force, only one partially trained infantry division, some battered combat airplanes, and their weary crews. There were no large aircraft repair bases and few mechanics. It was necessary, therefore, to give aircraft overhaul jobs to civilian organizations.[41]

From the recently occupied island of Timor, the Japanese were able to launch air attacks on Darwin, 510 miles away. General Brett insisted on keeping bomber aircraft as far north in Australia as possible so they could strike at Japanese targets in northern New Guinea, Rabaul, Salamaua, Lae, Timor, and the Celebes. A Japanese plan to capture Port Moresby, as well as Fiji and other islands, would have isolated Australia from its main supply line to the United States. Aircraft were stationed at Townsville, Darwin, Adelaide, and Perth, as well as at Brisbane, Melbourne, and Sydney.[42]

Because of the transportation problems, the urgent supply needs to support the bases in the north had to be met with air transport. Every airplane that went north from Melbourne (Laverton) was loaded to capacity, but there were not enough airplanes to carry the needed supplies. In addition to the need to supply Australian bases, efforts also were made to airlift supplies to the beleaguered forces defending the Philippines. Whenever an airplane could be spared, it was sent to the Philippines with badly needed food, ammunition, and medical supplies.[43]

To support the northern Australian bases, as well as those in Port Moresby, and to support the northern movement of combat aircraft from Laverton to Brisbane, an inland ferry route was established, running down the center of Australia, from Cloncurry in the north to Laverton in the south. Refueling depots also were established at Charleville and Daly Waters for those who had to fly short-range aircraft. A route from Townsville to Darwin by way of Cloncurry and Daly Waters was developed for aircraft such as fighters with a range of less than 1,000 miles. High-frequency direction-finding radio stations were located at Townsville, Cloncurry, and Darwin, all of which were stops on scheduled flights of Qantas before the war began.

General MacArthur Evacuated to Australia

In Australia, General Brett was advised by General Marshall that General MacArthur would call for a flight of long-range combat aircraft to

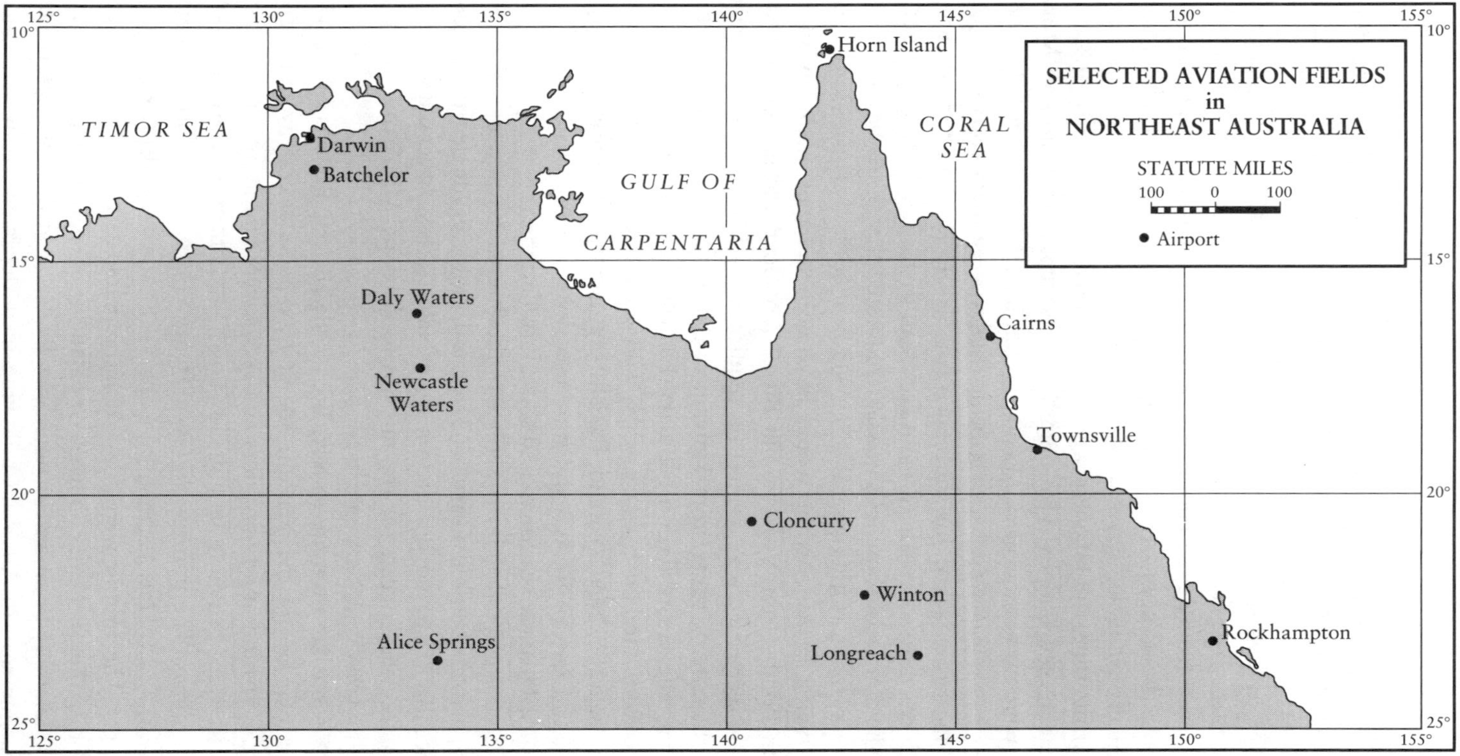

Selected aviation fields in northeast Australia.

transport a small group of passengers from Luzon in the Philippines to Australia prior to March 15. He interpreted this to mean that MacArthur had been ordered out of the Philippines.

The only long-range combat aircraft in General Brett's arsenal were the dozen B-17Cs and Ds that the 19th Bomb Group had evacuated to Australia from Java. These aircraft were in such bad shape that they should have been scrapped. Since they were the only long-range bombers available, they were kept flying.

At the time, the Japanese were on the other side of the Owen Stanley range in New Guinea. That natural barrier kept them from Port Moresby, which was their next invasion target, and the surviving B-17s, with their battle-weary crews, were being used to keep them away.

MacArthur asked for the best available airplanes in top condition, with the most experienced flight crews, to fly his family and staff out of the field at Del Monte. His message requested that B-24s be used if they were available. Otherwise, B-17s could be used.[44]

Obviously, MacArthur would have been unhappy with any of the 19th Bomb Group's B-17s, but there were no B-24s left in Australia. There seemed no way to meet his requirements. Using the newly opened southern ferry route from Hawaii, twelve new B-17Es had arrived in Townsville, Australia, on February 17. These aircraft were assigned to Vice Adm. Herbert F. Leary, USN, who commanded the waters of eastern Australia, New Zealand, British New Guinea, the Solomons, Loyalties, and Fijis (ANZAC) and were used by the Navy to support efforts against Japanese sea forces and shore installations.[45]

Brett attempted to borrow three of these relatively new B-17E aircraft assigned to Admiral Leary. The admiral, however, denied the request. Since Brett had no jurisdiction over Navy forces, he could not commandeer the aircraft for the mission to evacuate MacArthur from the Philippines.[46]

Without an alternate source, Brett ordered four B-17Ds of the 19th Bomb Group for the mission. The best available aircraft were assigned to the mission and their pilots and crews were among the most experienced, some of whom had already flown missions from Australia to the Philippines. The pilots were Capt. Henry Godman (the former pilot of 40-3097), Lt. Harl J. Pease Jr., Capt. G. F. Adams, and Lt. Kenneth D. Casper. The aircraft were checked and repaired as well as possible, considering their general condition, the paucity of spare parts, and the lack of availability of aircraft maintenance facilities. At Daly Waters, the first refueling stop in Australia following their departure from Melbourne,

Lieutenant Casper's airplane developed mechanical problems and was grounded.

Nothing was left undone. Weather reports were checked and rechecked before the remaining three aircraft took off from Darwin for Del Monte on March 13, 1942. Fifty miles north of Darwin, Captain Adams was forced to turn back because of engine trouble. And Henry Godman's airplane crashed off the coast of the Philippines (see chapter 3).

Only one of the aircraft reached its destination. The only B-17 still flying the evacuation mission was piloted by Lt. Harl Pease, one of the pilots who had ferried the first B-17s from the United States to Hawaii in May 1941, and subsequently pilot of another on the trans-Pacific flight to the Philippines from the United States as part of the 19th Group's transfer.

MacArthur waited at the Del Monte plantation clubhouse, expecting four new bombers to arrive and carry the group to safety in Australia. In addition to the general, the group consisted of his wife, their son and his Cantonese amah, Rear Adm. Francis Rockwell and his chief of staff, plus fourteen army officers. Much to their surprise, after waiting four days for their rescue aircraft, a lone B-17 touched down at the beleaguered airfield.[47]

The indignant MacArthur fired off the following message to Brett in Australia and General George Marshall in Washington:

> Only one of four planes arrived and that with an inexperienced pilot comma no brakes and supercharger not repeat not functioning stop This plane was returned to you by Gen. Sharp [Brigadier General William F. Sharp, commander of forces on Mindanao] since it was repeat not suitable for the purpose intended stop It is necessary that only the best planes and most experienced pilots of adequate service be employed for the transportation of such a party stop This trip is most important and desperate and must be set up with the greatest of care lest it end in disaster.[48]

While MacArthur's comments about the condition of the airplane were valid, Pease, while only a lieutenant, was not inexperienced. He was a veteran of many combat missions and had many flying hours of experience as a pilot of the B-17. (Killed in action on August 7, 1942, he was posthumously awarded the Congressional Medal of Honor.) Had MacArthur elected to accompany Pease on his return flight, he would have had a safe trip in spite of the condition of the airplane; however, the landing in Australia would have been exciting. Lieutenant Harry Schreiber was ordered to leave for Australia in Lieutenant Pease's airplane that had been rejected by MacArthur. Schreiber, who would become the navigator for General Brett after he acquired the Swoose, recalled Pease's memorable return flight from Del Monte to Darwin:

> If I remember correctly, there were 38 of us on the plane. I was directed to be the navigator and since we had no working superchargers and not enough oxygen for everyone, we flew back at 10,000 feet, going right down the line to Darwin, Australia, right over several islands, where we saw Japanese planes on the runways. Why they never came up to challenge us, I'll never know. We landed at Batchelor Field, about 60 miles south of Darwin, with no brakes. I can still remember barreling down the dirt runway, with Pease trying to slow us down by sweeping [the airplane] from side to side, and finally running through the stacks of inert bombs laid out at the end of the field. From here we were flown down to Laverton Field.[49]

Still faced with only the battered aircraft of the 19th Bomb Group from which to make his selection for an aircraft with which to evacuate MacArthur, Brett again made a plea for the new Navy B-17s. Apparently having heard from Washington in the interim, Admiral Leary quickly agreed to the loan of four airplanes.[50]

The four B-17E aircraft loaned to General Brett had been part of the 88th Reconnaissance Squadron of the 7th Bombardment Group. On December 7, 1941, the unit was on its way to reinforce the 19th Bomb Group in the Philippines. Their departure from the United States had been delayed two weeks while they waited for modification work on their airplanes to be completed. Finally, without ammunition, they departed before the work was done. The tail guns had not been installed and were packed in the airplanes. When attempts were made to install the guns in Hawaii, it was found that the guns were of the wrong type and would not fit.

The B-17E piloted by Frank Bostrom arrived over Hickam Field in Hawaii early that Sunday morning and was cleared to land by the control tower while the field was under attack by the Japanese. Noting that there was a war on, Bostrom climbed above the clouds, hoping to escape any attack on his unarmed craft. Japanese fighters shot at his B-17 three times that morning, damaging the fuel system. Losing fuel, Bostrom dropped through a hole in the clouds and landed safely on a golf course at Kahuka Point on the northeast corner of Oahu. Two days later, after repairs had been made, Bostrom took off from the golf course and landed at Hickam Field.

After spending the next two months at Hickam, Bostrom and the

88th Squadron of the AAF, under the command of Maj. R. H. Carmichael, were made part of Navy Task Force No. 17 operating with the carrier *Lexington*. In early February 1942, the squadron flew to Fiji by way of Christmas Island, Palmyra, and Canton. The squadron of B-17s operated out of Fiji for about a week, as part of a carrier task force scouting for Japanese sea forces. On February 17, the B-17Es flew to Townsville for a planned attack on Rabaul. That mission was canceled. On March 11, before the *Lexington* and the rest of the Navy task force moved into the Coral Sea, the B-17s of the 88th, following a similar raid by Navy aircraft from the *Lexington* and the *Yorktown* flew over the Owen Stanley range in New Guinea to bomb the Japanese at Lae and Salamaua, sinking two enemy ships, starting fires on four, and forcing one to be beached. This was to be the last mission of these B-17s as part of Navy Task Force No. 17.

When this unit was ordered to participate in the MacArthur evacuation, the copilot on board each B-17 was replaced with a pilot from the 19th Bomb Group who was familiar with operations at Del Monte. Lieutenant Edward Teats was assigned to Bostrom's airplane. Of the four B-17s loaned to Brett, only two left Australia for Del Monte. One had engine trouble and was forced to land en route to Batchelor Field, while the other aircraft remained at Batchelor Field as it lacked bomb-bay fuel tanks for the long overwater flight.[51]

The two remaining B-17s left Batchelor Field at 2 P.M. on March 16 and landed at Del Monte at 11:30 P.M., guided by light from two flares at either end of the field. General MacArthur and his family boarded Bostrom's B-17 and took off for Australia at 2:30 A.M. Landing at Batchelor Field at 10 A.M. on March 17, the MacArthur party disembarked and were subsequently flown on to Alice Springs by the B-17 that had not flown to Del Monte because of engine trouble. The other B-17 that did not participate in the evacuation was sent to Del Monte to retrieve the baggage.[52]

Arrangements had been made for two Douglas DC-3 aircraft borrowed from a commercial airline to carry MacArthur and the other evacuees to Melbourne from Batchelor Field, near Darwin. But MacArthur refused to fly any further. Advised that he would have to travel 600 miles over unpaved roads to reach the railhead at Alice Springs, MacArthur reluctantly agreed to fly that far.[53]

After more than a three-day train ride from Alice Springs, MacArthur arrived in Melbourne. In accordance with a prearranged plan, on March 18 General Brett turned over to him command of all U.S. forces in Australia.[54] Subsequently, the government of Australia and New Zealand nominated MacArthur as the supreme commander of the Allied Forces in the Southwest Pacific. General Brett became MacArthur's deputy for command of the U.S. Army Air Forces and then on April 20 of all Allied air forces in the Southwest Pacific.[55]

Unknown to General Brett, on March 21, within hours of his arrival in Melbourne, MacArthur sent a radio message to Washington that would mark the end of Brett's service in Australia and thereby extend the life of the Swoose. From his hotel, MacArthur sent a message stating that it was "most essential as a fundamental and primary step that Brett be released" from his assignment in Australia.[56]

Chapter 5

The Swoose in the News

Australian Sojourn and Fame

The Swoose's name probably first received media attention as the result of several articles written by Lee Van Atta, a war correspondent for the International News Service. The stories apparently captured the imagination of an American public looking for good news after the Pearl Harbor attack and the subsequent retreats of Allied forces throughout the Pacific.

Van Atta accompanied General Brett on many of his trips and was able to file elaborate stories about the adventures of the Swoose and its young pilot, Frank Kurtz. In one of his stories, Van Atta told of a takeoff with "twelve ranking Air Staff officers" during a raid by thirty-five Japanese Zeros. He went on to describe a hair-raising escape from the twelve Zeros pursuing the Swoose.[1]

Another of Van Atta's stories concerned a Swoose mission that included a takeoff from an 860-foot airstrip deep in mud to carry an injured soldier to a hospital 400 miles away. Still other Van Atta stories detailed the Swoose's "crash landing" in the Australian bush with twelve passengers—including three generals—and a recordbreaking flight from Australia to Hawaii to expedite a Royal Air Force officer's return to England.[2]

Another who detailed the Swoose's escapades in news stories during the Australian assignment was Col. John K. Gowen, then the USAF public relations officer in the Southwest Pacific, who also accompanied General Brett in the Swoose on many of its flights. Colonel Gowen had been General Brett's aide during his assignment in London in 1941.

Gowen wrote two stories that were widely used. One of these appeared in the *Boeing News* of September 1942, and the other in the *Air Force Times* of October 1942. They appear to have been written following General Brett's return to the United States. An earlier fact-filled story by Gowen was written during the Australian assignment and contained information typical of those initiated by military public information offices.[3]

Of course, the most widely read stories about the Swoose were contained in William L. White's bestseller, *Queens Die Proudly.* Written from information obtained from interviews with the Swoose's crew members following their return to the United States in August 1942, the book, although censored, told some of the stories of the 19th Bombardment Group at Clark Field on December 8, 1941. A condensed version of the book also appeared in *Reader's Digest.*

The stories filed by war correspondents also engendered a number of cartoon strips in newspapers across America, describing some of the events in the adventures of the Swoose and its crew. These too must have captured the imagination of the American public and furthered the fame of the Swoose and its pilot. While some of those stories written about the Swoose's early adventures in the Philippines were based on conjecture, those written during the time when it operated as General Brett's staff plane were basically accurate.

Brigadier General Ralph Royce and Brett alternated on the Swoose trips to advanced posts in the combat zone. On these trips, the Swoose carried fruit juices, candy, cigars, and cigarettes, as well as other necessities and luxuries to improve the morale of the airmen who lived and worked under primitive conditions.[4]

Record Flight to Hawaii

In May 1942, just after one of the missions to Port Moresby, the Swoose was loaned to Air Chief Marshall Sir Charles Burnett of the Royal Air Force, the ranking British air officer in Australia. For more than two years, Marshall Burnett, known as the "White Eagle," had been in command of the Royal Australian Air Force as chief of the Air Staff. But now he had been called back to England.[5]

The Swoose, with Lieutenant Kurtz as pilot and Colonel Gowen as passenger, was assigned to carry Marshall Burnett as far as Honolulu. Having started his career in aviation as a challenger of speed records, Kurtz planned to use the flight mission to break Pacific speed records set by the famous Australian airman Sir Charles Kingsford-Smith.[6]

On May 17, 1942, the Swoose and its two passengers were flown from Sydney, Australia, to Woodburne Air Field (Wellington), New Zealand, the southern terminus of the recently opened mid-Pacific ferry route, in 5 hours and 10 minutes.[7] This broke the 13-hour record for the 1,300-mile crossing of the Tasmanian Sea set in March 1933 by Sir Charles Kingsford-Smith.

While in New Zealand, the crew removed all of the guns and armor plate to reduce the airplane's weight. Since the route north to Honolulu would be outside the combat zone, armament would not be needed. The temporary floor in the bomb bay was removed, as well as the manual bomb hoists. In addition to reducing the weight of the airplane, Sergeant Varner arranged for members of the Royal New Zealand Women's Auxiliary Air Force to spend about 30 hours applying wax to the airplane's exterior. Kurtz felt that this added about 14 knots to the Swoose's cruising speed.[8]

Only one stop for fuel was made between New Zealand and Honolulu, at Canton in the Phoenix Islands, which lasted only one hour. The flight from Canton to Honolulu of 23 hours and 7 minutes broke another of Sir Charles Kingsford-Smith's records established in 1934, when he flew the same 3,150-mile route in 25 hours on his Brisbane-to-Oakland flight.[9]

Before leaving the airplane in Honolulu, Marshall Burnett added his testimonial by writing in red paint beneath the words, "It Flys," on the Swoose's logo, "I'll say it does." However, no photographic evidence exists to confirm any such alterations to Weldon Smith's original logo. On the return flight to Melbourne via Christmas Island and New Zealand the Swoose encountered heavy icing and was forced to carry the additional load because it no longer had any de-icing equipment.[10]

On the flight leg from Hawaii to Christmas Island, the Swoose carried a load of mail for the troops stationed on that isolated speck in the Pacific. Kurtz took great pride in being able to contribute to the joy of the troops at their long-delayed mail call.[11]

General Brett commented that MacArthur's headquarters took note of what normally would have been a matter of minor importance: the assignment of the Swoose to carry Marshall Burnett to Honolulu. He said headquarters, while ignoring such questions of importance to the conduct of the war as command, control of antiaircraft batteries, and promotions in the combat zone, on this occasion bombarded him with caustic notes and directives.[12]

A Future President's Adventure in the Swoose

By the end of March 1942, the survivors of the 19th Bombardment Group were headquartered in Mareeba, about 200 miles north of Townsville. From Mareeba they continued to fly long-range missions against the Japanese in northern New Guinea by staging through Port Moresby. They also were able to mount attacks on the big Japanese base at Rabaul in New Britain.

On May 7 and 8, a Japanese invasion fleet attempting to approach the Port Moresby area—the last Allied base on the western end of the island—was met and turned back by U.S. Navy carrier-based aircraft. Known as the Battle of the Coral Sea, this was the first fight in history between aircraft carriers, and it resulted in the turning back of the invasion force, permanently halting the Japanese drive by sea toward Australia.

The Swoose carried many important people during its Australian sojourn, and would in future years carry heads of state as well. One of its important passengers was aboard when the Swoose made a forced landing that could have changed the course of U.S. history had the airplane crashed.

President Roosevelt had asked Lt. Cmdr. Lyndon B. Johnson, then on leave from his seat in the U.S. House of Representatives, to make a fact-finding trip to the Southwest Pacific to check on the condition of troops under General MacArthur's command. The president feared that MacArthur's reports were unreliable because of the general's unhappiness with the situation in Australia. Roosevelt also wanted to check on rumors that MacArthur was treating even high-ranking Air Force officers with disdain.[13]

Johnson departed on his mission from the United States on May 7, 1942, and arrived in Sydney, Australia, at 10:30 on the morning of June 3, 1942. That same day, he boarded the Swoose for his inspection tour of Australia and a visit to the combat area at Port Moresby. Accompanying Johnson on his inspection were Brig. Gen. William F. Marquat of

MacArthur's staff, Lt. Col. Francis Stevens, and Lt. Col. Samuel Anderson. Marquat was a former Seattle reporter who had joined MacArthur's operations staff in 1937. During the subsequent occupation of Japan, he led efforts to restore Japan's war-ravaged industry, remaining on MacArthur's staff until 1951.[14]

According to Johnson's diary the Swoose departed Sydney at 10:45 A.M. on June 4 for the trip north that included stops at Brisbane, Rockhampton, MacKay, and Torrence Creek. They arrived at Townsville on June 7. The leg of the trip to Port Moresby and high adventure in a combat mission began on June 9, as the Swoose left Townsville for the 700-mile flight across the Coral Sea to Port Moresby, New Guinea. Of the Swoose's flight to Port Moresby, Johnson wrote in his diary that the group got up at 2 A.M., June 9, left for the airport at 2:30, and was in the air by 3:15. For three hours during the flight, they almost froze. Trying to get warm, Johnson wrote that he "stood up, beat my legs, stomped my feet, put on wind-breaker, sweater, fur coat, etc., to no avail."[15] That was a typical commentary on the inefficiency of military aircraft heating systems of the day.

Johnson took home movies on his trip, one of which had the following narrative of the visit to Australia and New Guinea:

> W. B. Courtney, Collier's war correspondent, in October issue says of his experiences with us: "Of course, anyone living day by day with sudden death, pilots—or war correspondents either, for that matter—can't afford superstitions. Aside from a horse chestnut you picked up, and a necktie you wore the day you soloed, a red and blue checkered handkerchief that someone dear gave to you long ago, you stuff your own pockets with a few 'conjurs.' Which brings up the first three pictures of this war that you'll never forget: You are in a B-17, flying through the night over the Coral Sea to New Guinea to catch an early morning 'show.' It is bitter cold, at 15,000 feet. The plane's stripped for action; flying without lights, inside or out. The floor's the only place to sit. Dim starlight through the roof windows, plus the natural accommodation of your eyes to the darkness, reveal your companions in various uneasy attitudes, cramped, stiff—and thoughtful. Some of them are going to fly in the dawn raid over Salamaua. The Colonel, for instance. You notice that he is sitting on your small handbag and you growl at him not to break anything. One hour later, he is dead—shot down into shark-infested sea. That night in your hut at Port Moresby, when you unpack your bag, you find your shaving mirror is broken."[16]

The Johnson party arrived at Port Moresby at 7:45 that morning. Shortly after disembarking from the Swoose, Johnson and his two traveling companions, Lieutenant Colonel Stevens and Colonel Anderson, were placed on board three separate twin-engine B-26 Marauders of the 22nd Bomb Group that were about to take off on a bombing mission over the Japanese-held airfield at Lae, on the northeastern coast of New Guinea. Johnson's airplane, "The Heckling Hare," was piloted by Capt. Walter H. Greer. Anderson's pilot was 1st Lt. Walter A. Krell and Stevens's pilot was 2nd Lt. Willis G. Bench. General Marquat flew in a B-26 piloted by Lt. R. R. Hatch.[17]

Because of a generator failure, the airplane carrying Johnson dropped out of formation before the target was reached.[18] It turned for home just minutes before the rest of the formation appeared, pursued by Japanese fighters. The B-26 carrying Stevens crashed into the sea, killing the occupants. The remaining B-26s returned safely.[19]

The B-26s were supposed to have followed a flight of B-25s to the target, the aerodrome at Lae. The B-25s were to bomb off to the side of the enemy airfield and draw the enemy fighters, while the B-26s arrived and bombed the airfield from low altitude. Unfortunately, the B-26s were late in following up and encountered the B-25s and their pursuing Zeros. The enemy aircraft left the B-25s and instead attacked the approaching B-26s.[20]

On June 18, when Johnson and Anderson met MacArthur in Melbourne, the general surprised the visitors with the Silver Star medal for their participation on the Lae mission. MacArthur posthumously awarded the Distinguished Flying Cross to Lieutenant Colonel Stevens.[21]

At 7:10 A.M. on June 10, the day after their arrival at Port Moresby, Johnson and the remaining passengers reboarded the Swoose for the return trip to Australia. Their final destination was Melbourne (Laverton Field). At 12:30 P.M. they arrived at Batchelor Field, their first stop in Australia. They drove from Batchelor Field to Darwin to spend the night.

The next morning at 7 A.M., they took off in the Swoose for the long flight across the rugged, desolate interior of the Australian continent. Their first refueling stop was scheduled to be Charleville, but this leg of the journey would come to a premature end. That afternoon, the Swoose made a forced landing on the rock-strewn Australian outback, near a sheep station known as Carisbrooke, about 48 miles from the town of Winton. The town was about 336 miles southeast of Cloncurry and 190 miles west of Longreach.

According to Johnson's itinerary, the grounded travelers stayed at Carisbrooke Station until 7:30 that evening, when they left by motor vehicle for the four-hour, 35-mile trip to Winton. In a story he filed with the International News Service, Lee Van Atta, one of two war correspondents aboard the Swoose, described the events as follows:[22]

Miracle Landing Spares General

Pilot of Fortress Lands on "Stamp" in Bush Country

United Nations headquarters in Australia, June 14—Capt. Frank Kurtz, United States Air Force hero, accomplished another in his list of brilliant feats yesterday when he brought his passenger-laden Flying Fortress down to a forced landing on the rock-strewn Australian desert.

By so doing, the former Olympic diving star from Glendale, California, saved the lives of two Generals, a United States Congressman now in the service, half a dozen other ranking officers, himself and his crew—not to mention the life of this correspondent.

After flying inspection tour of advance bases, our Flying Fortress was heading homeward early yesterday.

We carried a minimum load of gasoline to conserve supplies at our forward bases. And we went on, not knowing of the weather conditions because our bomber's radio was "dead" for reasons of security.

For eight hours we fought every weather element—electrical storms, roaring winds, and blistering rain—before our navigator announced that we had been blown off our course and apparently were lost over the desert.

Occupants of the plane included: Brigadier General Ralph Royce, Senior Air Staff Officer for the United Nations Air Commander Lieutenant General George H. Brett, Brigadier General Marquat of Seattle, anti-aircraft officer for United Nations Chief Commander General Douglas MacArthur, Lieutenant Commander Lyndon Johnson, youthful Texas Democrat and member of the United States House of Representatives, now in active service, Colonel Samuel Anderson of Greensboro, N.C., and Washington, D.C., general staff corps officer, Colonel Edwin Perrin, Deputy Chief of the Air Staff, W. B. Courtney, well known New York magazine writer.

Then there were Kurtz, his co-pilot, Lieutenant Marvin MacAdam[s] of Baltimore; his navigator, Lieutenant Harry Schreiber of Galveston, Texas, and myself. With only a few minutes' supply of gas left, Kurtz began circling, hoping to find an emergency landing spot. There were only rocks and the famed Australian bush below us and reaching ahead for miles.

Lands on Postage Stamp

Then, far off on the distant horizon we saw a small farm house. The cleared space by the farm house looked almost infinitesimal but Kurtz headed for it.

As the altimeter dropped below 1,000 feet, Kurtz ordered everyone to go to the tail of the bomber to give the ship better balance. From the tail we watched Kurtz and MacAdam[s] fight the battle to decide our fate and that of a $250,000 piece of Uncle Sam's fighting equipment. Seconds before we landed, Kurtz turned around, gave us a wink and shot up his right thumb cheerfully.

Then we were down. There was a tremendous bounce as we rode over a big boulder, but the plane stood that nicely. General Royce raced to the cockpit. "Thanks, Frankie!" he yelled, slapping Kurtz on the back. "That was the sweetest job I've ever seen."

From the farm house General Royce telephoned a United Nations base several hundred miles away for gasoline and help. It was arranged that Kurtz and his crew would try to get the plane off the next morning when the gasoline arrived. The remainder of our party would proceed to the nearest base by automobile to be dispatched to us.

For six hours we waited for signs of our relief party. The farm house was so small that only two of us were able to take advantage of its warmth at one time. Inasmuch as Generals Royce and Marquat got themselves engaged in a furious cribbage game by candlelight, the rest of our party shivered outside disconsolately and fought mosquitoes.

Johnson made a terrific lunge at one mosquito and suggested that someone write a song dedicated to him and entitled, "I Wish I Were Still on Capitol Hill." Our morale was sinking rapidly when we saw lights flickering far off in the desert. Finally aboard three automobiles of 1920 vintage, we set off for a village nearly one hundred miles away. Our road was a sheep path and our drivers had no conception of any speed limits. Courtney believed he had lost a leg going over our three hundredth obstruction, while Colonel Anderson claimed four kangaroos had passed through the car when we roared through a mosquito clump. To make things worse, the vehicle in which General Royce was riding broke down about halfway. We decided to continue by foot, with only General Royce's pocket flashlight to guide our footsteps. We had not gone far when Royce's light disclosed a husky rock python in the path. We returned headlong to our cars and patiently awaited repairs.

After four more hours we reached a sleepy village of two hundred or three hundred inhabitants only to discover that our base was at least another seventeen hours drive away. But Kurtz again saved the day. Early this morning his big fortress buzzed over the village. As Kurtz circled overhead, Royce said, "I'll bet he tries a landing here." Kurtz not only tried a landing but made it. We ran across the open field and gladly climbed back into the bomber which speedily brought us back to the base.

In an October 17, 1942, issue of *Collier's* weekly magazine, W. B. Courtney, the second war correspondent on the Swoose, described the same event in the following terms:

We're in another B-17, cruising aimlessly over the unbelievably empty never-never land of interior Australia. We're lost. Night fall is approaching and you all know—thirteen passengers and seven crew—that you've got to make a forced landing in the inhospitable wilderness in the next few minutes. The pilot—a youthful major, veteran of the Philippines and Java, not a day over twenty-five, you'd bet—is scanning the ground. His face is sober. Little beads of sweat on the bridge of his nose betray his feelings. He has a ship full of brass hats to add to his worries. He looks at you, behind the co-pilot's seat. He looks back into the plane at his passengers; stares down again, at the earth. Then, with a grin that suddenly dissolves the anxiety in his face, and a lilt that reminds you of Gracie Fields and her "aspidistra" song, he leans over to you, indicates all of Australia below us with an inclusive jerk of his head and says, "There's the biggest hunk of nothing in the world."[23]

Lyndon Johnson recorded his personal observations of the events that occurred on the Swoose flight to Melbourne from Port Moresby as follows:

Wednesday, June 10. Up at 5:30. Left Port Moresby at 7:10 a.m. Gen. Royce puts me in pilot's compartment. He takes controls. Pass over Horn and Thursday Island. 8:55 a.m. flying at 5,000 feet, heavy overcast, we try out guns. Very comfortable flying—still trying guns. Land at Batchelor at 12:30. Batchelor is 40 miles from Darwin.

Thursday, June 11. Up at 5:30, left Darwin at 7:05. Beautiful takeoff. Lovely sunrise. Thought of Miss Jesus plenty. Now over desert. It's 10:10 the time our bombs were to drop on Lae. We are going through middle of Australia en route to Charleville. At 11:00 we discover that we are lost due to arrive Gloncurry [*sic*] but can't find it. Then 4 hours of roaming—from 2:30 to 3:30 very tense. Three Generals in pilot's cabin, Andy and I looking at each other. We circle pasture and take bearing. We climb, we circle. Now we are looking at parachutes—now [*sic*] place to land—select windmill and pasture. Kurtz then moves all to tail—down we come bump a bomb bum. We made it. All out doors. Flies by the million, beer, maps, natives then telephone. Five hour wait, wrecks pick us up. Terrible ride. 48 long miles to Winton—North Gregory Hotel (Adams Hotel) Ham and eggs and drink—to bed at 12. Up at six. What a day. (Tough shaving—no bath—plenty mosquitoes. Off to Longreach.) Hope this better day.

Friday, June 12. Up at six. Shaved, breakfast and off to plane which had gotten gas at five. Off to Longreach at 8 a.m. Fine flying still desert. Land at Longreach. General Royce leaves us at 11. We are off to Melbourne and civilization. Due Melbourne at 5:30. Courtney in pilot's seat. We have 1600 gallons of gas—yesterday taught us. Had good tail wind. Arrived Melbourne 4:00.

In a conversation with the author, forty-six years after the event, Harry Schreiber, the Swoose's navigator, added his recollection of the flight with Johnson.[24] On the return flight to Melbourne, they had departed Port Moresby and landed at Darwin for refueling. The airplane, loaded with thirteen passengers, forced the navigator to share his small compartment in the nose with a couple of newspaper people and their photographic equipment. They had taken off from Batchelor Field with less than a full load of fuel. At the time it was standard practice to limit the fuel load to minimize drain on fuel stores at each refueling stop in Australia.

In the tight quarters of his crowded compartment, and lacking navigation aids, Schreiber laid out a dead-reckoning course designed so that the airplane would pass 30 miles west of the true course he wanted to follow to Charleville, the next refueling stop. This procedure would keep him well over land and allow a turn to the left upon reaching the estimated time of arrival (ETA), bringing the plane over the station at Charleville. During the trip, various passengers were invited to take over the controls and handle the big airplane. Of course, these maneuvers may have contributed to the navigator's problems.

When possible, the navigator of an airplane flying by dead-reckoning is required to take several celestial sightings to aid in updating his position. The airplane's position over the earth's surface is determined from these and other calculations. As Schreiber took his sightings of the sun, he reported to Kurtz that each of the readings differed significantly from the previous readings, making the observations useless for calculating their position. The cause of the spurious readings was attributed to a loose set-screw in the navigator's octant, the delicate instrument used for observing the geometric relationship of celestial bodies to the earth.[25]

During these early days of the war, radio silence was required of all Australian ground stations and aircraft; it was not even possible to get a routine report on weather conditions. As the ETA approached, Schreiber called Cloncurry for a radio bearing so that he could correct his course to that station. Knowing that the Swoose had VIPs on board and that the aircraft was west of his station and therefore not an enemy airplane, the ground radio station gave them a bearing. Because Schreiber was expecting a steering course to the station, he advised Kurtz to turn to the compass reading.[26]

Thirty minutes later, recognizing that they were flying 180 degrees from the course they wanted, Schreiber advised the pilot that a 180-degree turn was necessary. By then, they had about three hours of fuel remaining and were about 200 miles southwest of Cloncurry, another of the midcontinent refueling depots.[27]

The weather was clear and the crew had been in the air about six hours as Kurtz brought the Swoose down to 5,000 feet from his cruising altitude of 15,000 feet and began flying a box search pattern to locate Cloncurry, or some other navigational landmark. Finally, with about one hour and 15 minutes of fuel remaining, and only 40 to 50 minutes until sunset, Kurtz elected to make a landing rather than subject his VIP cargo to the further risk of a forced landing at night.

Kurtz picked a relatively smooth area near some farm buildings where his landing run would end up a slight incline, to help shorten the landing roll. During his landing approach, Kurtz noticed out of the corner of his eye what appeared to be a long, straight dirt road near the town of Winton. It was there that his passengers were taken and he planned to pick them up at the road the next day.

Soon after the Swoose landed, members of the Carisbrooke sheep station greeted them and arranged for the passengers to be taken to the station, and driven from there to Winton about 35 miles away over an unpaved road. After his passengers had departed, Kurtz and his crew lifted the tail of the Swoose and carried it up the incline so that their takeoff the next morning would be downhill. They cleared the takeoff path of the rocks and boulders that they were able to move by hand. The crew also serviced the airplane as best they could, from low-octane automobile fuel supplies stored at the sheep station. This gasoline doubled the fuel load already in the Swoose's wing tanks.[28]

The next morning, the Swoose took off downhill and flew on to retrieve its passengers at Winton, the sleepy village referred to in Courtney's report. The Swoose and its recovered load of VIPs took off from the dirt road at 8 A.M. on the morning of June 12 for the relatively short flight to Longreach, the nearest refueling station. By 11:10 that same morning they were on their way to Melbourne, where they arrived at 4:20 P.M.[29]

Brett's Combat Problems

Compelled to send fighter pilots into combat with fewer than 10 hours of experience in an airplane type, Brett's task was complicated by the number and types of U.S. aircraft in Australia.[30] The number of aircraft in General Brett's arsenal was beginning to grow as a result of the opening of the South Pacific ferry route and from the cargo holds and decks of ships carrying crated aircraft. In addition to the B-17, the aircraft inventory now included such diverse types as the Douglas A-20 Havoc twin-engine bomber, the Douglas A-24 single-engine attack bomber the

Navy called "Dauntless"; the North American B-25 Mitchell twin-engine medium bomber; the Martin B-26 Marauder twin-engine medium bomber; the Bell P-39 and P-400 Airacobra single-engine fighters (the P-400s had been manufactured for the British but were repossessed by the United States for shipment to Australia following the attack on Pearl Harbor); as well as the ubiquitous Curtiss single-engine, liquid-cooled P-40 Warhawk, and an assortment of transport aircraft.

Many of these aircraft types produced unique operational problems. For example, the P-39 engines would sputter and wheeze as the pilots tried to get enough altitude to reach overflying Mitsubishi bombers at 25,000 feet. In a desperate attempt to attack, the pilots would fire their guns at the top of their climb in the hopes of hitting one of their targets before falling off in a spin from the lack of power. The faster, more maneuverable Zeros had high ceilings as well.

To increase their combat range, one squadron of fighters stationed at Port Moresby was stripped of armor and everything else except one .50-caliber machine gun. When a raid came, the squadron was held on the ground until the last minute, whereupon they would then use their planes as decoys for the Japanese aircraft to follow until their fuel was low. Kill ratios for this squadron were about seven Japanese to one of the Allies. The A-24 dive bombers should not have been used; however, they saw action in a desperate attempt to stop the Japanese. Casualties among the A-24 pilots were exceptionally high.

The stubby-winged Martin B-26 was in its test stage in Australia. It was known as the "Flying Prostitute," because the plane had no visible means of support. It was feared by some that if one of the B-26's two engines failed on takeoff, the plane would crash. One day General Brett made six takeoffs in the nose of the B-26 to convince the pilots (even the veterans) that if he could take it so could they.[31]

On July 1, 1942, the Swoose was flown from Laverton to its new home base at Brisbane, where MacArthur had moved the general headquarters. On this flight, General Brett was accompanied by Col. John K. Gowen Jr., Maj. Roscoe T. Nichols Jr., and Capt. John F. DeVos. The crew was composed of Capt. Frank A. Kurtz, 1st Lt. Harry J. Schreiber, 2nd Lt. Marvin L. MacAdams, M. Sgt. Roland A. Boone, T. Sgt. Charles T. Reeves, S. Sgt. Edgar W. English, and Cpl. Aubrey J. Fox.

On July 26, 1942, after a tenuous relationship with General MacArthur and his staff, Brett was advised by MacArthur that he was to be replaced by Maj. Gen. George C. Kenney. General Kenney had been advised he was replacing Brett on July 11.[32] Kenney, an old friend of Brett's from their earlier days at Wright Field in Dayton, Ohio, had arrived in Australia on July 28, two days before the friends met. That evening, at Brett's invitation, Kenney borrowed the Swoose for a quick inspection trip to Port Moresby, New Guinea, and the airfields near Townsville. With Kenney on board, the Swoose took off from Brisbane at 11 P.M. that same evening, arriving at Townsville four hours later.[33]

At Townsville, they picked up Maj. Gen. Ralph Royce, Brig. Gen. Ennis C. Whitehead, and an Australian civilian named Robinson. Shortly after daybreak New Guinea was sighted, and at 7 A.M. the Swoose landed at Seven-Mile Strip, just north of Port Moresby. According to Kenney, after he deplaned, the Swoose departed for Horn Island, off the northeast coast of Australia, to avoid the daily morning Japanese air attacks launched from Lae, Salamaua, and Buna on the north coast of New Guinea.[34]

Seven-Mile Strip was normally used only for refueling for the Australian-based B-17s, B-25s, and B-26s on their missions north. The Swoose thus escaped a noon raid on the base at Port Moresby by twelve enemy bombers, escorted by fifteen fighters; only four minutes of warning preceded the attack.

The Swoose returned to Port Moresby early the next morning (July 31) to recover its passengers for the return flight to Townsville. That same afternoon, they flew to Mareeba, the air depot at Charter Towers, where the 19th Bombardment Group was then based. Later that same day, they were airborne again for the return trip to Brisbane.

As happened many times in the history of the Swoose, its prospects rested precariously. The airplane was already obsolete. At the time when General Brett was ordered to return to the United States, the Swoose could not have lasted much longer under the stress of operational conditions in a foreign war zone. In far-off Australia the gallant, aged, patched-up airplane was probably destined for the same conclusion as many of its former contemporaries, to become a valuable source of critical parts for later model B-17s that were now carrying the war to enemy strongholds in the north. But once again fate had other plans for the Swoose.

The regular shuttle flight from Hawaii that had been due to arrive in Sydney on August 1 had been temporarily withdrawn to provide higher priority service between Honolulu and San Francisco. Since Brett had been ordered to return to the United States without delay, he had to find an alternate airplane for the trip.

Brett approached Kenney with a request that the Swoose and its crew be used for the flight. Following Kenney's agreement, on July 30, 1942, the day he was officially relieved from his assignment in Australia, Brett visited General MacArthur, the commander-in-chief, South West Pacific Area, to ask for his approval to utilize the Swoose and its crew for the trip to the United States.

Brett agreed to return the airplane as soon as possible, if it was in suitable condition for the long trans-Pacific flight. However, he pointed out to MacArthur, the airplane was obsolete and would probably need a complete overhaul of its engines and superchargers before it could be made ready for the return flight. As for the crew, Brett stressed that as combat veterans they had significant potential as instructors in USAAF technical schools. General MacArthur agreed that as former chief of Allied Air Forces, General Brett should return to the United States in his own airplane. He left to Brett's good judgment the decision regarding the airplane's return.

At dawn on August 4, 1942, the Swoose, piloted by the newly promoted Maj. Frank Kurtz, with General Brett and Col. E. S. Perrin aboard, departed Australia for the last time. Upon his arrival in Washington, Brett asked that MacArthur's headquarters be advised that the Swoose was unfit for further operational service and would remain in the United States.[35]

Three days after the Swoose left Australia, the Allied offensive began with the First Marine Division's invasion of Guadalcanal and Tulagi in the Solomon Islands, about 600 miles east of New Guinea. The B-17Es used in support of that operation were originally built for the British. Still in their original British camouflage paint, the aircraft were flown to New Caledonia from Hawaii in July by the 11th Bombardment Group.[36] It would be more than another year before the ground offensive in New Guinea would begin, when paratroopers were dropped behind enemy lines on September 7, 1943.

Homeward Bound

General Brett estimated that while the Swoose was assigned to him during his Australian tour, the aircraft flew an average of 150 hours a month. Its crew and the airplane had performed with great reliability, which probably is directly attributable to the excellent maintenance provided by the crew and its ground-support personnel. During the next phase of its history, the airplane and its pilot became well-known heroes to the people at home.

On August 4, 1942, leaving the combat zones of the Southwest Pacific, the Swoose was about to establish still another new speed record across the Pacific to the United States. The homeward bound flight from Brisbane, Australia, to Hickam Field in Hawaii, and then to Hamilton Field near San Francisco on August 7, took 36 hours and 10 minutes of actual flying time. This remarkable flight set a record from Australia to the U.S. mainland that later was broken by a Consolidated C-87, the cargo version of the B-24. Carrying Gen. Hap Arnold, it made the trip in 35 hours and 53 minutes when it landed on October 1, 1942. The Swoose became the first combat bomber to return from the war zone to the United States.[37]

The transcontinental flight to its new home base at Bolling Field in Washington, D.C., started at Hamilton Field where, sixteen months earlier the Swoose had embarked on its flight westward to Hawaii and subsequently across the Pacific. Heading east from Hamilton Field, the Swoose now had another passenger; Mrs. Mary Devol Brett joined the list of passengers. On August 10, 1942, the Swoose landed in Omaha. When the plane departed the next morning, Mrs. Margo Kurtz was also on board the flight carrying the veterans of the Pacific war to Washington. The Swoose landed in Washington on August 12 after flying 47 hours from Brisbane.[38]

On August 17, 1942, the Swoose was flown from Bolling Field to Miami, Florida. On August 20, 1942, the Swoose was flown to the Army Air Force repair facility at the Middletown Air Depot outside of Harrisburg, Pennsylvania, where it remained until August 26. Apparently, General Brett remained in Miami, for on August 22 the first public announcement was made of his arrival in the United States. On that day, he addressed a graduating class at the Army Air Force Technical Training Command in Miami Beach. It was not until September 16 that MacArthur announced that Brett had been replaced by Kenney.[39]

On August 29, with General Brett on board, Kurtz and the Swoose were en route on another transcontinental flight when some maintenance work was performed at the North American plant in Wichita, Kansas.[40] From Wichita, they flew to Lowry Field in Denver, Colorado, where it was announced that Brett would tour the United States and visit aircraft manufacturers and Air Force commands to give them the benefit of lessons learned in the Southwest Pacific. Accompanying General Brett and his regular flight crew were Colonel Perrin, Lt. Col. L. B. Kelly, and Maj. John F. DeVos.

On August 31, the Swoose and its crew flew from Denver to the airplane's birthplace, the Boeing Aircraft Company in Seattle.[41] The tour of cities and military installations was interrupted when the Swoose returned to Bolling Field on September 30, 1942, preparatory to being flown on October 20 to the Middletown Air Depot for repairs, where it remained for six days before returning to Bolling Field. In his memo to General Arnold of September 7, 1942, Brett commented that the airplane "has already spent at least forty percent of the time since its return, in depots getting new superchargers and getting repaired or checked."

Chapter 6

Diplomatic Operations

The Swoose Becomes a Diplomat

The transfer of General Brett and the Swoose to the Panama Canal Zone began on November 6, 1942, when, with Kurtz at the controls, they departed Bolling Field for Miami, en route to Albrook Field in the Canal Zone. The Swoose landed in Panama on November 9 at 1:20 A.M. after the flight of 1,380 miles in six hours from Miami. On the trip to Panama, General Brett was accompanied by Major DeVos and Capt. Francis J. Fitzpatrick. Captain Schreiber was the navigator, and 1st Lt. Marvin L. MacAdams was the copilot. The enlisted men in the crew were Roland A. Boone, Harold M. Varner, and Charles T. Reeves.

Brett replaced Lt. Gen. Frank Andrews as the new commanding officer of the Caribbean Defense Command with headquarters at Quarry Heights, Canal Zone. At that time, the Canal Zone was considered the most fortified place on earth. Charged with protecting the critical link between the Atlantic and Pacific, the Army was also charged with providing "effective support of Ecuador, Colombia, Venezuela, and the

Central American Republics" and with "occupying within forty-eight hours notice strategic interior cities with troops transported by air."[1] The Good Neighbor Policy and international protocol required that Brett attend the inauguration of South American government heads. There were enough of these alone to make his job a traveling one.

The Swoose's next recorded flight was on November 16, 1942, when it departed Albrook Field carrying General Brett on an inspection tour of his command. Apparently that was to be the last trip aboard the Swoose for some of Brett's original crew. Extra crew members were carried who would later be recorded as members of the Swoose crew.

In addition to the passengers, the following are listed as crew members in the official records of the Headquarters, Caribbean Defense Command: Lt. Col. Frank Kurtz, pilot; 1st Lt. Marvin L. MacAdams, copilot; 1st Lt. Martin Peterson, extra copilot; Capt. Harry J. Schreiber, navigator; 1st Lt. Stanley Nast, extra navigator; S. Sgt. Albert D. Woods, radio; M. Sgt. Harold M. Varner, engineer; T. Sgt. Charles E. Watt, extra engineer; S. Sgt. John C. Crawford; S. Sgt. C. Tourney; and Pfc. H. G. Seekatz. In addition to General Brett, the passengers were as follows: Maj. Gen. Davenport Johnson; Brig. Gen. Henry C. Ingalls; Capt. F. J. Fitzpatrick, General Brett's aide; and Adm. Clifford E. Van Hook.

In January 1943, the Air Force adopted a new prefix for combat-type aircraft that no longer were suitable for their primary mission, but still could serve other purposes. The prefix was "R," for "restricted" status. The restriction was applied to every Army combat-type airplane built prior to Pearl Harbor. And so, the Swoose became an RB-17D.

Also in January, Kurtz returned to the United States where on August 27, 1943, he was named commander of the 463rd Bomb Group at Lakeland Army Air Field, Florida.[2] This would not end his relationship with the original Swoose, for, as we will see, Kurtz played a significant role in the aircraft's subsequent history.

At Lakeland Army Air Field, on February 3, 1944, Margo Kurtz broke a bottle of champagne over the nose of a new B-17G, christening it the "Swoose." Lieutenant Charles Reeves would be its bombardier—the only other original Swoose crew member to be assigned to the new airplane. Piloting this second airplane to be named the Swoose and as part of the Fifteenth Air Force in Italy, Kurtz would fly sixty missions, bombing targets in eleven countries.[3] The appearance of the Swoose in the European Theater gave the original Swoose an added, but spurious, aura as a combat airplane that served in two separate war zones, since some who saw the airplane in Europe believed it to be the original Swoose.[4]

In July 1943, General Brett appointed Capt. Martin F. Peterson of Spokane, Washington, to become his new aide-de-camp and Frank Kurtz's replacement as pilot of the general's Swoose. Peterson, a high school teacher prior to entering the military service, was a 1938 graduate of the University of Idaho. Peterson had attended Army Air Force flying schools at Randolph and Brooks fields in Texas, where he won his wings in July 1941. He had previously served as the pilot for Maj. Gen. Hubert R. Harmon, the commander of Army Air Forces in the Caribbean area. The Swoose crew at the time of Peterson's appointment included the copilot, Capt. Benjamin Wardwell, and Stanley Nast, the navigator.[5]

Latin America was composed of twenty-one independent countries, and one of Brett's responsibilities was to personify the U.S. Good Neighbor policy among all those countries except Brazil, which was outside his sphere. Of vital importance to the United States in the region were such strategic raw materials needed for the war effort as tin, copper, and petroleum. While all Latin American countries cooperated in hemispheric defense, there was also strong pro-German sentiment. In 1941, German or German-controlled airlines had been serving five of the ten South American republics. Later, their operations were hampered by a shortage of planes, spare parts, and pilots.

Other very practical considerations were part of the Good Neighbor policy to improve relations with Latin America and the defense of the Caribbean area that controlled the Atlantic approaches to the Panama Canal. Close and cordial relations with the Latin American countries were very important to defending the Canal, as well as the Western Hemisphere. Under General Brett, training programs were conducted in Panama for Latin American aircraft technicians. Pilots from those countries were trained in the United States.

General Brett and his Swoose were used extensively to maintain good relations with countries of the region. They appeared on formal visits to help celebrate national holidays. During these visits heads of state were given orientation flights aboard the Swoose. Latin American military chiefs and their staffs were encouraged to reciprocate by visiting General Brett in Panama. Many of these dignitaries received aerial tours of Panama as passengers in the Swoose. Trips made by other distinguished passengers, such as visiting members of the U.S. Congress, journalists, and sometimes the children of foreign politicians, were widely reported in the press—with the Swoose always mentioned.

The Swoose led a hectic life, carrying General Brett and the U.S. flag to the various countries of the Southern Hemisphere, Central America, and the islands of the Caribbean. All these activities, of course, were covered widely by the press and sometimes by newsreels. On numerous other trips, the Swoose carried U.S. military inspection teams to destinations within the theater, without General Brett. From time to time, the Swoose and its crew were placed at the disposal of certain Latin American and Caribbean governments, for such reasons as medical emergencies or other appropriate situations. The Swoose helped to foster a spirit of harmony and cooperation among those countries and the United States. One-time dignitaries hosted by General Brett, including Cuban president Fulgencio Batista and Nicaraguan president Anastasio Somoza, were allowed to fly the Swoose for 15 minutes from the copilot's seat, during which they managed to execute a few gentle turns.[6]

Jack Crane, another of the Swoose's pilots in Panama, recalled that he liked to conclude General Brett's goodwill visits with a final salute in the form of a low, high-speed pass over the flight line, ending with a steep climbing turn. He said he can still hear the general on the interphone saying, "Get it down, Jack, get it down." Recalling those occasions, Crane expressed his delight with a sigh and "Ahh, those were the days."

From newspaper reports, the Swoose could be tracked to Miami on December 18, 1942. It was in Trinidad on February 5, 1943, in Quito, Ecuador, February 16, and San Juan, Puerto Rico, on February 25. It carried Brett and Lt. Gen. V.A.H. Sturdee, head of the Australian military mission in Washington, to the Canal Zone on March 3.[7]

On March 27, 1943, General Brett and the Swoose left Panama for San José, Costa Rica, on an official three-day visit. In addition to others, two International News Service reporters were included among the passengers. They visited Bogotá, Colombia, on April 8, and Santiago, Chile, on May 14, en route to Lima, Peru. The crew at the time included Capt. Martin F. Peterson, pilot; Capt. Ben Wardlaw, copilot; Lt. Homer "Buck" Rogers, copilot; Capt. Stanley Nast, navigator; crew chief T. Sgt. Charles E. Tourney; and S. Sgt. Alfred J. Chappel as engineer/mechanic. Later that year, Peterson was promoted to major, Tourney to master sergeant, and Chappel to staff sergeant.[8]

In June 1943, the Swoose brought three West Point cadets to Panama. One was Gen. Brett's son, Devol Brett, who would later become a major general in the U.S. Air Force.[9]

A previously unreported crew member of the Swoose surfaced in a news report describing an untimely death.[10] A cocker spaniel pup (named "Swank" by General Brett) had been killed by an automobile while being walked. The puppy was reported to have traveled in the Swoose with the general and Captain Peterson or Captain Wardlaw and Lieutenant Rogers.

Lowell Thomas, the well-known news analyst and lecturer then affiliated with the National Broadcasting System, was the passenger on July 9, 1943, when General Brett piloted the Swoose on an inspection flight over the Canal and its fortifications. Thomas was impressed by the performance of the battle-scarred bomber.

On July 17, 1943, nine generals were photographed with the Swoose at the Sixth Air Force Headquarters in Panama, after six of them returned from a trip to an outlying base. On August 1, three Swoose crew members were awarded Air Medals for their part in carrying out long-range patrol flights over the Pacific and Caribbean approaches to the Panama Canal, prior to their assignments to the Swoose. Many of the flights were under adverse conditions. Each man was credited with at least 200 hours of patrol time. The award went to captains Wardlaw and Nast and Major Peterson. After serving as the pilot of the Swoose since January 1943, Maj. Martin F. Peterson left the airplane in September 1943 to return to the States for reassignment.[11]

New Pilot—The Swoose Becomes a Swan

Having been checked out in the airplane by Frank Kurtz before he left, Capt. Jack J. Crane was selected to be the pilot of the Swoose on September 28, 1943.[12] After Peterson's departure, Crane would serve longer in that capacity than any who had ever flown the airplane. While he was only 24 years old, Crane had nearly three years of service in Panama and held the Air Medal for overwater patrol flight duty.[13]

Following graduation from college with a degree in aeroengineering, Crane entered the service in July 1940 as an aviation cadet and won his wings at Maxwell Field, Alabama, in February 1941. He was assigned to the 74th Bombardment Squadron at Albrook Field, and later served with the 20th Transport Squadron at France Field in the Canal Zone.[14]

Following the breakout of war in 1941, Crane was assigned to the 3rd Bombardment Squadron at Rio Hato in Panama, and later in the Galapagos Islands where he flew antisubmarine patrols. Crane subsequently became engineering and assistant operations officer of the Sixth Air Force Headquarters Squadron at Albrook. He also was assigned to serve as flying aide to Maj. Gen. Davenport Johnson, commander of the Sixth Air Force, and to Maj. Gen. Hubert Harmon, which was his assignment when the Swoose landed at Albrook, bringing General Brett, the new commander of the Caribbean Defense Command. By then, Crane had considerable experience flying the B-18, C-47, and the B-17, both B and E models.

Since the Swoose was assigned to the Sixth Air Force Headquarters Squadron for maintenance, Kurtz and Crane met each time Kurtz came in to fly the Swoose. It was Crane who checked out Kurtz in the C-49B, the AAF designation for an Eastern Air Lines DC-3 requisitioned by the Air Force and used frequently for flights by the Caribbean command.[15]

By the time Crane was selected to pilot the Swoose, he had made a few check flights in the Swoose with Peterson, beginning on August 8, 1943. Crane made his first trip as pilot on September 28. His copilot at the time was 1st Lt. Homer Rogers. The crew chief was M. Sgt. John Crawford, with M. Sgt. C. Tourney as assistant crew chief and engineer. S. Sgt. Alfred J. Chappel, Sgt. Alfred E. Frye, and Sgt. Jerry R. Grimes were all mechanics and engineers, while Cpl. Wallace K. Carter, Pvt. Glenn Cutshall, Pvt. Edward Chambers, Pvt. Myer E. Eccles, Sgt. Franklin B. Nice were all mechanics. M. Sgt. Joseph Schwab was the radio operator.[16]

From that time, Crane was aboard the Swoose for every flight while he and the airplane were stationed in Panama. Crane soon learned that General Brett was very attached to the weatherbeaten, drab-camouflaged airplane. While it wasn't impressive in appearance, the Swoose seemed to Crane to have some symbolic significance to the general, which Brett never discussed.[17]

Crane, who was promoted to major in January 1944, described the interior of the Swoose as stark, "with a few salvaged, thinly padded airline seats bolted to a crude plywood floor in the aft section of the fuselage. A long bench occupied one side of the radio compartment." Apparently these were the modifications made at Laverton, Australia, when the Swoose was first made ready for assignment to General Brett. To make up for the poor heating system, many blankets were needed by passengers on long flights.

When Crane took over he found that the engines were in good condition, and the turbo-superchargers made for reliable operations from high-altitude airfields such as those at Bogotá, Quito, and La Paz. One side of the bomb bay was filled with a 500-gallon fuel tank that gave the airplane a 2,200-gallon fuel capacity. With that load, it was possible to fly for 12 to 13 hours at 200 to 220 MPH, ideal for the long, nonstop flights necessary to cover all of South and Central America and the Caribbean, as well as the Galapagos Islands in the Pacific.[18]

Apparently the "bathtub" gun housing on the underside of the fuselage had been removed at some point after the Swoose arrived in Panama on November 9, 1942. Photographs show the belly gun housing as General Brett arrived to take up his duties there. In a photograph taken on June 22, 1943, the gun housing has been removed.

Homer Rogers recalled that he came up with the idea to have the flags painted on the nose. Sometime between October 1943 and February 23, 1944 (when the Swoose was in the hanger for repair), the camouflage exterior paint had been removed. Photographs taken on February 3, 1944, show the Swoose in its natural aluminum finish.[19]

Based on Crane's flight logs, the Swoose averaged about 50 to 55 hours a month in the air, or 1,200 hours for the two years he was pilot. The Swoose was out of service for overhaul and modification for three months starting on February 24, 1944. During that time General Brett used a stripped B-17E assigned to the Sixth Air Force Headquarters for a few long flights, but mostly he flew in the more comfortable Eastern Airlines DC-3 (C-49B).[20]

In early February, while the Swoose was having one of its required periodic inspections at the Albrook Field depot, numerous small cracks were found in the main spars of both wings, between the landing gear attachments and the fuselage. While the cracks themselves were not bad enough to permanently ground the airplane, severe corrosion was found on both the interior structure and exterior skin of the wings. Corrosion also was found in the horizontal and vertical stabilizers and on the underside of the aft section of the fuselage. Based on these conditions it was decided that the aircraft no longer was reparable, and should be junked.[21]

General Brett was very disturbed to hear that the Swoose would have to be abandoned. Knowing of Brett's strong feelings, Crane began checking all potential ways to save the airplane. He discovered that the biggest problem was replacing the inboard wing panels. All other parts could be reworked by depot personnel.

Since the wing design of the B-17 had remained unchanged since the first model of the aircraft had been produced, any B-17 wing could be used to replace the damaged wing structure. Crane recalled that before the B-17Es had come to Albrook, antisubmarine patrols were conducted by B-17Bs, which had been maintained at the now abandoned France Field Air Depot, across the isthmus from Albrook Field.

The B models released by the newly arrived Es had been flown to Amarillo Army Air Field in Texas, and were no longer available as a source of cannibalized spare parts to repair the ailing Swoose. On the remote chance that he might yet find some spare parts, Crane toured the old France Field depot, which now was being used for dead storage. In a dark corner of a storage shed he made a monumental discovery—a pair of open crates resting side by side which contained two spanking new B-17B inboard wing panels. Somehow they had been overlooked in the move to Albrook, or they had been left for return to supply stores in the United States. At any rate, there were no records to indicate they had even existed.

General Brett was delighted by Crane's discovery. The deal soon was consummated with the depot's commanding officer, a Colonel Munro, to begin the overhaul of the Swoose on a low-priority basis, relative to other essential work at the depot. Plans also were made to update the Swoose to B-17E standards wherever practical.[22]

In addition to the wings, other details about the different models of the B-17 were also similar. The B-17D tanks provided for 1,246 gallons in each wing, while the B-17B fuel capacity was 1,241 gallons. The difference between the B and D model wing tanks came from the use of self-sealing tanks that were introduced in the later models. Crane recalled that the B-17B tanks could be serviced with a total of 2,492 gallons, rather than the 2,452 gallons provided for in the specification, or about 10 hours total of flying.[23]

The crated B-17B wings at France Field were barged through the Panama Canal and trucked to the depot at Albrook Field. There they were installed on the Swoose. In addition to replacing the wing panels, crews removed and reworked the entire empennage. There had been a number of crude patches scattered over the vertical and horizontal stabilizers, which Frank Kurtz attributed to repairs of combat damage. The Swoose also had bullet hole patches on its fuselage, tail, and control surfaces.[24] Since the tail had been replaced in Australia, the patches must have covered wounds suffered by its donor.

Basic changes also were made to the electrical system to provide for installing improved, alternating current, autosynchronized instrumentation that had been developed and made standard on later B-17s. To provide the required AC power, two DC-to-AC inverters were installed in the cockpit on the pilot's side.[25]

The radio communications system remained unchanged. Very high frequency (VHF) radio was quite new at the time and virtually unknown in U.S. aircraft flying in South America. The low-frequency radio was adequate for contacting control towers, radio range reception, and radio direction-finding in that area of the world. The radio operator was relocated to the flight deck, and made responsible for handling weather reports, airways clearance, and official messages on the high-frequency equipment.[26]

The automatic flight control equipment (AFCE) of B-17s was coupled to the Norden bombsight and the electrically operated automatic pilot to provide a steady platform during bombing runs. When the bombardier required small adjustments in the aircraft, position signals were fed to the automatic pilot from the bombsight controls. Though the Swoose no longer had a bombsight, the bombsight stabilizer, which housed the gyros for the automatic pilot, and all the fittings, wiring, and plumbing related to the AFCE remained. After much discussion, it was decided to eliminate the entire autopilot system. This would allow for the removal of most of the associated hardware and instrumentation. As a result of this decision, the Swoose would have to be manually controlled in flight forever after.

Removing the AFCE hardware in the vicinity of the former bombsight location opened up a large area of the former bombardier's compartment in the nose. That area was converted into a roomy semi-circular seating area, an ideal place for visiting dignitaries to get an unobstructed view. General Brett often would sit there with his guests and point out areas of interest as they flew at low altitudes along the length of the canal. These one-hour tours never failed to impress visitors.

Other changes to the Swoose's interior included the construction of a larger, more substantial floor in the passenger compartment, which was then covered with carpeting. The number of oxygen tube outlets was increased in the cabin and finished wood panels were installed along the side, greatly improving the general appearance of the interior. Passengers and crew were still required to suck oxygen from tubes directly into their mouths. Draw curtains were installed to cut the glare from the large side windows. The lavatory area at the rear also was improved. A floor was built in the right side of the bomb bay and on it a stove and ice box were installed. The old, odd assortment of passenger seats was removed and replaced by attractive, uniform seats scavenged from a wrecked Beechcraft C-45. While the appearance and comfort level of the passenger compartment was significantly improved, the Swoose remained cold, drafty, and noisy during flight.[27]

For the exterior, during the overhaul, all corroded or worn skin was replaced. Some time after the overhaul, the Swoose's original segmented plastic nose cone was removed and replaced with the two-piece nose used on the B-17G, to give passengers an unobstructed view. The old B-17D wheels, with their troublesome bladder-activated brakes, were removed and replaced with B-17E wheels and tires. The new wheels, tires, and brakes added greatly to operational safety, as the Swoose routinely landed on short dirt, gravel, and grass runways.[28] The reworked Swoose now could be operated from a 2,500-foot landing strip.

During the overhaul, the skin previously installed to cover the hole left by the "bathtub" gun compartment was removed. The resulting cavity was bridged by installing several formers and stringers to provide longitudinal and lateral reinforcement of the fuselage. The area was then covered on the outside by new aluminum skin, riveted to the new structural members. On the inside of the airplane the new, reinforced flooring covered the cavity.

Crane was surprised to see the flimsy repairs that had been made earlier, at the time the "bathtub" had been removed. He recalled that the Swoose had shown a slight directional instability that he had attributed to a misalignment in the replacement tail assembly installed in Australia. After the overhaul, the instability disappeared and the airplane could be trimmed to hold a true and steady course with hands off the controls. While other factors could have caused the instability, a primary reason might have come from the flexing of the aft fuselage under air loads due to the loss of structural rigidity from incomplete repairs made immediately after removal of the "bathtub."

Because of the low priority, it took three months to complete the Swoose's makeover. But, for the second time, it had been saved from the scrap pile. After all the repairs and modifications had been made, the unpainted Swoose was hand-polished by a crew of volunteers who were rewarded with a short flight around the Canal Zone. According to Crane, "There were at least twenty men and we had some of them standing on the catwalk of the bomb bay for the takeoff and landing, to balance the airplane." On its shiny nose, the Swoose now had the flags of the seventeen countries it had visited.[29] On May 30, 1944, when the Swoose returned to flight status, it was a thing of beauty, "a true queen of the skies," according to Crane. The Swoose was now a swan, in spite of its name. Crane had given it a flight test for 2 hours and 10 minutes and declared the Swoose ready for service.[30]

In June 1944, the Swoose, now a glistening airliner in her polished, natural metal finish, flew nonstop from Albrook Field in the Canal Zone to San Antonio, Texas in 9 hours and 26 minutes, for an average speed of 197 MPH for the 1,900-mile trip. While no speed record could be claimed, there were none who could recall a similar flight over land and water between the two Americas.

The crew for that novel flight was composed of Capt. Jack J. Crane (pilot), 1st Lt. Homer C. "Buck" Rogers (copilot), Capt. Stanley C. Nast (navigator), M. Sgt. John C. Crawford (crew chief), M. Sgt. C. E. Tourney (assistant crew chief), and M. Sgt. Joseph M. Schwab (radio operator). Other members of the Swoose crew were S. Sgt. Alfred J. Chappel (assistant engineer/mechanic), and sergeants Jerry R. Grimes and Franklin B. Nice (mechanics). Two former members of the ground crew who made the trip as passengers were staff sergeants L. T. Waldron and G. A. Accoe.[31] There is no record of any other passengers on this flight.

Crane's experiences with both the early and later model B-17s caused him to note only slight differences in their flight characteristics, although the later models had greatly increased weight aft of the wings because of the increased length of the fuselage, the greater size of the tail structure, and the heavy ball turret on the underside of the rear compartment. Since the early models were extremely light in the tail, the added weight in the E and subsequent models made for improved weight distribution. The later models were "a piece of cake" to land, and easily managed by a single pilot.[32]

While the Swoose was a stable airplane to fly, with no bad habits, it was so nose-heavy in the landing configuration with the flaps down that a three-point landing was possible but not advisable. On final approach, as flaps were being lowered, the copilot had to rotate the elevator trim tab wheel in increments, on command from the pilot as flying speed slowly reduced to final approach speed.[33]

The safest landing attitude, according to Crane, was on the main landing gear with the tail low. Achieving a three-point landing required so much tail-down trim that if a go-around should be necessary, a sudden application of power could result in a dangerous nose-high attitude unless the elevator trim tab was quickly and correctly adjusted. All of this made a coordinated two-man effort essential. Word had it that General Brett and the Swoose had a close call on an aborted landing some time in the past and he did not want the airplane flown by pilots unaware of its landing idiosyncrasies.[34]

On September 16, 1944, with General Brett on board, the Swoose made the first of three trips to Santiago, Chile. This first flight was made to permit U.S. participation in that country's Independence Day celebration. General Brett also visited Peru on this ten-day South American trip. In addition to the Swoose, three B-24s, a C-47, and a UC-67, the transport version of the Douglas B-23 Dragon, were used to carry fifty-five officers to Santiago.[35] They left from Los Cerrillos Airport on September 19. On long trips such as this, the crew generally consisted of ten members, which left space for only six or seven passengers. The Swoose crew for the Santiago flight was Maj. Jack Crane, pilot; Capt. Charles W. Nall, copilot; Capt. Stanley Nast, navigator; M. Sgt. John Crawford, crew chief; S. Sgt. Alfred Chappel, assistant crew chief; and M. Sgt. Charles Schwab, radio operator.

About a week after returning to the Canal Zone, Crane was surprised to see a syndicated newsreel of the Swoose's Chilean arrival at the base theater. Newsreels normally were shown before the feature film in motion-picture theaters of the day, and in this case the voice of the newscaster was in Spanish.

The Swoose made subsequent flights to Santiago in January 1945 with Crane and Nall at the controls. In September 1945 a third trip was made. In June 1945, the beautiful "Swoose" carried General Brett and a contingent of Latin American representatives to San Francisco for the signing of the United Nations charter.[36]

A review of Jack Crane's flight log indicates that the Swoose flew 1,194 hours while he was the assigned pilot. For the eleven-month period from November 1942 to September, 1943, when the Swoose was flown in Panama first by Frank Kurtz and then by Peterson, the flying pattern was about the same—an average of around 50 hours per month. So, during assignment in Panama, the Swoose is estimated to have flown at least 1,750 hours.

On September 5, 1945, Maj. Jack Crane last flew the Swoose, ending a relationship that began August 8, 1943. Crane served as General Brett's Swoose pilot longer than anyone else. Because of Crane's personal intervention, the Swoose had been saved for posterity for a second time. The modifications and overhaul conducted as a result of his personal efforts would help the Swoose to survive the neglect it would face in the next few years. Crane's successor as the pilot of the Swoose was Capt. Charles Nall. Apparently Nall was to be the last of Brett's Swoose assigned pilots, as its career as a regular member of the U.S. Air Force was about to end.

Chapter 7

The Long Road Home

Homecoming

In March 1944 while the Swoose was undergoing its overhaul at the Albrook depot, a new crew member joined General Brett's crew. He was Charles W. "Chuck" Nall, a twenty-five-year-old first lieutenant assigned as the copilot to replace Ben Wardlaw who died in the crash of a single-engine Vultee BT-13 near Rio Hato, Panama.[1]

Nall entered the Army Air Corps in June 1939 as an enlisted man. After graduation from the Air Corps School of Photography in Denver he was assigned for a short time to March Field in California where he became acquainted with 1st Lt. Frank Kurtz, a public information officer at that installation. Accepted into the Aviation Cadet program, Nall graduated in the Class of 42J and received his pilot's wings at Roswell, New Mexico. Following transition training in four-engine aircraft, he was assigned to the 74th Bomb Squadron in Panama and soon thereafter to the 74th Squadron flying the B-17F. It was from there that Jack Crane selected him to fill the copilot's position in the Swoose.

On March 17, 1944, Crane flew Nall to his new assignment at Albrook Field. Here he joined the other members in the flight test section of the Headquarters, Caribbean Defense Command. That section had responsibility for providing air transportation to the headquarters staff.

Assigned to the flight test section were a number of different aircraft types that were used to transport staff to various locations in the Caribbean, South and Central America, and to various locations in the United States. In addition to the Swoose, the section was assigned a Beech C-45, North American B-25, Douglas C-49, Boeing B-17E, and a Douglas UC-67 (one of several B-23s that had been modified as a transport). Like other pilots assigned to the section, Nall flew many of these during his tour.

Nall's first flight in the Swoose took place on June 2, 1944. In that first month the Swoose was flown more than 26 hours. On July 24, 1944, Nall was first logged as the pilot of the Swoose for one hour. In the months that followed, Crane and Nall shared more and more of the first pilot's duties. In September 1945 when Crane left, Chuck Nall was to become the last of the Swoose's assigned pilots.

With the surrender of Nazi Germany on May 7, 1945, flying activity in the Caribbean Defense Command began to wind down. On August 6, 1945, the B-29 Enola Gay ushered in the atomic age when it dropped the first atomic bomb over the city of Hiroshima, Japan. The devastation wrought by that and the one dropped over Nagasaki in the tenacious enemy's homeland essentially brought the tragic war to an end on Tuesday, August 14, 1945.

With the surrender of the Axis powers, demobilization of the U.S. military might began immediately as the American public clamored for the return of its citizen soldiers. To expedite demobilization, separation centers were established at many locations throughout the country and other facilities were established to collect and dispose of the airplanes that had been part of the greatest air armada the world had ever seen.

With the coming of peace General Brett, after more than 35 years of military service, was scheduled to return to the United States to retire. The Swoose was scheduled to be decommissioned and disposed of in accordance with government policies established for surplus war material.

Captain Nall had received his orders to return to the States for discharge when, in the midst of his preparations to leave, General Brett asked him to postpone his departure. The general asked Nall to fly him and the Swoose back to the United States and to remain as the pilot for about two additional weeks as he wished to visit a number of locations

Top: Pictured during a stop at Asunción, Paraguay, in November 1939 is one of the Y1B-17s that participated in the flight of the second Goodwill Mission to South America. First Lieutenant Henry C. Godman, who would become the pilot of the Swoose, is third from right. Under the nose gun turret is a flat glass panel through which the optical bombsight was aimed. (*Source:* Courtesy H. C. Godman.) **Bottom:** The B-17D. One of the Swoose's sister aircraft. Externally, it did not differ from the C model except for the newly installed cowl flaps. (*Source:* Courtesy Boeing.)

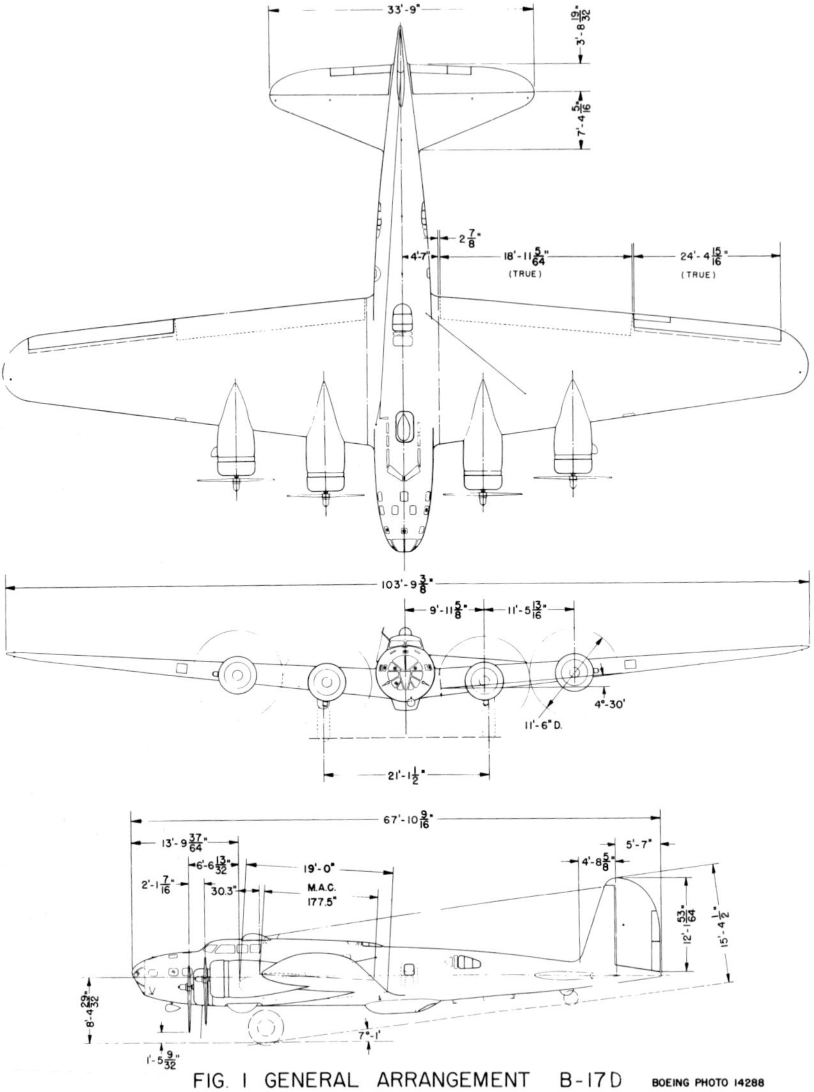

FIG. 1 GENERAL ARRANGEMENT B-17D BOEING PHOTO 14288

Dimensions of the B-17D. (*Source:* Courtesy Robert C. Mikesh.)

Top: The B-17D looking aft from near the rear entrance. The inward-opening waist gunner's windows and machine-gun mounting posts are on the left and right. In the center of the fuselage, toward the rear, is the commode. Part of the opening to the "bathtub" gun blister can be seen in the foreground. (*Source:* Courtesy Boeing.) **Bottom:** Looking down on the rear-firing twin .50-caliber gun installation. The gunner had to kneel to aim and fire the guns. (*Source:* Courtesy Boeing.)

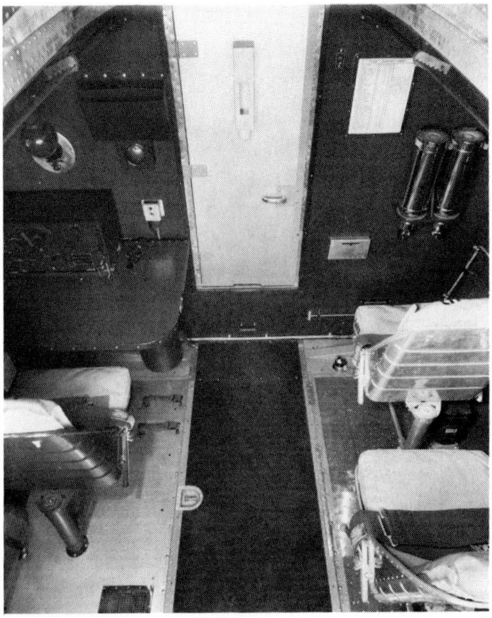

The B-17D radio compartment. The liaison receiver and telegraph key are shown on the operator's table. The door in the floor opens to the camera compartment. (*Source:* Courtesy Boeing.)

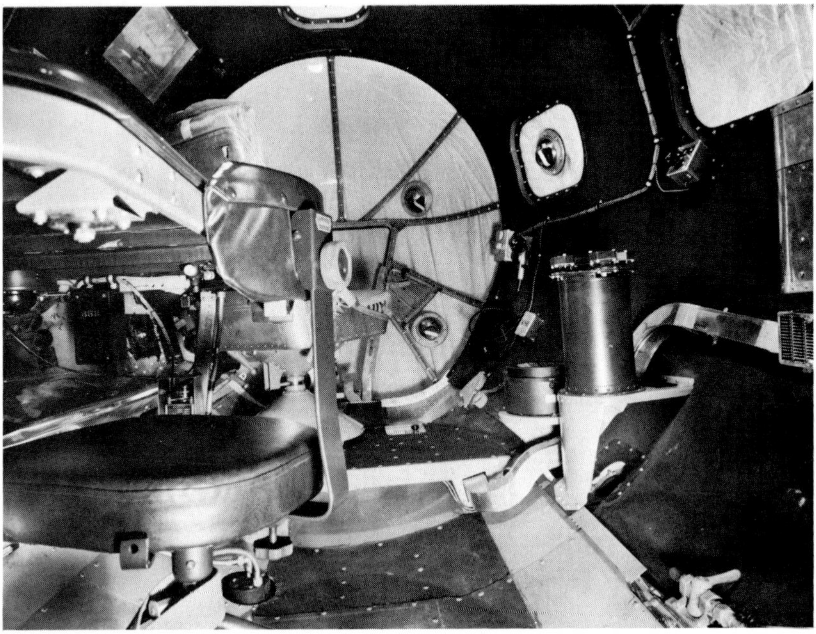

Navigator and bombardier positions in the nose. On the left is the navigator's table. The bombardier's chair can be seen in the nose. The cylindrical-shaped device on the right is the mount for the drift meter and forward of that is an Aperiodic compass. Gun sockets in the nose are for the single .30-caliber gun stowed in the compartment. (*Source:* Courtesy Boeing.)

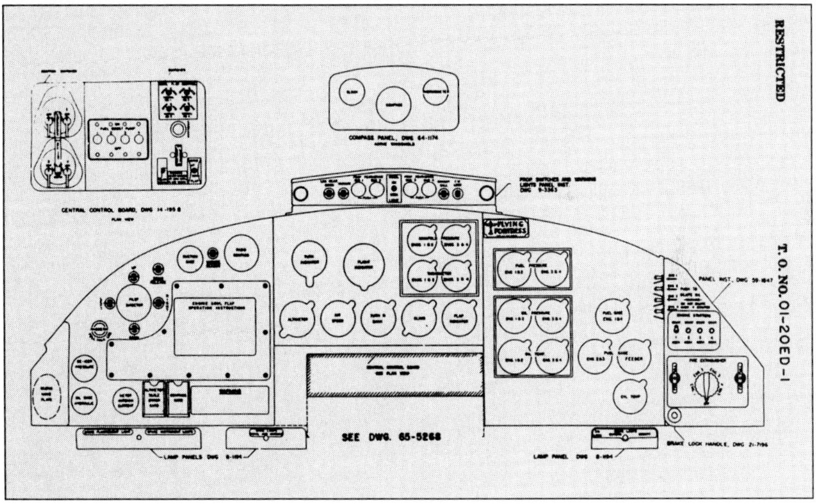

Top: The B-17D flight deck. The instrument panel arrangement in the Swoose differed from that shown. However, the arrangement of switches and controls on the pedestal between the seats is the same. The vertically aligned wheels on either side of the pedestal control the elevator trim tabs. The box of switches near the floor is the autopilot altitude control. The wheel in the floor is the rudder trim tab control. The lever in the floor to the left of the pedestal is the rudder and elevator lock. The lever to the right is the tail wheel lock. (*Source:* Courtesy Boeing.) **Bottom:** The pilot and copilot's instrument panel as installed in the Swoose. (*Source:* Courtesy Boeing.)

Top: Men of the 19th Bombardment Group who flew the first U.S. ferry mission of combat aircraft to an overseas U.S. base. On May 13, 1941, they flew twenty-one B-17Ds from Hamilton Field, California, to Hickam Field in the Territory of Hawaii. One of those airplanes would become known as "The Swoose." (*Source:* USAF photo.) **Bottom:** The 14th Bombardment Squadron at Port Moresby, Papua, New Guinea, on September 9, 1941, en route to Clark Field. The B-17 in the foreground carrying the number "21" is 40-3097, which would become the Swoose. The tail numbers still carry the 11th Bombardment Group designation. (*Source:* National Museum and Art Gallery, Papua, New Guinea, courtesy Bruce D. Hoy.)

Top: Aerial photograph of Clark Field on August 26, 1939. No appreciable changes to the landing field had been made when the 14th Bombardment Squadron landed there two years later. (*Source:* NASM photo 85-16207.) **Bottom:** Clark Field, September 1941. Officers of the 14th Bombardment Squadron shortly after their pioneering flight from Hawaii. Standing *(left to right)* are Pelly Dittman, Morris N. ("Moe") Friedman, unidentified, unidentified, Carl Epperson (navigator of 40-3097), unidentified, unidentified, unidentified, Emmett C. O'Donnell, Colin P. Kelly, Donald M. Keiser, Weldon H. Smith, Edward C. Teats, unidentified, unidentified. Kneeling *(left to right)* are: P. R. Tarbutton, Robert S. Clinkscales (copilot of 40-3097), Richard T. Carlisle, unidentified, unidentified, Guiford R. ("Monty") Montgomery, Henry C. Godman (pilot of 40-3097), J. P. Ferry, C. J. Holdridge, and three unidentified individuals. (*Source:* Courtesy H. C. Godman.)

The crew of B-17D 40-3097 shortly after their flight from Hawaii to Clark Field. Standing *(left to right)* are: Robert S. Clinkscales (copilot), Henry C. Godman (pilot), and Carl Epperson (navigator). Kneeling *(left to right)* are: S. G. ("Junior") Brooks (radio operator–gunner), John A. Wallach (bombardier), Norman P. Michelson (radio operator–gunner), Coley L. James (engineer-gunner), and H. E. Weist (engineer-gunner). (*Source:* Courtesy H. C. Godman.)

Top: This view of aircraft parked at Clark Field in November 1941 is from the family quarters area, used by the flight officers since the families had been evacuated. In the foreground are decoy aircraft resembling P-35s. A number of unpainted B-17s are parked in the open. The airplane under the arrow is 40-3097. (*Source:* Courtesy H. C. Godman.) **Bottom:** A 14th Bombardment Squadron B-17 visiting the fighter base at Iba, Luzon, in November 1941. (*Source:* Photographed by William R. Wright of the 17th Pursuit Squadron. Courtesy William Bartsch.)

Top: Aircraft parked at Del Monte shortly after December 15, 1941. Painted and unpainted B-17s are shown. The dark tail in the center is that of 40-3097. To the right is a B-18 with the tail of another B-18 to its right. (*Source:* Courtesy H. C. Godman and William Bartsch.) **Bottom:** Crew quarters at Del Monte. The field had no other housing and no aircraft maintenance facility. (*Source:* Courtesy H. C. Godman.)

Top: B-17D 40-3097 at Del Monte, camouflaged with bamboo to hide it from aerial observation. Now painted with camouflage paint to keep the sun from reflecting off the skin, its color was described as "swampy green and brown." The number "21" in black appears to have been restenciled after the airplane was painted. The individual in the photograph is Henry C. Godman. (*Source:* Courtesy H. C. Godman.) **Bottom:** The field at Darwin as seen from an approaching B-17 of the 19th Bombardment Group. On one night's takeoff, a kangaroo bolted into the airplane's landing lights and it appeared as a man to the pilot. (*Source:* Photographed by Edward M. Jacquet.)

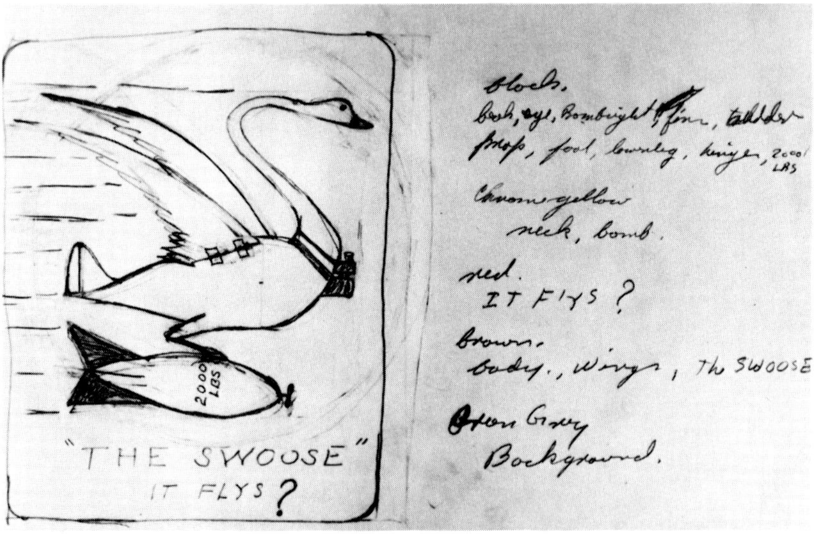

Top: Singosari airfield, Malang, Java. This photograph was taken from a Dutch single-engine biplane about 20 minutes after a Japanese strafing raid. The remains of a B-17 that was parked in its protective revetment can be seen scattered about. (*Source:* Photographed by Edward M. Jacquet.) **Bottom:** Believed to be the original sketch and color specification prepared by Weldon H. Smith for the logo he applied to B-17D 40-3097. (*Source:* Weldon H. Smith collection, courtesy of his daughters.)

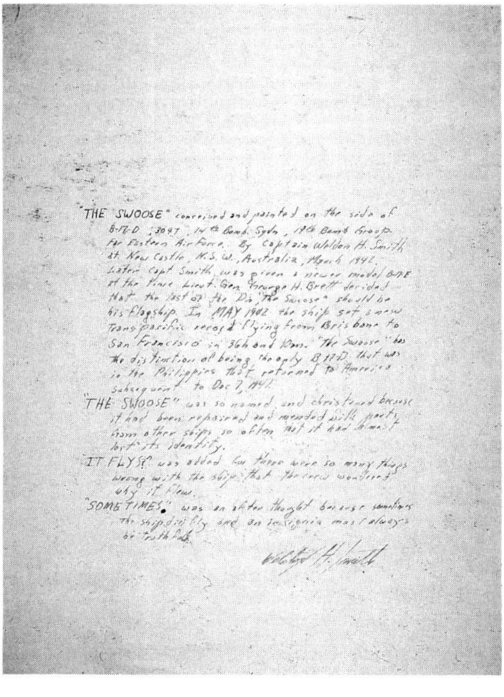
"THE SWOOSE" conceived and painted on the side of B-17-D, 3047, 14th Bomb. Sqdn, 19th Bomb Group. Far Eastern Air Force. By Captain Weldon H. Smith at New Castle, N.S.W., Australia, March 1942. Later Capt Smith was given a newer model ONE at the time Lieut. Gen. George H. Brett decided that the last of the D's, "The Swoose" should be his flagship. In MAY 1942 the ship set a new Trans-pacific record flying from Brisbane to San Francisco in 36 h and 10 m. "The Swoose" has the distinction of being the only B17D that was in the Philippines that returned to America subsequent to Dec 7, 1941.

"THE SWOOSE" was so named and christened because it had been repaired and mended with parts from other ships so often that it had almost lost its identity.

"IT FLYS?" was added for there were so many things wrong with the ship that the crew wondered why it flew.

"SOME TIMES." was an after thought because sometimes the ship didn't fly and an insignia must always be truthful.

Weldon H. Smith

Top: Painting of the Swoose logo presented to Mrs. C. A. "Mother" Tusch on May 1, 1943. This rendition of the logo was probably painted by Weldon Smith following his return to the United States. **Bottom:** A note found on the back of the logo presented by Weldon Smith to "Mother" Tusch. (*Source:* NASM archives.)

Top: General George Brett's B-24A "Arabian Knight" at Teheran in December 1941 en route from Cairo, Egypt, to Australia. After the Arabian Knight was destroyed on the ground by the Japanese air attack on Broome, Australia, the Swoose was selected to replace it. (*Source:* Courtesy Lt. Gen. Devol Brett, USAF [Ret.].) **Bottom:** Taken in Australia in 1942, this photograph of Harry J. Schreiber shows the Swoose logo, probably as it was originally applied to the airplane by Weldon Smith. (*Source:* Harry J. Schreiber collection.)

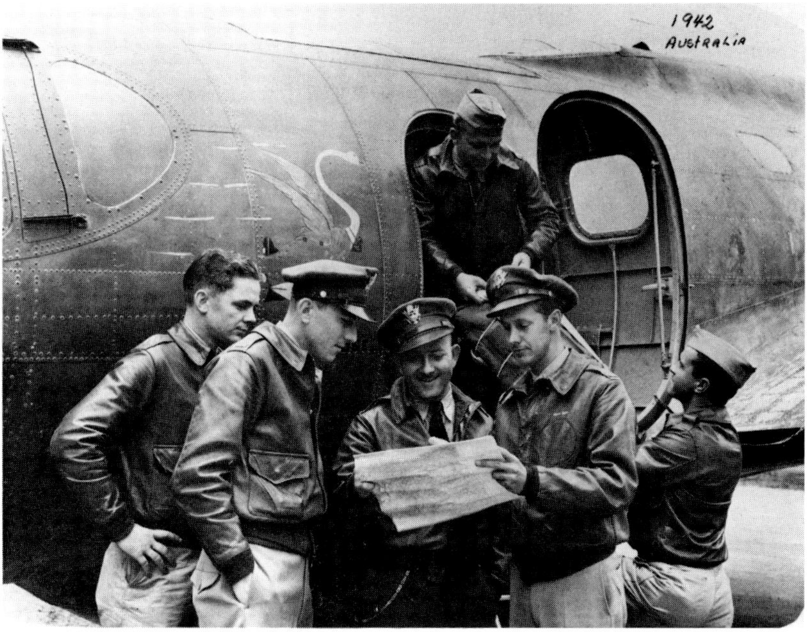

The first of several crews to serve General Brett on his many trips in the Swoose *(left to right)*: Cpl. Aubrey Fox, 1st Lt. Marvin L. MacAdams, 1st Lt. Harry J. Schreiber, Capt. Frank Kurtz, M. Sgt. Roland A. Boone, T. Sgt. Charles T. Reeves (in the doorway). (*Source:* Harry J. Schreiber collection.)

The crew of the Swoose and its passenger at Hickam Field on March 17, 1942, following their recordbreaking crossing of the Pacific. Weldon Smith's logo shows evidence of being altered. What can be seen of the logo shows "99—THE" followed by words hidden from view to have been added in front of "THE SWOOSE." The new words may have been a reference to "Ole 99," the name given to Frank Kurtz's B-17, destroyed on the ground at Clark Field on December 8, 1941.

Top: Lyndon B. Johnson, thirty-sixth president of the United States, is shown at Port Moresby on June 10, 1942, preparing to continue his inspection tour of the Southwest Pacific. The replacement tail assembly installed at Laverton can be seen for the first time. (*Source:* Harry J. Schreiber collection.) **Bottom:** The Swoose at its birthplace, Boeing Field, Seattle, Washington, on August 31, 1942, during General Brett's transcontinental tour of U.S. facilities. The airplane had undergone repairs at the Middletown Air Depot in Pennsylvania before the tour began. It appears that the rudder was replaced or given a new coat of paint. (*Source:* USAF photo.)

Top: General George Brett at the controls of the Swoose as they prepare to leave Seattle on August 31, 1942. (*Source:* Courtesy Boeing.) **Bottom:** Close-up of the Swoose logo, with new alterations, on August 31, 1942. (*Source:* Courtesy Boeing.)

Comic strip depicting some of the Swoose's adventures during its service in Australia after it was assigned to General Brett. The strip was published in the Sunday (September 12, 1942) edition of many of the nation's newspapers. The reference to the airplane's arrival in the Philippines as described in the second panel is in error.

Top: The second Swoose, B-17G 42-31844, assigned to the Fifteenth Air Force in Italy. Before its departure for combat in Europe, it was christened by Margo Kurtz in ceremonies at Lakeland, Florida, on February 3, 1944, after it had been assigned to her husband. A replica of Weldon Smith's original logo was painted in a white circle on the right-hand side of the fuselage and the nose sections. (*Source:* USAF photo, courtesy Frank Kurtz.) **Bottom:** As shown in this 1943 photograph taken at Albrook Field, the transformation of the Swoose has begun. Now known as a RB-17, the bathtub gun housing has been removed from the underside of the fuselage as was the observation dome in the cockpit ceiling. The new national insignia appears for the first time. (*Source:* USAF photo, from the collection of Jack J. Crane.)

Top: The left rear quarter of the Swoose taken at Albrook Field in early 1943. The crew at the time was Capt. Martin F. Peterson, Capt. Stanley E. Nast, 2nd Lt. Benjamin Wardlaw, M. Sgt. Joseph M. Schwab, S. Sgt. Robert R. Alexander, and Technician V. Tolentino. (*Source:* USAF photo, from the collection of Jack J. Crane.) **Bottom:** The Swoose in Panama in March 1943. The crew at this time includes *(left to right):* Cpl. Pete L. Maria, T. Sgt. Charles E. Tourney, Capt. Benjamin Wardlaw, Capt. Martin F. Peterson, unidentified. Kneeling are M. Sgt. Joseph Schwab and Lt. Homer Rogers. Captain Stanley Nast is in the doorway. (*Source:* Courtesy John H. Crawford.)

Top: Radio commentator and author Lowell Thomas is shown with General Brett on July 9, 1943, following an aerial tour of the Canal Zone. (*Source:* Courtesy Charles Nall.)
Bottom: First flag scheme painted on the nose of the Swoose. The words painted above the fourteen flags read, "FLAGS OF THE COUNTRIES WE HAVE VISITED." The crew members at Albrook Field on June 22, 1943 are *(left to right):* Capt. Martin F. Peterson, Capt. Benjamin Wardlaw, Lt. Homer C. Rogers, and an unidentified individual. Kneeling are *(left to right):* M. Sgt. John H. Crawford, an unidentified person, and M. Sgt. Joseph Schwab. (*Source:* USAF photo.)

In 1944 the crew constructed a motorized cart to replace the bicycle formerly used to haul supplies to and from the Swoose. Shown are *(left to right):* S. Sgt. Alfred E. Frye, M. Sgt. Alfred J. Chappel, Pvt. Glenn Cutshall, M. Sgt. Charles E. Tourney, Cpl. Wallace K. Carter, and an unidentified person. (*Source:* Courtesy John J. Crawford.)

Top: The metamorphosis of the Swoose continues. In this photograph the paint applied in 1941 had been partially stripped. Master sergeants Charles E. Tourney and John H. Crawford are in the right waist gunner's window. (*Source:* Courtesy John J. Crawford.) **Bottom:** The camouflage paint has been almost totally removed in this photograph of February 3, 1944. Black paint remains on the propellers. A new flag configuration on the nose can be seen here as the Swoose taxis to its parking place at Albrook Field. (*Source:* Collection of Jack J. Crane.)

Major Jack J. Crane and the Swoose with a new flag configuration. (*Source:* Collection of Jack J. Crane.)

Top: General Brett admires a newly painted logo that replaces the original Weldon Smith logo painted in Australia in 1942. (*Source:* Collection of Jack J. Crane.) **Bottom:** The Swoose over Albrook Field in June 1944, following major overhaul and extensive modifications completed on May 30. With its polished natural aluminum finish, the old bomber is a sleek airliner. (*Source:* Courtesy Lt. Gen. Devol Brett, USAF [Ret.].)

Top: A new configuration of flags can be seen in this photograph at Albrook Field in the summer of 1944. The airplane's flight and ground crews standing are *(left to right):* Capt. Stanley Nast, M. Sgt. Alfred J. Chappel, M. Sgt. Joseph M. Schwab, Maj. Jack J. Crane, M. Sgt. John H. Crawford, M. Sgt. L. H. Mullikin, and Capt. Charles Nall. The ground-crew members shown in the front row could not be unidentified. (*Source:* Collection of Jack J. Crane.) **Bottom:** The Swoose at Miami Army Air Field, Florida, in June 1945. The B-17E wheels are evident, as is the new air scoop in the roof of the nose compartment. (*Source:* USAF photo.)

Top: Rescued from the B-17 graveyard at Kingman, the Swoose was flown to March Field before being flown to Los Angeles for a ceremonial presentation to the city as a proposed war memorial. Pictured is General Brett's original crew of the Swoose at March Field before their flight back to Kingman. (*Source:* USAF photo.) **Bottom:** The flag configuration appears to have been altered to accommodate the newly applied olive-drab paint applied at March Field as shown in this photograph taken on April 1, 1946, at Mines Field, Los Angeles. The B-17F clear plastic nose installed at Albrook Field can also be seen. (*Source:* Harry J. Schreiber collection.)

Top: Lieutenant Colonel Henry C. Godman and, on his right, Maj. Weldon H. Smith at the Los Angeles ceremonies on April 6, 1946. (*Source:* Courtesy H. C. Godman.) **Bottom:** On the trip to Chicago, the Swoose stopped at Hamilton Field, California, the first of three such stops. General Henry H. "Hap" Arnold, wartime chief of the Army Air Forces, is shown as he visits the airplane there. (*Source:* Courtesy Boeing.)

The last crew to fly the Swoose. On December 2, 1953, this crew from Kelly Air Force Base, Texas, ferried the plane from Pyote to Andrews Air Force Base outside of Washington, D.C. From left to right are civilians Edward Flowers and James Wilcox, along with Maj. Richard T. Saxe and Maj. William Pelton, the pilot and copilot. (*Source:* USAF photo, courtesy Richard T. Saxe.)

Top: The Swoose in July 1956, parked at the museum's holding area at Andrews Air Force Base. Unprotected and unguarded, it remained here for more than seven years before it was disassembled and trucked to the museum's restoration and storage facility at Silver Hill, Maryland. (*Source:* Courtesy Robert C. Mikesh.) **Bottom:** The work of vandals and time have ravaged the interior of the Swoose shown in this 1981 photograph taken at the Paul E. Garber Restoration Facility at Silver Hill, Maryland. (*Source:* Courtesy Robert C. Mikesh.)

On November 16, 1989, Henry C. Godman visited his old war comrade, the Swoose, as it rested in a cradle at Silver Hill, Maryland, waiting for restoration so that it can take its historic place among the displays of the National Air and Space Museum. A B-17D plastic nose has been reinstalled. (*Source:* Courtesy H. C. Godman.)

across the country. Many in the Swoose crew had also received orders that would lead to their discharge from the military service or reassignment to other duties. General Brett asked Nall to select from among these people those that could accompany the Swoose on its last flight back to the States.

Orders were issued on October 13, 1945, for the Swoose and its crew to leave Albrook Field the next day and proceed to Albuquerque, New Mexico, and then to Los Angeles, San Francisco, and back to Albuquerque. From there each individual was directed to proceed to a specifically designated separation center for discharge or to a reception center for reassignment.

In addition to General Brett, those assigned to participate in the last mission of the Swoose were Capt. Charles Nall, pilot; 1st Lt. Thurman A. Seaton, copilot; 1st Lt. Burell E. Jones, navigator; M. Sgt. John Crawford, crew chief; M. Sgt. Lovell H. Mullikin, radio operator; and T. Sgt. Glenn W. Cutshall. The passengers on the flight were S. Sgt. Pete L. Meria (General Brett's long-time personal aide), Capt. Oliver D. Washburn, T. Sgt. Andrew E. Evans, and Sgt. Forcelledo y Suarez, a member of the ground crew.

The Swoose departed Albrook Field for the last time and began its homeward-bound journey at eight on the morning of October 15, 1945. The trip would prove to be a memorable barnstorming peacetime mission of unusual proportions for the veteran combat airplane, a fitting end to a unique airborne career that had begun four years earlier as a cataclysmic war was about to envelope the world.

The flight line at Albrook Field was lined with troops who had participated in the farewell ceremonies for the departing General Brett. When he climbed aboard the Swoose, he took his place in the pilot's seat, started the engines, taxied out to the runway, and made a thrilling takeoff. According to Captain Nall, immediately after leaving the ground, with the landing gear still in the down position, Brett put the Swoose into a very tight turn and made a couple of low passes over the flight line that, as he recalled, brought the troops to their knees. Following the departure from Albrook Field, General Brett returned to his seat in the rear compartment and with Nall at the controls they set a course for the first stop on their journey, Guatemala City, Guatemala. That flight lasted 4 hours and 45 minutes.

Two days later, at 7:05 on the morning of October 17, the Swoose left its last foreign port of call and headed north to its next destination, Kelly Field outside of San Antonio, Texas. The Swoose touched down on U.S. soil at 2:10 on the afternoon of October 17, 1945, thus ending more than four years of foreign duty.

For the next two weeks the Swoose would criss-cross the continental U.S. with the general verbally providing Captain Nall with his next destination a day or two before they were scheduled to depart. Each time, these travel plans seem to have been dependent on a telephone call made by the general. On October 18 they left Kelly Field at 9:05 in the morning. After flying 4 hours and 40 minutes the Swoose touched down at Kirtland Army Air Field, near Albuquerque, the prewar home of the 19th Bombardment Group.

The next destination was unusual. General Brett asked Nall to land as close to Sergeant Meria's home in Los Angeles as possible. The sergeant had been the general's personal aide for a number of years and he wished to expedite his trip home. Nall selected the airport at Glendale, California, where he landed at 11:05 on the morning of October 19, after a 3-hour and 35-minute flight from Kirtland Army Air Field. The runway at Glendale was just wide enough to accommodate the four-engine bomber's wheel spread. It was probably the first time a four-engine airplane had landed there. The Swoose dropped off the sergeant and was back in the sky a short 25 minutes after its wheels had touched down on the runway at Glendale. Their destination on this leg of their barnstorming journey was San Francisco, 75 minutes away.

San Francisco played a continuing role in the history of the Swoose. It was from nearby Hamilton Field, on May 13, 1941, that the Swoose had left the United States for Hawaii and combat service in the Southwest Pacific. Piloted by Frank Kurtz, it had returned to Hamilton Field on August 8, 1942, after its fame was established in the war zone. It had returned again with Frank Kurtz at the controls during General Brett's tour of the continent later in 1942. In 1944, with Crane and Nall at its controls it spent Christmas Day at San Francisco. In June 1945 it brought a delegation of Latin American representatives to this city for the historic signing of the United Nations charter. Though no one knew it at the time, years later the Swoose would again visit the San Francisco area during a unique flight mission with Frank Kurtz as the pilot and many of the old crew from its earlier days "down under."

The Swoose remained in San Francisco from October 19 until October 22, 1945, when it was used by Col. Bernard A. Schriever, later to become commanding general of the Air Force Systems Command. On that day the Swoose was flown for 6 hours and 20 minutes on a trip that made stops at Orange County Army Air Field near Santa Anna, California, and Bakersfield before returning to San Francisco.

The Swoose and General Brett left San Francisco on October 24, 1945, for a 5-hour and 15-minute flight to Kirtland Army Air Field in New Mexico. The following day they were once again airborne on their cross-country tour, en route to New Orleans, where they landed after a 5-hour flight.

Early on the morning of October 26, the Swoose was headed on a course that would take it to the Army air field at Marietta, Georgia, a flight of 2 hours and 30 minutes. After remaining overnight they departed for the Smyrna Army Air Field at Smyrna, Tennessee, a flight of 1 hour and 5 minutes. On the ground for only 40 minutes, they were airborne once again. Two hours and fifteen minutes after the departure from Smyrna they landed at the airport in Akron, Ohio. The next day, October 28, the Swoose landed at Bolling Field in Washington, D.C., after a 1-hour and 20-minute flight. It remained there until October 31 when the Swoose and its crew headed once again for Smyrna. As before, the stop in Smyrna was a short one. After a stay of 1 hour and 35 minutes, they took off for Marietta. The following day, at 8:15 in the morning, they left Marietta with Miami, Florida, as their next destination. Arriving at 11:35 they stayed until 3:10 that afternoon before departing for Tallahassee. The next day took them back to Marietta and New Orleans.

The last leg in the homecoming air voyage that began in Panama on October 15 started at 9:25 on Saturday morning, November 3, 1945, when Captain Nall retracted the landing gear of the Swoose for the last time after lifting off from the field at New Orleans. After flying his last mission of 5 hours and 35 minutes he taxied the veteran aircraft to its parking place on the flight line at Kirtland Army Air Field.

Farewells were exchanged among the crew as they all went their separate ways. General Brett and Captain Nall left the flight line for the visiting officers quarters. When they arrived, Brett made a request that could have changed the future course of the Swoose's unique existence. He asked Nall to return to the flight line and arrange to have the airplane's painted logo and multi-flag display removed. He expressed a fear that the Swoose would be exploited after it was declared surplus government property. So many men had participated in the airplane's history that it was unlikely that their individual contributions could be properly recognized. Accordingly, the general wanted the now-famous Swoose to be destroyed at the end of its useful life in the same manner as so many others of similar fame. Without the unique markings, the general felt that the airplane would be unrecognized and without ceremony be processed into metal scrap along with the other obsolete war birds.

Nall returned to the flight line to comply with the general's request. Removal of the paint would require a solvent and other materials, such as servicing stands. The crew had already left and Nall looked for assistance from personnel normally available on the flight line. He recalled that there was a football game in the area that afternoon and he could not find anyone to help him. Without appropriate support and supplies, the task was impossible to accomplish. Before abandoning the task he tried to remove the painted markings with a razor blade but found that approach impractical.

Forced to abort the unsuccessful attempt, Nall returned to report his failure to General Brett, who was having dinner. Nall gave a very brief report on his inability to have the paint removed as had been requested. The general told Nall that he would arrange to have the work done later, since he planned to use the airplane again before it was released. Nall subsequently departed for the separation center at Camp Attebury, Indiana, where he was separated from military service.

The general obviously failed in his attempt to destroy the airplane's identity and thereby frustrate those who would want to save the Swoose from destruction and the scrap heap. In a memorandum for the record dated January 25, 1949, Robert C. Strobel, the associate curator of the National Air Museum, wrote of General Brett's strong feelings that all of the historical facts and background concerning the Swoose would be untold and that only a small part of its history would be recounted in efforts to memorialize the airplane.

Retirement and Decommissioning

It has not been possible to reconstruct General Brett's travels after Nall parked the Swoose on November 3, 1945, and the next reported event in the airplane's history on December 1, 1945. General Brett has written that the Swoose remained his personal airplane until December 1, when he flew the airplane himself on his last mission, a round-trip between Albuquerque (Kirtland Army Air Field) and Los Angeles.[2] Following his retirement, Brett made his home in Winter Park, Florida.

Much of the greatest air fleet the world had ever known disappeared in a five-square mile patch of Arizona desert—Kingman Army Air Field, which had become Storage Depot 41, the largest of five such depots operated by the War Assets Administration. In December 1945, the Swoose was but one of the thousands of surplus military aircraft arriving from all parts of the world, sometimes at the rate of one a minute.

Kingman received over 5,500 aircraft and about one-third of them were B-17s. Another third was made up of B-24s, while the remainder included A-20s, B-25s, B-26s, P-38s, and P-63s.[3]

Stretching along six and one-half miles of U.S. Route 66, the aircraft were parked row after row. Some were legendary combat aircraft like the Swoose. A few were recently manufactured and had but very few flying hours. Most of the latter would be sold intact and flown away for commercial or foreign government service. But for battle-scarred airplanes like the Swoose, the end would be ignominious. They were stripped of their equipment and crushed into scrap metal. Finely engineered, costly aircraft were converted to ordinary junk.

The forsaken aircraft began arriving at Kingman on October 10, 1945. Some of the four-engine aircraft limped in after flying from their overseas stations. Others arrived from air bases in the United States. After they landed, their U.S. insignias were painted out and they were taxied through the mesquite to line up in a row of similar types awaiting their fate. Those aircraft with 100 or fewer hours of flying time were given preservation treatment intended to protect them from corrosion, sand, and weather.

A standard price for each airplane, regardless of flying time, was set by the War Assets Administration. A B-17 Flying Fortress or B-24 Liberator could be purchased for $13,750. A B-25 Mitchell medium bomber's price was $8,250, and a Lockheed P-38 Lightning brought $1,250. B-32s and the new A-26 were $2,000 each. The Northrup P-61 Black Widow night fighter could be purchased at Kingman for $6,000 and the Republic P-47 Thunderbolt for $3,500. The Curtiss P-40, whose earlier version fought in the Philippines on December 8, 1941, could be bought for $1,250. A Douglas A-24, the Navy's Dauntless dive-bomber whose earlier models were so troublesome to General Brett in Australia, was priced at $1,650.

Before the airplanes were offered for sale, they were stripped of any confidential equipment, which included bombsights, radar, and radio gear. Aircraft too decrepit to fly again were stripped of engines and propellers. All instrumentation and saleable equipment was taken out of the structure before the crushing began. One contractor bought 5,437 of the old airplanes for $2.78 million (and recovered the purchase price from the sale of the residual fuel drained from their tanks),[4] about $500 a piece while another took 475 for $55,425.68 or about $117 for each of an assortment of war birds including 133 four-engine bombers.

Standing on the desert floor at Kingman, the Swoose was destined to follow other famous planes on the path to an anonymous end in the jaws of a metal crusher. But, for the third time in its life, the Swoose would be saved. In March 1946, it would undergo a refurbishment of sorts in preparation for what was supposed to be one last flight. Another historic airplane at Kingman at the time was the B-29 Enola Gay, which had dropped the atomic bomb on Hiroshima. It was claimed by the Smithsonian Institution and also saved from the crusher.

The Swoose: A War Memorial

The Swoose's road to a home in the Smithsonian's National Air Museum began with a conversation between Frank Kurtz and his copilot, as they flew a Beech C-45 to Alaska early in 1946. Colonel Kurtz at the time was stationed in Washington, D.C., at the Air Transport Command headquarters. Kurtz's copilot in the C-45 mentioned in the course of conversation that he recently had flown the Swoose from Albuquerque to the War Assets Administration at Kingman.[5] Frank Kurtz had been searching for the Swoose since the end of the war. After making an instrument landing at the Kodiak Naval Air Station in Alaska, Kurtz arranged to get a call through to Los Angeles, where he contacted John J. Garland, a prominent local businessman. Garland immediately contacted Fletcher Bowron, the mayor of Los Angeles, and the wheels were put in motion that would lead to the purchase of the Swoose by the city of Los Angeles.[6]

Garland had been the first to suggest that the Swoose be acquired by the city of Los Angeles as a war memorial. In December 1944, Kurtz had been dispatched on a Treasury Department–sponsored six-week, 6,000-mile war bond tour of the western states. As Colonel and Mrs. Kurtz were flying on a commercial flight from Tucson to Burbank (the next stop on that tour), they met John Garland. Later on the tour, the Kurtzes also met Mayor Bowron, who, along with members of the Chamber of Commerce, had given them a homecoming welcome.

Government policy made special provisions for granting the sale of surplus war material at a token cost to communities and academic organizations for ground-instruction purposes or, in the case of airplanes and ships, for war memorials.

On March 2, 1946, a week after Kurtz called John Garland from Alaska, the mayor of Los Angeles requested the Swoose for permanent display, as an object of historical importance and a memorial to those who lost their lives during World War II.[7] The airplane was to be housed in an exhibition room to be built as part of the grandstand structure of a swimming tank adjacent to the Los Angeles Memorial Coliseum.[8]

At the same time, arrangements had been made through Air Force channels for assistance in preparing the Swoose for its presentation to the city. Kurtz arranged for Harold Varner and Roland Boone, his old crewmates who had since been promoted to commissioned Air Force officers, to leave their assigned bases and be placed on detached service at March Field. From there, they were assigned to temporary duty at Kingman, where they joined Kurtz. Frank, Margo, and the crew lived in an abandoned barracks on the field for a time while the Swoose was prepared for flight.[9]

One can imagine their surprise as they gazed at the new "Swoose." It had been more than three years since they last saw "their" airplane. The group had come to Kingman with the objective of refurbishing the airplane to its combat configuration and to make it airworthy for one last flight to Los Angeles. But they found a quite different Swoose—whose exterior was more that of a sleek airliner than a scarred veteran of battle that was to be christened as a war memorial. The condition of the airplane's interior when Kurtz and his party arrived on the scene at Kingman is not known. However, it was standard practice to remove all flight instrumentation and equipment in preparation for reducing old airplanes to scrap, and it was reported that this process had begun before the city of Los Angeles claimed it for $350.[10]

Over the next few weeks, a 25-hour inspection was performed and some of the recently removed instruments were replaced for a flight to March Field under visual flight rules (VFR), which govern the conduct of flight under visual conditions. Kurtz took a test flight from Kingman to Las Vegas and then back to Kingman in order to detect any faults. When he found none, the airplane was refueled and then flown to March Field.[11]

Little could be done at March Field to return the demilitarized airplane to its combat configuration, but apparently a quick coat of olive drab and black paint was applied to cover the gleaming, polished aluminum skin, giving the Swoose more of the desired combat-weary appearance.

The grouping of flags painted on the right side of the nose was apparently masked over during the painting, and the natural aluminum skin that showed through between the flags was painted white to cover the aluminum. In connection with this cosmetic alteration, the words over the group of flags were changed. After the overhaul in Panama, the words painted above the flags were: "THE LANDS THE SWOOSE HAS VISITED." At March Field, the words applied over the white background were: "FLAGS OF THE COUNTRIES SWOOSE HAS VISITED."[12] The Swoose logo, aft of the door on the right side, seems to have been untouched by the new paint job. Following the Albrook overhaul, that logo appeared as a circle. When originally painted by Weldon Smith in Australia, the logo was painted directly over the camouflage paint.

The Swoose remained at March Field until early in April, when Kurtz flew it back to Kingman for the formal flight to its new home in Los Angeles. Festooned with large replicas of the signature of each of General Brett's original crew on its fuselage, the Swoose lifted off from Kingman on April 6, 1946, with a radio reporter transmitting from the airplane as it flew to Los Angeles.[13]

Miraculously the Swoose had escaped demolition once again, and now was winging its way through the sky toward a new home in Los Angeles, where the airplane would become a war memorial on public display. At the controls were Col. Frank Kurtz, with Mrs. Kurtz in the seat normally occupied by the copilot. Mayor Bowron sat in the copilot's seat during the approach into Los Angeles. Arthur E. Rogers, father of both Margo Kurtz and Kurtz's former copilot in Panama (as well as his brother-in-law), Homer "Buck" Rogers, was on board, having been invited to fly from Kingman to Los Angeles.[14] Many of the original crew who had served with General Brett in Australia also were on board. They were Maj. Harry J. Schreiber, Capt. Harold Varner, Capt. Rowland Boone, and Maj. Charles T. Reeves.[15] Missing were Sgt. Aubrey Fox, and Lt. Marvin MacAdams, who was killed in 1943.

Following the short flight, the airplane landed at Mines Field, the Los Angeles municipal airport, where it was greeted by a gathering of 3,000 people who had come to celebrate Army Day. Standing on the speakers' platform for the transfer ceremony were Mayor Fletcher Bowron, Serge F. Bailey Jr., regional director for the War Assets Administration, and Colonel Kurtz. Bailey formally transferred the airplane to the city. Since the terms of the transfer prohibited the Swoose from ever flying again, it was thought by all those present that the airplane had at last found a permanent home, where it would be enshrined for future generations to see.[16]

Among the large crowd at this historic event were Lt. Col. Henry Godman and Lt. Col. Weldon H. Smith, who waited out of the rain under the wing of a parked airplane. Seeing their old friend again stirred in them memories of lost comrades and trying days in the Philippines and Southwest Pacific during those early days of the war. They were probably happy to know this relic of their past would now be saved for posterity. General Brett, however, expressed his continuing concern for the Swoose's history—he felt that the full history of the Swoose was not recognized by those involved in the ceremony in Los Angeles.[17]

There were other unrelated and contrasting Army Day activities on the day the old veteran Swoose arrived in Los Angeles. Nearby at Muroc Army Air Field, the new experimental aircraft, the "Flying Wing," was put on display. Meanwhile, at March Field, the new Lockheed jet-propelled airplanes were demonstrating their aerial capabilities.[18]

Saved Again—Operation Valhalla

In January 1947, during a visit to "The Hangar," a cottage museum in Berkeley, California, maintained by C. A. "Mother" Tusch, Paul Garber, curator of the National Air Museum, first learned of the Swoose when he saw a framed painting of the Swoose logo hanging on the wall. The painting by Weldon Smith included a caption that detailed some of the airplane's history.[19] Unknown to Garber, Robert C. Strobel, then associate curator of the National Air Museum, had attempted to obtain the Swoose in 1947 when he was chief of the Air Force Technical Museum in Dayton, Ohio.[20]

When he learned the airplane's future might be in jeopardy, Kurtz contacted Grover Loening, a long-time friend who was then on the Smithsonian's Board of Regents. Loening said he would immediately contact Paul Garber of the Smithsonian and apprise him of the situation. Conversations began with Paul Garber, Frank Kurtz, and the mayor of Los Angeles to initiate formal plans for the city to turn the Swoose over to the National Air Museum.

In May 1948, Garber visited the neglected B-17, sitting alone in a hangar with birds' nests in its control surface hinges. Following his return to Washington, Garber initiated correspondence with the airport manager, Clarence Young, which finally led to the transfer of the airplane to the National Air Museum.[21] Following an investigation of methods to get the Swoose into the museum's collection, it was agreed that the most effective way would be under its own power, if at all possible.

In September 1948, Loening called Paul Garber to advise him that Frank Kurtz was then assigned to Air Force Headquarters in

Washington, in the policy division of the Directorate of Plans and Operations. Loening thought that Kurtz might be able to help in getting the airplane flown to the museum's holding facility in the old Douglas Aircraft Company's DC-4 assembly building at the Chicago Orchard Airport in Park Ridge.[22] With the cooperation of Maj. Gen. E. M. Powers, the USAF representative on the National Air Museum Advisory Board, and through Frank Kurtz's efforts, the Air Force agreed to restore the Swoose to flyable condition for the flight to Orchard Park even though the airplane was no longer Air Force property.[23]

At Garber's request, the Civil Aeronautics Administration's (CAA) regional office in Los Angeles conducted a visual inspection of the Swoose and found the airplane in "fair" condition. They estimated that it would take two mechanics about three weeks to make it airworthy. Among the observations they noted, the tail wheel tire had blown out, the main landing gear tires were badly worn, and the left elevator trim tab and left aileron needed repair or replacement. The engines had last been run about eight months earlier and the oil had drained. The bottom cylinders were full of oil.[24]

Following a visit to Los Angeles, Frank Kurtz arranged for his old crew chief, now Capt. Rowland Boone of the Twelfth Air Force, to conduct a survey of the airplane. On December 9, 1948, Captain Boone advised Kurtz of the results of an inspection conducted December 6.[25] Boone had found the Swoose covered with dust and grime accumulated in the two years since its arrival. All the fuel had been drained, which dried out the fuel tanks and caused cracks around the fuel tank drain cocks. He doubted that the left inboard fuel cell could be used, and could not be sure of the others until they had been serviced with gasoline. Because the fuel had been completely drained, the rubber diaphragms in the carburetors no longer were serviceable, and the carburetors would have to be replaced, although there was a possibility that soaking them in gasoline for several days might make them operational. The supercharger compressor wheels were free, but the supercharger oil also had been drained from the system.

The general condition of the fuel and oil hoses was better than one would expect. Some, however, like the rubber hose connections on the engine push rod tubes, would have to be replaced. The electrical system seemed to be in working order, but Boone felt they probably would encounter some trouble with engine-starter solenoids, generators, and relays.

Boone also found a number of instruments missing from the cockpit instrument panel. While he could not at the time identify all that had been removed, Boone did note that the vacuum gauge, compass, clock, and free air temperature gauge were among the missing. An observer who had gone out to the airport to photograph the Swoose before it took off January 22, 1949, was invited on board following the completion of preflight tests. He noted that "most of the instruments had been stolen." Apparently Boone had not been able to replace many of the instruments he had noted were missing in his initial inspection.

The major communications equipment still was installed and appeared to Boone to be intact, but he could not determine whether they would operate. As noted earlier by the CAA, Boone felt that the landing gear tires and tubes had to be replaced. Since the hydraulic fluid had been drained, he could not determine the condition of the brake cylinders and the emergency hand pump. Since the airplane was being supported by wing jacks, the condition of the fully extended oleo struts could not be assessed, although they did not show signs of rust. The aircraft control systems seemed to be operational when Boone moved them. However, repairs would have to be made to the damaged left and right ailerons and the trim tab on the left elevator. Birds' nests were found in a number of places, which Boone felt might be a problem—the tenants would have to be evicted.

Upon reading Boone's report, Frank Kurtz realized that significant effort would be required by the Air Force to make the airplane ready for a flight to Chicago. He presented the problem to General Powers. Plans to return the Swoose to airworthiness went forward with Air Force precision. At the time, Kurtz had planned to obtain machine guns, bombs, and bomb racks to put the old relic back in as near combat condition as possible.[26]

In the meantime, the CAA agreed to grant necessary certification to clear the airplane. On December 17, 1948, Captain Boone and an Air Force detachment from March Field began the reconditioning of the Swoose in preparation for a flight to March Field, where additional work would be undertaken for the flight east to Chicago.

On Christmas Eve, 1948, Captain Boone notified Colonel Kurtz that the airplane was ready for testing. Kurtz had planned to fly the Swoose for three hours of "slow time" and land at March Field for a planned 48-hour shakedown and final check before returning the airplane to Los Angeles and the start of the final flight east.[27]

Frank Kurtz and Paul Garber left Washington for Los Angeles in an Air Force B-25 on January 19, 1949. Because of weather delays en route, they did not arrive at Mines Field until Saturday, January 22. They met with the airport manager and proceeded to the vicinity of the Pan American Airways hangar, where the Swoose was moored outside in the rain. For two days, with Kurtz in the pilot's seat once more and Boone occupying the copilot's position, they made extensive tests of the Swoose's engines in order to detect any malfunctions that could impact the safety of flight.[28]

Having assured himself that each of the four engines was performing satisfactorily, Kurtz then got permission from the tower to make taxi runs along the main runway to test the operation of the wheels and brakes, the general response of the airplane, and the reaction of its instruments. After four such runs, two more runs were made with the airplane allowed to be aloft to an altitude of five or ten feet to test the flight controls and integrity of the landing gear.[29]

About 4:00 P.M. on January 22, 1949, following the test runs, the Swoose was cleared to taxi to the runway for takeoff and a VFR flight to March Field. With Paul Garber in the copilot's seat, the plane climbed to between 5,000 and 6,000 feet, the flight profile being limited because of the overcast. Garber handled the controls briefly after Kurtz turned the airplane toward March Field, where they landed without incident. Frank Birely, a friend of Kurtz's, was also on board for the flight to March Field. Following the landing, as Kurtz entered a taxiway, the tail wheel blew out.[30]

The Swoose was turned over to Air Force maintenance crews for further work. The cursory information in the airplane's maintenance record included a notation that on January 22 the aircraft flew 1 hour and 35 minutes with Kurtz as pilot. Evidently this entry covered the flight to March Field from Los Angeles. The pilot's reported discrepancies were:

> #4 oil temperature running too cool. #4 tach 200 RPM slow. #3 voltage regulator cannot be adjusted low enough. Magnetic compass 30 degrees off. Command transmitter too weak. No pitot tube heat. Turbos wired in open position. Tail wheel tire weak.[31]

The following Monday, January 24, Paul Garber and Frank Kurtz met with Mayor Bowron, and the formal transfer of the airplane to the custody of the Smithsonian Institution was consummated.[32] The words used by the mayor at the airport ceremony were:

> At this time I should like to turn over to the Smithsonian Institute [*sic*], whom you—Paul E. Garber represent as Curator of its National Air Museum—the historic and immortalized B-17, "The Swoose." I am making this presentation on

behalf of the city of Los Angeles, its Airport Commission and its citizens. This is a memorable occasion to we in Los Angeles who have had "The Swoose" under our care at the Municipal Airport.

I don't have to remind you of this famous warplane's record—how it survived the enemy's attack from the time of the Pearl Harbor bombardment until the war ended in the Pacific. It is a symbol of our fighting Air Force—the greatest the world has known.[33]

The next day, January 25, 1949, Kurtz and Garber began their return trip to Washington in the B-25. The Swoose remained at March Field, which had been the airplane's first home after it was built in 1941 and assigned to the 19th Bombardment Group. The Swoose truly had returned home. En route to Washington, Garber and Kurtz stopped in Omaha where, on January 26, they made a broadcast tape at a local radio station detailing the history of the Swoose and its proposed flight to the National Air Museum.[34]

Upon his return to Washington, Garber reported that the Swoose appeared to be flyable and its delivery to Park Ridge by air still seemed practical. He outlined considerations being given to a plan for flying the Swoose east to Chicago via Hamilton Field (San Francisco), Seattle (Boeing Field), Rapid City, Denver, Omaha, Dayton, Cleveland, Patterson, N.J., and Washington, D.C. The purpose of this long, meandering flight path was to contact the makers of the airframe and engines "to advertise the history and present performance of this historic plane, and at the same time obtain publicity for the National Air Museum."[35]

This extended flight plan did not come to fruition and a shorter, more direct route was selected, but not without attendant publicity. On March 18, 1949, a letter was sent to the Chicago Chamber of Commerce advising them that the Swoose would soon be flown east by Col. Frank Kurtz and its original wartime crew, and that it would be placed in the National Air Museum's storage facility at Park Ridge. The storage area was described as Building 6, Chicago—Orchard Park, Higgins, and Mannheim Roads, Park Ridge. According to the letter, the storage facility already contained a large number of airplanes destined for exhibition "when our proposed new building is ready."

The Swoose remained at March Field for two months. It was subjected to preflight inspections on January 23 and 30. In February, preflights were recorded on the seventh, tenth, fifteenth, and twenty-first days of the month. Preflights were run on March 2, 4, 11, and 18.[36] During that time the problems noted by Kurtz on the January 22 flight were corrected. A number of other defects were detected during the inspections of the airplane while at March, and some of these were also corrected.

No mention of missing instruments was made in the maintenance inspection record; however, a newspaper reported that the airplane was not equipped for instrument flying.[37] It may be assumed from subsequent documentation made in May 1953 that most of the flight instruments noted by Boone to be missing during his inspection in Los Angeles were replaced by March Field maintenance crews.

The last recorded entry made by March Field crews showed only the following discrepancies, considered to be minor and not affecting the Swoose's airworthiness: "Slight fuel leak around the bottom of #2 inboard fuel tank. Tail wheel tire worn. Oxygen system inoperative, wrong regulators."[38]

On March 4, 1949, a 25-hour inspection was completed and only the discrepancies noted above were carried forward. It was noted in a local newspaper that the main landing gear tires had been replaced.[39] Although the airplane remained at March Field for several more days, no further entries were made in the maintenance inspection record. The cover of that document shows that any subsequent entries were transferred to a new form, which is missing.

The Swoose remained at March Field until March 23, 1949, when Colonel Kurtz flew a return trip to Los Angeles for a public ceremony marking the airplane's official departure from the city. The ceremony took place at 1:30 P.M. when, in the company of the manager of the Los Angeles Department of Airports, Clarence Young, Mayor Bowron gave the airplane over to Frank Kurtz for delivery to the Smithsonian Institution facility in Chicago.[40]

On Saturday, March 26, as twelve North American F-51s of the Air National Guard flew overhead as a guard of honor, the Swoose departed Los Angeles for the last time, buzzing several large air fields en route to northern California. With a leaking fuel tank, a boot in its worn tail wheel, and with one of its doors wired shut, the Swoose began its last transcontinental adventure by first flying to Hamilton Field near San Francisco.[41]

Less than two months short of eight years earlier, and as a spanking new airplane, B-17D 40-3097 had departed from the same Hamilton Field for the journey westward—first to Hawaii, and subsequently to high adventure and fame in the air battles in the Philippines and the Southwest Pacific, and then a legendary tour of duty in the Western Hemisphere.

The crew for the last departure from Hamilton Field were part of Colonel Kurtz's crew that had served General Brett in Australia. In addition to Kurtz, they were Maj. Harry Schreiber, Maj. Charles Reeves, Capt. Harold Varner, and Capt. Rowland Boone. Also on board was the Los Angeles newspaper columnist, Vincent X. Flaherty.[42]

Prior to its departure from Hamilton Field, at 12:50 P.M. on March 27, the Swoose was visited by Gen. Henry H. "Hap" Arnold, wartime chief of the Army Air Force, who now lived in retirement nearby. Later that day, after its compass had been replaced, the Swoose took off on the next leg of the planned flight to Chicago. On its way out, the Swoose was flown low over General Arnold's house. He came out and saluted the airplane as it dipped its wing in a final tribute.[43]

The Swoose's first scheduled stop was Las Vegas. However, Kurtz found the airplane behaving so well that he elected to continue on to Albuquerque, where the Swoose landed at 6:45 P.M. MST, after just under five hours of flying.[44] The unscheduled stop at Kirtland Air Force Base in Albuquerque was a sentimental one for both the crew and the airplane. The crew had trained there before leaving for the Pacific with the 19th Bombardment Group in October 1941. Colonel Kurtz had been the commander of the base in 1945. As for the Swoose, it had made its last landing there with General Brett at the controls on December 1, 1945, before being flown off to an appointment with a metal crusher at Kingman Air Field.

After a 4-hour and 40-minute flight from Kirtland, the now-legendary Swoose settled down on the runway at Offutt Air Force Base near Omaha at 4:40 P.M., Monday, March 28. The Swoose was met by Mrs. Kurtz and the Kurtzes' four-year-old daughter, Swoosie. Swoosie, who was born on September 6, 1944, was named after the airplane her father piloted in Australia and Panama. Frank Kurtz recalled that following her birth in Omaha, Mrs. Kurtz was visited by three newspaper reporters. When one asked the name of the newborn, one of the other reporters is quoted as saying, "Well, she's the new Swoose, we'll call her 'Swoosie.'" Thus the airplane now had a living namesake. Swoosie Kurtz is now a stage, screen, and television actress and continues to use that name.[45]

On the morning of March 29, 1949, the Swoose left Offutt Air Force Base for the short hop to the Omaha Municipal Airport, where it was exhibited to the public throughout the day. Mrs. Kurtz and Swoosie accompanied the crew on the flight.[46]

After being entertained by the local chamber of commerce, the crew reboarded the Swoose on March 31, 1949, for the last time. The takeoff from the municipal airport was scheduled for 12:15 that afternoon.

After circling the city for 20 minutes, Kurtz was scheduled to point the Swoose in the direction of Chicago. It was the final leg of a journey that had started on January 22, 1949, when the Swoose had left the Los Angeles municipal airport for March Field. The plan for this last flight called for a flyover of Des Moines, Iowa, and then on to Joliet, Illinois, where it was met by three Douglas B-26s of the Illinois National Guard, who escorted the Swoose to Chicago. The aircraft landed at Orchard Park Airport at 3:30 P.M. to appropriate fanfare.[47]

The arrival in Chicago was duly noted in the newspapers. Preparations had been made for a reception honoring the Swoose, "the only bomber that was in World War II from start to finish," and its crew. The local papers reported that plans were made for school children to be taken on tours to the airport to see the "battle-scarred veteran."[48]

With this milestone, the Swoose ended its affiliation with Frank Kurtz and the others of the crew, one that had first begun in Australia in April 1942. Walter M. Male of the Smithsonian's National Air Museum, in charge of the museum's storage hanger, took charge of the Swoose upon its arrival in Chicago. As had been the case in Los Angeles, it was again thought that the Swoose's flying days were over. Male commented that the noble airplane would be stored in the hanger for at least five years before being disassembled and crated for shipment to the newly planned air museum to be constructed in Washington.[49]

The Swoose Odyssey Continues

The *New York Times,* in its editorial of April 11, 1949, commenting on the Swoose's retirement, said, "Last week, the last B-17 of the pre–World War II vintage still flying—'Swoose'—hung up its propellers. The Swoose rested in its hangar with other artifacts of aviation awaiting shipment to Washington and public display in the new facility being planned for that purpose." That was not to be, nor was the Swoose to become forever bound to the ground. Fate had failed to permanently ground the airplane at Laverton, Australia, and again in Panama. Against all odds it rose into the sky again at Kingman before it could be destroyed. Grounded by government edict, it had again spread its wings skyward after a long stay in Los Angeles. Chicago was to be no different.

On June 27, 1950, Pres. Harry Truman ordered the U.S. Air Force to Korea after North Korea invaded the South. On June 30, he approved air strikes against the North. The fighting would last until July 27,

1953, and it involved as many as 112,738 members of the USAF, 2,360 of whom would be killed.[50] To support the Korean "police action," the Air Force decided that it needed the former Douglas Aircraft Company assembly hangar where the Swoose and other Smithsonian aircraft were housed. Arrangements were made for an Air Force crew to fly the Swoose from Chicago to Pyote Air Force Base in Texas. Air Force maintenance crews at O'Hare Air Force Base had removed the Swoose from storage and on January 10, 1952, they completed a 100-hour airworthiness inspection. The Swoose was then test-flown and cleared for a one-time flight to Pyote with the left and right wing feeder tanks blocked off.[51]

The airplane was flown to Tinker Air Force Base near Oklahoma City on January 18. The pilot, Lt. Col. Jack Williams, noted in the aircraft inspection and maintenance record (AF Form 1) that the top hatch blew off on takeoff. Other noted discrepancies included that the right and left fuel feeder tanks were blocked off, the number 2 and 3 turbo supercharger controls were "off" in the forward position while the number 1 and 4 controls were "off" in the aft position.

The top hatch was replaced at Tinker. On January 18, serviced with 755 gallons of fuel, the Swoose flew on to Pyote, Texas, in 2 hours and 35 minutes. The pilot for that flight was Capt. Floyd O. Bock.[52] The airplane and its engines were subsequently placed in storage status and parked outdoors alongside the Enola Gay.

The Last of the Last Swoose Flights

Almost two years later, the Swoose was reclaimed from its outdoor storage and prepared for its final flight to Andrews Air Force Base near Washington, D.C. On November 23, 1953, work had begun at Pyote Air Force Base to remove the Swoose from storage and restore it for that last flight to Washington and its home in the collection of the Smithsonian Institution. After much work, the airplane received a flight test on December 2.[53]

The Swoose was cleared for its last flight with the following problems not related to flight safety: the engine fire extinguishers were not winterized; the anti-icing system was disconnected; the "G" files (airplane records) were incomplete; no de-icer boots were installed (they had been removed in the Southwest Pacific); the clock was removed; vacuum, fuel, and oil hoses were deteriorated; and the oxygen system was disconnected. Other notes included the fact that the tires were weather-checked and that the SCR 274 Radio Compass was inspected for low-band reception only and would not "home." (Photographic evidence shows that the antenna had been removed.) The number 1 transmitter was set on 3105 Kc in lieu of 4495 in compliance with Technical Order 01-1-297. The turbo controls for number 2 and number 3 engines were "off" in the forward positions, while "off" for number 1 and number 4 was in the aft positions. The feeder fuel tanks were blocked, and an item indicated that the control surfaces were satisfactory for the one-time flight to Washington. The Swoose also carried on its last flight deteriorated oil hoses, an erratic engine tachometer (number 3 engine), an erratic manifold pressure gauge (number 4 engine), and an inoperative engine generator (number 2 engine).

The airplane was weighed on November 18, and a weight and balance form prepared. The weight and balance form showed the basic airplane weight to be 30,991 pounds and, with 140 gallons of oil, five crew members, and 800 gallons of fuel, the takeoff weight was 37,841 pounds (when new, the B-17D weighed 30,707 pounds empty and had a gross weight of 46,174 pounds).[54]

The crew for the last Swoose mission came from Kelly Air Force Base near San Antonio. The pilot was Maj. Richard T. Saxe and the copilot was Maj. William A. Pelton. They were accompanied by a civilian crew from Kelly's flight test branch made up of James Wilcox, Edward Flowers, and Edmund Peres.[55] Saxe had copiloted his first B-17 in 1942 and had flown over the North Pole with famous polar veterans Bernt Balchen and Sir Hubert Wilkins. As part of Air Force projects "Parkway" and "Icicle," Saxe had flown a number of missions to the Arctic. More recently, he had been flying C-124 cargo runs at Kelly.

Major Gen. Clements "Concrete" McMullen, commanding general of the San Antonio Air Materiel Area, recalling Saxe's affection for B-17s, had asked him to accept the challenge of getting the Swoose out of the sands at Pyote and to try to fly it to Washington for the Smithsonian. Saxe accepted the challenge and selected the crew. When Saxe and crew arrived, they found the Swoose with its unique logo still vividly showing on the fuselage, despite the corrosive effects of the sandstorms to which it had been subjected at Pyote. According to Saxe, the aircraft had no instruments to speak of. There was no air-speed indicator or rate-of-climb indicator. Only the magnetic and gyro compasses remained. A lash-up oil pressure and temperature gauge were installed by the ground crew, along with replacement air-speed and rate-of-climb indicators. A low-frequency radio was made available for air-to-ground communications.

The airplane had no navigation lights. Without navigation instruments and appropriate communications equipment, the Swoose would have to be flown in daylight, under visual flight rules, and by dead-reckoning all the way to Washington.[56]

On the morning of December 2, 1953, the crew boarded the Swoose for the purpose of making ground taxi tests. The airplane handled well, so they decided to take off on the first leg of the long trip to Washington. Several relatively short legs would be required because the fuel supply was limited as the two feeder fuel tanks in the wings were blocked off.

The Enola Gay was sitting at the end of the Pyote runway when the Swoose left the ground with 1,000 gallons of gasoline in its tanks. As a salute to the famous carrier of the first atomic bomb to be dropped, Saxe flew low over the famous B-29. As Saxe pulled the Swoose up in a climbing turn, the ceiling hatch in the flight crew compartment came off. (This was the second time the hatch had come off since the Swoose left Chicago.)[57]

The crew flew on to their next stop at Laredo, Texas. There they refueled the airplane, ate sandwiches, and prepared for takeoff on the next leg to Ellington Air Force Base in Houston. Before that takeoff, as Major Pelton, the copilot, was setting the parking brakes, he accidentally pulled a fire extinguisher handle instead of the parking brake, discharging the CO2 fire extinguisher into the number 4 engine compartment.[58] (Jack Crane, one of the Swoose's former pilots, remarked that something like this always happened when there was too much rank in the cockpit.)

En route to Ellington, still flying with the open hatch, they encountered a heavy downpour. The rain poured through the opening and flooded the floor of the flight crew compartment. At Ellington on December 3, after the hatch was replaced and the Swoose serviced with fuel and oil, they pressed on to Maxwell Air Force Base outside Montgomery, Alabama. At Maxwell, the front spark plugs on the number 4 engine were replaced to correct rough running and an excessive drop in RPM during ground checks.[59]

On December 3, during the flight from Maxwell to McGhee Tyson Field at Knoxville, Tennessee, the Swoose, stripped of much of its normal weight of fuel and equipment and helped along by a tail wind, averaged a striking 230 MPH. However, as it approached Knoxville, a series of inflight engine problems appeared that could have brought the last mission of the Swoose to a premature and catastrophic end.

The old radio was receiving only a single station out of Raleigh, North Carolina, and the crew was navigating by reference to visual features on the ground, when about five miles out of Knoxville the number 1 engine began to shake and lose power. The number 2 engine already was spewing oil. The Swoose landed at McGhee Tyson with the number 1 propeller feathered. After repairing the oil leak in number 2, the last crew of the Swoose took off for its final destination, Andrews Air Force Base, feathering the number 1 engine once again shortly after takeoff.

In the fading daylight, about 50 miles from Washington, an oil line on the number 3 engine broke and that engine was shut down, its propeller feathered. Attempts to restart the number 1 engine proved futile. With the remaining two operating engines, they pressed on. About 10 minutes before final approach, the number 2 engine started to act up.

The Swoose was losing power and vibrating severely. Saxe was forced to shut down and feather engine number 2. With only engine number 4 running (whose fire extinguisher had been depleted at Laredo), amazingly (though the airplane was very light), the Swoose was still apparently able to hold its altitude.

Saxe set the course for landing so that the flight path carried the Swoose over the Potomac River as long as possible, to give him the option of ditching the airplane in the river should it become necessary. The Swoose did not fail them. The very lightweight airplane responded to its controls, until Saxe spotted the runway lights at Andrews, where he landed at dusk on December 5, 1953, four days after the departure from Pyote.[60] When the single remaining engine had been shut down, and with the Swoose resting safely on the ground with smoke rising from its tired, overworked engine, the old bird had at last flown its final mission.

The impact of the hair-raising experience suffered by the ferry crew of the Swoose can best be demonstrated by their mode of travel back to San Antonio. While the flight crew, Saxe, and Pelton, returned by commercial air, Wilcox, Flowers, and Peres took a train.

Home without a Roof

The Swoose was unceremoniously towed from the flight line at Andrews to an unguarded area far from all base activities, where it joined other Smithsonian airplanes parked among the weeds. There it remained in exile, unvisited except by a few brave souls who would venture to the area from time to time to view these relics from the past.

Apparently, among those visitors were some who collected souvenirs. Collectors completely ravaged the airplane. Much of the pilot's and copilot's instrument panels were removed, along with other small items that could easily be carried off. Jack Crane wrote to the museum expressing his alarm over the situation, after reading of the sad state of the Swoose "rotting away in outdoor storage."[61] Others also expressed concern as did an Air Force lieutenant with a passionate interest in these airplanes. In 1956, he obtained media support from the *Washington Post, Air Force Times,* and syndicated news reporters which brought pressure to bear for improving the care of these relics of the war in the air. (Fate would one day put that former lieutenant, Robert C. Mikesh, on the museum staff with responsibility as the curator and for the well-being of the Swoose and the other historic airplanes in the collection.) Finally recognizing that the Swoose was deteriorating and being vandalized at its outdoor location at Andrews, in April 1961 officials had the Swoose disassembled and its component parts trucked to what is now known as the Paul E. Garber Preservation, Restoration, and Storage Facility in Suitland, Maryland, where it is currently stored out of public view.

On July 19, 1966, Pres. Lyndon Baines Johnson signed into law an act (Public Law 89-509), which changed the name of the National Air Museum to the National Air and Space Museum and authorized the construction of a new museum building. The building, 635 feet long, 225 feet wide, and almost 83 feet high, was designed to display air and space artifacts.

Ten years later, on July 1, 1976, during the celebration of the nation's Bicentennial, the new Smithsonian National Air and Space Museum was opened on the Mall in Washington. This new museum failed to provide adequate space for displaying aircraft larger than the Douglas DC-3 in the half of the facility dedicated to aeronautics. So, large numbers of the aeronautics department's artifacts remained at the Garber facility.

People had said in the past that it would never fly again, but the Swoose led a charmed life and defied attempts to assign it eternally to the ground. Now, with its fuselage stored in one building while the preserved engines are in another, and its wings in still another, the Swoose is permanently at rest, awaiting a day when it will be restored to dignity and displayed to the public in a new National Air and Space Museum annex.

The Swoose is in good hands. Though the lack of restoration

resources and the unavailability of exhibition space will postpone its rebirth, it has been saved for posterity and will not go the way of so many other important, historically significant aircraft that have been lost forever. On the day the Swoose is restored, it will again tell of the exploits and times of those who took part in the air operations of World War II. The brave men of the 19th Bombardment Group and the other mortals who flew in the airplane will be gone by then, but the Swoose will survive as a reminder of the part they played in the defense of the free world.

Appendix A

Headquarters, 19th Bombardment Group (H) GHQ AF March Field, Riverside, California

May 10, 1941
SPECIAL ORDERS
:
No. 89)

Extract

1. Pursuant to authority contained in Letter, WD, File AG 210.482, (4-9-41), Subject: Orders, dated April 9, 1941, and 3rd Indorsement, Headquarters, 1st Bombardment Wing, GHQ AF, March Field, Riverside, California, dated April 18, 1941, the following named personnel:

Crew No. 1

Lt Col Eugene L. Eubank, 0-10580, AC
1st Lieut Kenneth R. Kreps, 0-21493, AC
2nd Lieut John W. Chiles, 0-377514, AR

This is the roster of 19th Bombardment Group personnel who participated in the May 1941 flight from Hamilton Field, California, to Hawaii.

2nd Lieut William A. Cocke, Jr., 0-22801, AC
1st Lieut Elbert D. Reynolds, 0-21570, AC
T/Sgt Charles K. Smith, 6102050, Hq & Hq Sq, 19th Bomb Gp (H) GHQ AF
M/Sgt Raymond C. Lane, 6526355, Hq & Hq Sq, 19th Bomb Gp (H) GHQ AF
T/Sgt Ruffus R, Nicholas, 6230961, Hq & Hq Sq, 19th Bomb Gp (H) GHQ AF
S/Sgt Frank A. Carroll, 6137776, Hq & Hq Sq, 19th Bomb Gp (H) GHQ AF

Crew No. 2

Major David R. Gibbs, 0-17165, AC
Captain Cecil E. Combs, 0-20121, AC
Captain Edwin B. Broadhurst, 0-20744, AC
1st Lieut Robert F. Hardy, 0-21517, AC
2nd Lieut James A. Worrell, Jr., 0-377836, AR
T/Sgt Anthony Holub, 6541498, Hq & Hq Sq, 19th Bomb Gp (H) GHQ AF
T/Sgt Leslie O. Stone, 6825520, 30th Bombardment Group (H) GHQ AF (Atchd)
Sgt Homer H. Hammond, 6755430, Hq & Hq Sq, 19th Bomb Gp (H) GHQ AF
S/Sgt Theodore L. Miller, 6557809, Hq & Hq Sq, 19th Bomb Gp (H) GHQ AF

Crew No. 3

Lt Col Thomas W. Blackburn, 0-10814, AC
1st Lieut John E L. Huse, 0-21777, AC
1st Lieut Sam Maddux, Jr., 0-21589, AC
1st Lieut Raymond V. Schwanbeck, 0-21589, AC
1st Lieut Alvino V. Reyes, 0-380564, AR
M/Sgt Edgar W. Gardner, R-779698, 30th Bombardment Group (H) GHQ AF (Atchd)
S/Sgt William K. Hollingsworth, 6825961, 30th Bombardment Group (H) GHQ AF (Atchd)
Corp Morris E. Taylor, 6950938, 30th Bombardment Squadron (H) GHQ AF
T/Sgt Sidney J. Willis, 6521723, 30th Bombardment Group (H) GHQ AF (Atchd)

Crew No. 4

Major Budd J. Peaslee, 0-17061, AC
Captain Charles B. Westover, 0-20746
1st Lieut Ben I. Funk, 0-21506, AC
2nd Lieut Cuthbert L. Moseley, Jr., 0-377814, AR
2nd Lieut Jay M. Horowitz, 0-409900, AR
M/Sgt Ballard B. Small, R-326531, 30th Bombardment Squadron (H) GHQ AF (Atchd)
S/Sgt James A. Leckbee, 6563756, 41st Bombardment Group (M) GHQ AF (Atchd)

S/Sgt Franklin J. Trammell, 6564880, 30th Bombardment Group (H) GHQ AF (Atchd)

Pvt 1cl Anthony E. Jumia, 6911488, 30th Bombardment Group (H) GHQ AF (Atchd)

Crew No. 5

Captain Charles B. Dougher, 0-18581, AC

1st Lieut Ernest G. Ford, 0-22382, AC

1st Lieut James L. Travis, 0-21578, AC

2nd Lieut Melvin A. McKenzie, 0-374167, AR

2nd Lieut George B. Berkowitz, 0-409896, AR

S/Sgt Louis Hirsch, 6067630, 30th Bombardment Group (H) GHQ AF (Atchd)

T/Sgt John O. Fleming, 6537402, 30th Bombardment Squadron (H) GHQ AF (Atchd)

M/Sgt Hugh J. Marth, 6488763, 30th Bombardment Squadron (H) GHQ AF (Atchd)

S/Sgt Peter E. Shook, 6658245, 30th Bombardment Squadron (H) GHQ AF (Atchd)

Crew No. 6

Captain Douglas W. Cairns, 0-19129, AC

1st Lieut Jack Adams, 0-22338, AC

1st Lieut Arthur A. Aro, 0-368736, AR

1st Lieut Clifford S. Heflin, 0-22617, AC

2nd Lieut Francis B. Rang, 0-409905, AR

S/Sgt Albert C. Kissinger, 6814614, 41st Bombardment Group (M) GHQ AF (Atchd)

M/Sgt Frank W. Lytle, 6553898, 41st Bombardment Group (M) GHQ AF (Atchd)

M/Sgt Phillip P. Monroy, R-816699, 41st Bombardment Group (M) GHQ AF (Atchd)

Crew No. 7

Major Archibald Y. Smith, 0-15422, AC

1st Lieut James F. Starkey, 0-22439, AC

1st Lieut Robert C. Whipple, 0-22082, AC

1st Lieut Patrick W. McIntyre, 0-21495, AC

2nd Lieut Anthony E. Oliver, 0-409904, AR

T/Sgt Harry McHayes, 6645625, 32nd Bombardment Squadron (H) GHQ AF

T/Sgt Francis G. Denery, 6699071, 32nd Bombardment Squadron (H) GHQ AF

S/Sgt Myron S. Ficke, 6555983, 41st Bombardment Group (M) GHQ AF (Atchd)

Sgt Richard J. Barrett, Jr., 6714692, 32nd Bombardment Squadron (H) GHQ AF

Crew No. 8

Major Robert F. Tate, 0-17128, AC
1st Lieut Frank A. Kurtz, 0-22473, AC
2nd Lieut Lorin L. Johnson, 0-395164, AR
1st Lieut Arnold T. King, 0-359939, AR
2nd Lieut Charles J. Stevens, 0-409907, AR
S/Sgt Lloyd O. Gilbert, 6561158, 30th Bombardment Group (H) GHQ AF (Atchd)
T/Sgt Lloyd A. Severson, 6745013, 32nd Bombardment Squadron (H) GHQ AF
Corp Leonard F. Stuart, 6820712, 32nd Bombardment Squadron (H) GHQ AF
M/Sgt Walter E. Banas, R-352689, 30th Bombardment Group (H) GHQ AF (Atchd)

Crew No. 9

1st Lieut Ralph W. Rodieck, 0-22333, AC
1st Lieut Warner W. Croxton, Jr., 0-21957, AC
2nd Lieut James S. Park, 0-395257, AR
2nd Lieut John R. Maney, 0-22871, AC
2nd Lieut Leo G. Clarke, Jr., 0-409897, AR
M/Sgt Verl A. Shelley, 6506575, 32nd Bombardment Squadron (H) GHQ AF
T/Sgt Herbert H. Van Bibber, R-27217, 30th Bombardment Group (H) GHQ AF (Atchd)
S/Sgt Sterling P. Bone, 6257179, 32nd Bombardment Squadron (H) GHQ AF
Pvt 1cl Donald T. Ostlund, 6932103, 32nd Bombardment Squadron (H) GHQ AF

Crew No. 10

1st Lieut Kenneth H. Gibson, 0-22410, AC
2nd Lieut Charles E. Blankenhorn, 0-395110, AR
2nd Lieut Paul E. Cool, 0-395119, AR
2nd Lieut Glenn H. Boes, 0-392741, AR
2nd Lieut Charles E. Dewey, 0-393124, AR
M/Sgt William A. Wilson, R-2133740, 32nd Bombardment Squadron (H) GHQ AF
Sgt Otto J. Seidl, 6914117, 30th Bombardment Group (H) GHQ AF (Atchd)
S/Sgt Gerald P. Wilson, 6565370, 32nd Bombardment Squadron (H) GHQ AF
S/Sgt Edwin M. Rueffer, 6550189, 41st Bombardment Group (M) GHQ AF (Atchd)

Crew No. 11

Major Leo W. De Rosier, 0-17005, AC
Major Charles B. Overacker, Jr., 0-17007, AC
1st Lieut Harmon Lampley, Jr., 0-21792, AC

2nd Lieut Edwin H. Graham, Jr., 0393110, AR
2nd Lieut John W. Cox, Jr., 0-409898, AR
S/Sgt Wyndolyn E. Burgess, 6246578, 32nd Bombardment Squadron (H) GHQ AF
Sgt Dean H. Amholt, 6569943, 32nd Bombardment Squadron (H) GHQ AF
Sgt Robert M. Clark, 656584, 41st Bombardment Group (M) GHQ AF (Atchd)
T/Sgt Stephen J. Jerbic, 6654981, 32nd Bombardment Squadron (H) GHQ AF

Crew No. 12

Major Hilbert M. Wittkop, 0-15006, AC
1st Lieut Max R. Fennell, 0-350822, AR
2nd Lieut Harl Pease, Jr., 0-395306, AR
1st Lieut Edwin S. Green, 0-22330, AC
2nd Lieut Kenneth L. Akins, 0-392729, AR
M/Sgt Jesse C. McConnel, R-203791, 41st Bombardment Group (M) GHQ AF (Atchd)
S/Sgt Joseph J. Benkovic, 6893392, 93rd Bombardment Squadron (H) GHQ AF
S/Sgt Ross E. Watkins, 6833782, 93rd Bombardment Squadron (H) GHQ AF
Pvt 1cl Jean A. Byers, 6291071, 93rd Bombardment Squadron (H) GHQ AF

Crew No. 13

1st Lieut Arthur W. Schmitt, 0-21606, AC
2nd Lieut Harold J. Larson, 0-395124, AR
1st Lieut Elliot Vandevanter, Jr., 0-21989, AC
1st Lieut William J. Bohnaker, 0-22357, AC
2nd Lieut William S. Warner, 0-409909, AR
T/Sgt Gerald J. Slorf, 6763912, 30th Bombardment Group (H) GHQ AF (Atchd)
S/Sgt Joseph J. Claud, 6379966, 93rd Bombardment Squadron (H) GHQ AF
Sgt Ralph E. Anderson, 6857722, 93rd Bombardment Squadron (H) GHQ AF
Corp Victor J. Lorber, 6974283, 93rd Bombardment Squadron (H) GHQ AF

Crew No. 14

Major Thomas W. Steed, 0-17331, AC
1st Lieut Benoid E. Clawe, 0-21902, AC
1st Lieut John W. Carpenter, III, 0-21790, AC
1st Lieut Dean C. Hoevet, 0-22248, AC
2nd Lieut George M. Markovich, 0-409903, AR
T/Sgt Roy W. Irwin, 6215344, 41st Bombardment Group (M) GHQ AF (Atchd)
Corp Earl L. Rice, 6915529, 30th Bombardment Group (H) GHQ AF (Atchd)
Pvt 1cl Arthur E. Norgaard, 6571986, 93rd Bombardment Squadron (H) GHQ AF
T/Sgt William E. Wood, 6236292, 93rd Bombardment Squadron (H) GHQ AF

Crew No. 15

1st Lieut James W. Anderson, 0-22398, AC
1st Lieut Walter R. Ford, 0-370271, AR
2nd Lieut Edward L. Burge, 0-373488, AR
2nd Lieut Charles H. Hansen, 0-393115, AR
2nd Lieut Harry J. Schreiber, 0-342137, AR
S/Sgt Robert H. Cochrane, 6872071, 93rd Bombardment Squadron (H) GHQ AF
S/Sgt Jack P. Floyd, 6249596, 30th Bombardment Group (H) GHQ AF (Atchd)
Sgt William E. King, 6281545, 93rd Bombardment Squadron (H) GHQ AF
Pvt 1cl Jack W. Douglas, 6580266, 93rd Bombardment Squadron (H) GHQ AF

Crew No. 16

Major Jack W. Wood, 0-17488, AC
1st Lieut George W. Rogers, 0-364008, AR
1st Lieut Robert R. Little, 0-21917, AC
2nd Lieut Earl R. Tash, 0-374475, AR
2nd Lieut William F. Meenagh, 0-374475, AR
T/Sgt George L. Marsh, 6526011, 41st Bombardment Group (M) GHQ AF (Atchd)
Pvt 1cl Robert A. Hiron, 6581742, 93rd Bombardment Squadron (H) GHQ AF
Pvt 1cl Charles C. Kovacs, 6281713, 93rd Bombardment Squadron (H) GHQ AF
S/Sgt Jacques J. Deckers, 6721138, 93rd Bombardment Squadron (H) GHQ AF

Crew No. 17

Major Truman H. Landon, 0-17268, AC
1st Lieut James W. Chapman, 0-22481, AC
1st Lieut Maurice A. Morgan, 0-373909, AR
2nd Lieut Richard C. Hutchinson, 0-22802, AC
2nd Lieut Edgar D. Whitcomb, 0-409910, AR
M/Sgt Horace K. Hunsberger, R-629767, 38th Ren Aq (H) GHQ AF (Atchd)
S/Sgt Lawrence B. Velarde, 6555983, 38th Ren Aq (H) GHQ AF (Atchd)
S/Sgt Albert E. Brawley, 6252117, 38th Ren Aq (H) GHQ AF (Atchd)
Sgt Joseph J. Bruce, 6910319, 38th Ren Aq (H) GHQ AF (Atchd)

Crew No. 18

Major Elder Patteson, 0-17958, AC
2nd Lieut Francis B. Carlson, 0-22876, AC
1st Lieut Adam K. Breckenridge, 0-21815, AC
1st Lieut Bourne Adkinson, 0-22342, AC
2nd Lieut Theodore J. Boselli, 0-377349, AR
M/Sgt Richard M. Tennant, R-1003793, 6th Ren Sq (M) GHQ AF (Atchd)
S/Sgt Melvin D. Zajic, 6859921, 38th Ren Aq (H) GHQ AF (Atchd)

T/Sgt Charles F. Needels, 6536482, 38th Ren Aq (H) GHQ AF (Atchd)
Corp Clyde W. Nowlin, 6667130, 38th Ren Aq (H) GHQ AF (Atchd)

Crew No. 19
Captain Dwight O. Monteith, 0-20127, AC
1st Lieut William N. Vickers, Jr., 0-359104, AR
1st Lieut Lee B. Coats, 0-22383, AC
2nd Lieut Bruce G. Allen, 0-395101, AR
2nd Lieut Homer R. Taylor, 0-409908, AR
T/Sgt Ernest J. Barker, 6120734, 2nd Ren Sq (H) GHQ AF (Atchd)
T/Sgt Roy H. Coulter, 6783075, 38th Ren Aq (H) GHQ AF (Atchd)
Corp Donald K. Hassig, 6291068, 39th Ren Aq (H) GHQ AF (Atchd)
Pvt 1cl Raymond R. Joslin, 6578322, 38th Ren Aq (H) GHQ AF (Atchd)

Crew No. 20
Captain Don O. Darrow, 0-20429, AC
1st Lieut Clair E. Ryan, 0-280274, AR
1st Lieut John K. Carr, 0-22452, AC
1st Lieut Hewitt T. Wheless, 0-323879, AR
2nd Lieut Walter E. Seamon, Jr., 0-409906, AR
T/Sgt Edgar A. Geisler, 6509097, 6th Ren Sq (M) GHQ AF (Atchd)
S/Sgt Roy W. Donaldson, 6563456, 2nd Ren Sq (H) GHQ AF (Atchd)
Sgt Leslie H. Wells, 6865252, 6th Ren Sq (M) GHQ AF (Atchd)
S/Sgt Robert L. Sturdavent, 6833698, 6th Ren Sq (M) GHQ AF (Atchd)

Crew No. 21
Captain James C. Jensen, 0-291625, AR
1st Lieut Conrad J. Herlick, 0-21599, AC
1st Lieut Raymond T. Swenson, 0-369714, AR
2nd Lieut Ralph A. Reeve, 0-23395, AC
2nd Lieut Thomas W. Finnie, 0-373698, AR
M/Sgt Stanley Modzeleski, R-655236, 2nd Ren Sq (H) GHQ AF (Atchd)
S/Sgt Roy E. Kaden, 6570168, 6th Ren Sq (M) GHQ AF (Atchd)
Corp Clain W. Smith, 6577784, 6th Ren Sq (M) GHQ AF (Atchd)
Sgt William J. Bendig, 6570083, 6th Ren Sq (M) GHQ AF (Atchd)

will proceed by military Aircraft on or about May 12, 1941, from March Field, Riverside, California, to Hamilton Field, or other suitable Airport in the San Francisco Bay area; thence to Hawaii on temporary duty for the purpose of ferrying twenty-one (21) B-17D Airplanes to Hawaii; thence all personnel involved will return by Army or Navy transport to the United States; thence will proceed by rail, from port of debarkation to their proper stations.

Duties to be performed at Hamilton Field or other suitable Airport in the San Francisco Bay area, being exceptional will require more than seventy-two (72) hours for their performance, a delay of not to exceed fifteen (15) days is authorized.

In lieu of subsistence, a flat per diem of $6.00 is authorized for travel by military Aircraft for officers and enlisted men, and for the period of temporary duty outside the continental limits of the United States except while traveling on a Government vessel, in accordance with existing law and regulations.

The Quartermaster will furnish the necessary rail transportation for officers and enlisted men. It being impracticable for the government to furnish cooking facilities for rations, the Finance Department will pay to the above named enlisted men, in advance, the monetary travel allowance as prescribed in Table II, paragraph 2 a, AR 35-4520, at the rate of $3.00 per day for rations for one (1) day each.

The travel directed is necessary in the military service. Payment when made is chargeable to Procurement Authorities:

Officers: FD 1463 P 5-06 A 0410-01
Enlisted Men: FD 1463 P 7-06 A 0410-01

By order of Lieut Colonel EUBANK:

/s/t K. R. KREPS
1st Lieut., Air Corps,
Adjutant.

OFFICIAL:
/s/t K. R. KREPS,
1st Lieut, Air Corps,
Adjutant.

Appendix B

Headquarters, 14th Bombardment Squadron Hickam Field, Territory of Hawaii

SPECIAL ORDERS) Hickam Field, T.H.
: 2 September 1941.
Number 203)

9. Each of the following-named Officers, Air Corps, and Aviation Cadets, is, effective 2 September 1941, relieved from further assignment and duty with the 5th Bombardment Group (H), Air Corps, this station, and assigned to the 11th Bombardment Group (H), Air Corps, this station, and with the concurrence of the Commanding Officer, 11th Bombardment Group (H), Air Corps, this station, is assigned to the 14th Bombardment Squadron (H):

First Lieutenant George E. Schaetzel (0-21640),
Second Lieutenant Ernest C. Wade (0-411744),
Second Lieutenant Stanley Cottage (0-420870),
First Lieutenant Henry C. Godman (0-21664),
Second Lieutenant Robert S. Clinkscales (0-401370),

Special Orders 203, dated September 2, 1941, listing the names of personnel transferred from the 5th Bombardment Group and other elements of the 11th Bombardment Group to the newly equipped 14th Bombardment Squadron (H) about to fly from Hawaii to the Philippines.

Second Lieutenant Carl E. Eperson (0-420872),
First Lieutenant Guilford R. Montgomery (0-22397),
Second Lieutenant Curtis J. Holdridge (0-417633),
Aviation Cadet Robert S. Wasson, 18014495,
Second Lieutenant Donald M. Keiser (0-22816),
Second Lieutenant James P. Ferrey (0-352477),
Second Lieutenant Donald D. Robins (0-401307),
Second Lieutenant Francis K. McAllister (0-420874).

10. Each of the following named Officers, Air Corps, and Aviation Cadets, 11th Bombardment Group (H), Air Corps, this station, is, with the concurrence of the Commanding Officer, 11th Bombardment Group (H), relieved from further assignment and duty with the organization shown after his name, and assigned to the 14th Bombardment Squadron (H):

First Lieutenant Edward C. Teats (0-342513), 42nd Bomb. Sq. (H), AC,
First Lieutenant Weldon H. Smith (0-22363), 26th Bomb. Sq. (H), AC,
Second Lieutenant Morris N. Friedman (0-401146), 26th Bomb. Sq. (H), AC
Aviation Cadet Addie W. Hayman, 18009495, 26th Bomb. Sq. (H), AC,
Captain Colin P. Kelly (0-20811), 42nd Bomb. Sq. (H), AC
Aviation Cadet Joe M. Bean, 19049351, 42nd Bomb. Sq. (H), AC,
Second Lieutenant Francis R. Thompson (0-401547), 50th Recon. Sq. (H), AC,
Second Lieutenant John B. Wright (0-420880), 50th Recon. Sq. (H), AC.

11. Each of the following named Officers, Air Corps, and Aviation Cadets, is, effective 2 September 1941, with the concurrence of the Commanding Officer, 11th Bombardment Group (H), Air Corps, this station, relieved from further assignment and duty with the 14th Bombardment Squadron (H), and is assigned to the Headquarters and Headquarters Squadron (H), 11th Bombardment Group (H), Air Corps, this station:

Captain Marshall R. Gray (0-20792),
First Lieutenant Charles O. Allan, Jr. (0-367335),
First Lieutenant Rolle E. Stone (0-383747),
First Lieutenant Clarence P. Tokarz (0-363812),
Second Lieutenant John M. Atkinson (0-413558),
Second Lieutenant Jack C. Clark (0-401369),
Second Lieutenant William S. Cope (0-411695),
Second Lieutenant Vincent N. Crane (0-401375),
Second Lieutenant Theodore S. Greene (0-413592),
Second Lieutenant William G. Ivey (0-417146),
Second Lieutenant Willis E. Jacobs (0-417147),
Second Lieutenant Jay J. Jordan (0-417154),
Second Lieutenant Daniel H. Judd (0-417155),
Aviation Cadet Edwin J. Lanigan, 11020734,

Aviation Cadet James W. Bushee, 6917783,
Aviation Cadet Sidney I. Darden, 18037530.

12. Captain William P. Fisher (0-20461), Air Corps, having been assigned to the 18th Bombardment Wing, Air Corps, Hickam Field, T. H., pursuant to paragraph 14, Special Orders No. 216, Headquarters Hawaiian Department, cs, and having reported at this station this date, is, effective 2 September 1941, assigned to the 11th Bombardment Group (H), Air Corps, this station, and with the concurrence of the Commanding Officer, 11th Bombardment Group (H), is assigned to the 14th Bombardment Squadron (H).

13. Major Ernest Moore (0-18445), Air Corps, having been attached to the 18th Bombardment Wing, Air Corps, Hickam Field, T. H., for duty, pursuant to paragraph 15, Special Orders No. 216, Headquarters Hawaiian Department, cs, and having reported at this station this date, is, effective 2 September 1941, attached to the 11th Bombardment Group (H), Air Corps, this station, and with the concurrence of the Commanding Officer, 11th Bombardment Group (H), is attached to the 14th Bombardment Squadron (H).

14. Major Gordon A. Blake (0-18389), Air Corps, is, effective 2 September 1941, relieved from further assignment to the Headquarters and Headquarters Squadron, 18th Bombardment Wing, Air Corps, Hickam Field, T. H., and assigned to the 11th Bombardment Group (H), Air Corps, this station; and with the concurrence of the Commanding Officer, 11th Bombardment Group (H), is assigned to the 14th Bombardment Squadron (H).

15. Captain Donald D. Flickinger (0-19677), Medical Corps, having been attached to the 18th Bombardment Wing, Air Corps, Hickam Field, T. H., for duty with the Air Corps, pursuant to paragraph 16, Special Orders No. 216, Headquarters Hawaiian Department, cs, is attached for duty, effective 2 September 1941, to the 11th Bombardment Group (H), Air Corps, Hickam Field, T. H., and with the concurrence of the Commanding Officer, 11th Bombardment Group (H), Air Corps, this station, is attached to the 14th Bombardment Squadron (H).

By command of Brigadier General Rudolph:

F. Green,
Major, A.G.D.,
Asst. Adjutant General.

OFFICIAL:
F. Green,
Major, A.G.D.,
Asst. Adjutant General.

DISTRIBUTION: "H" 105 Copies-Plus: 1-CF HAF; 1-0 Sec HAF; 1-Ea 0 Conc; 5-Post Sig 0; 20-5th Gp; 20-11th Gp.

Appendix C

Headquarters Hawaiian Department Fort Shafter, Territory of Hawaii

In reply refer to:
AG 201- Godman, Henry C. (Off) 4 September 1941

SUBJECT: Orders.
TO: Commanding General, Hawaiian Air Force, Hickam Field, T. H.

First Lieutenant Henry C. Godman (0-21664) - - - - - Air Corps, Hickam Field, T. H., in compliance with radiograms, The Adjutant General's Office, 30 August and 3 September 1941, is relieved from assignment and duty in the Hawaiian Department, effective on date of departure, is assigned to the Philippine Department, will proceed by Government Airplane from Hickam Field, Territory of Hawaii, on or about 5 September 1941, to Clark Field, Fort Stotsenburg, Philippine Islands, via such intermediate landing points as may be necessary or directed by this Headquarters, and will report to the Commanding Officer, Clark Field, and the Commanding General, Philippine Department, for duty with the Air Corps. In lieu of subsistence he will be paid a flat per diem of

---

Orders dated September 4, 1941, transferring Henry C. Godman (and the 14th Bombardment Squadron) from Hawaii to the Philippines.

six dollars ($6.00), in accordance with existing law and regulations, for the period of travel by Government Airplane, for any other necessary travel (except by Government steamship) and for delays of not to exceed thirty (30) days each, hereby authorized, for temporary duty at intermediate landing points, all travel and temporary duty being of an exceptional nature which may require delays in the continuous journey of more than seventy-two (72) hours, and under circumstances which render it impracticable to carry facilities for messing and shelter. The travel directed is necessary in the military service. FD 1437 P 1-06, 3-06 A 0410-2.

By command of Lieutenant General SHORT:

Robert H. Dunlop,
Colonel, A.G.D.,
Adjutant General.

DISTRIBUTION:
CG HAF
CG Hickam Field
CG Philippine Dept.
Officer named
File

Appendix D

Officer's Roster 14th Squadron Clark Field

Officer's roster for the 14th Squadron at Clark Field before the arrival of the 19th Bombardment Group, dated October 17, 1941.

Maj. E. O'Donnell
Capt. W. P. Fisher
Capt. B. Hubbard
Capt. C. P. Kelly
1st Lt. H. C. Godman
1st Lt. G. R. Montgomery
1st Lt. G. E. Schaetzel
1st Lt. D. M. Keiser
1st Lt. J. P. Ferrey
2nd Lt. J. M. Bean
2nd Lt. R. T. Carlisle
2nd Lt. S. Cottage
2nd Lt. H. Dittman
2nd Lt. C. E. Everson
2nd Lt. M. N. Friedman
2nd Lt. T. S. Greene
2nd Lt. E. W. Hayman
2nd Lt. C. J. Holdridge
2nd Lt. R. T. McAllister
2nd Lt. D. D. Robins
2nd Lt. P. R. Tarbutton
2nd Lt. F. R. Thompson
2nd Lt. E. C. Wade
2nd Lt. R. F. Wasson
2nd Lt. J. B. Wright
2nd Lt. P. S. Miller
2nd Lt. G. E. Evans
2nd Lt. C. L. Bowman

Appendix E

Air Echelon Headquarters 19th Bomb Group (H) AFCC Albuquerque, New Mexico

Orders transferring the 19th Bomb Group and their airplanes from Albuquerque, New Mexico, to Clark Field in the Philippine Islands.

October 17, 1941

SPECIAL ORDER
No. 1

Corrected Copy

Extract

1. Pursuant to authority contained in letter W.D. File AG 370.5 (9-17-41) MC-C-M, Subject: Movement of Air Corps and Air Corps Service Units to the xxxxxxxxxxxxx dated September 18, 1941 and Letter WD File AG 370.5 (10-7-41) MC-C-M, Subject: Movement of Air Corps Units dated October 9, 1941, and 2nd. Indorsement, Headquarters 4th Air Force, Riverside, California dated October 13, 1941, the following named personnel:

Crew No. 1

Lt. Col. Eugene L. Eubank - 0-10580
1st Lt. Kenneth R. Kreps - 0-21493
2nd Lt. Melvin A. McKenzie - 0-374167

Sgt. Raymond W. Furnald - 6556239
Tech Sgt. Rufus R. Nicholas - 6230961
Sgt. Howard Pack - 6264846
Sgt. Lloyd Worth - 6862566
S/Sgt. Homer H. Hammond - 6755430
Pfc. Henry Korzzak - 6579517

Crew No. 2
Arthur W. Schmitt (1st Lt.) - 0-21606
1st Lt. Warner W. Croxton - 0-21957
2nd Lt. Edwin H. Graham - 0-393110
M/Sgt. Raymond C. Lane - 6526355
T/Sgt. Anthony Holub - 6541498
Sgt. William C. Jones - 6268715
Cpl. Frank S. Monaghan - 6580288
S/Sgt. Theodore L. Miller - 6557809
Pfc. Lloyd C. Belcher - 6566173

Crew No. 3
2nd Lt. William A. Cocke - 0-22801
2nd Lt. Edson J. Sponable - 0-398528
2nd Lt. John W. Chiles - 0-377514
Avn Cadet William N. Carrithers, 18000659
S/Sgt. Alden L. Lackie - 6554524
T/Sgt. Madison B. Blair - 6553864
Cpl. Warner E. Brewer - 6297825
Pfc. Jack S. Anderson - 6296271
Pvt. Fred G. Templin - 6914489

Crew No. 4
1st Lt. Patrick W. McIntyre - 0-21495
Edward J. Bechtold (2nd Lt.) - 0-417686
2nd Lt. Glen H. Boes - 0-392741
Avn. Cadet Butler H. O. Lauterbach 19049356
S/Sgt. Clayton E. Manners - 6899040
Cpl. Oline D. Light - 6915682
Cpl. Garland W. Lawson - 6914301
Pfc. Alma B. Mills - 658115
Pfc. Joe H. Sikes - 6386668

Crew No. 5
Major Birrell Walsh - 0-18109
2nd Lt. Robert R. Meyer - 0-416325
2nd Lt. Jay M. Horowitz - 0-409900

Avn. Cadet Ralph Howard - 18004590
S/Sgt. Henry S. Baier - 6524288
Benjamin F. (Sgt.) Kimmerle - 6293452
Cpl. William W. Williams - 6576079
Pfc. Howard M. Gilliland - 6579271
M/Sgt. Charles K. Smith - 6102050

Crew No. 6
1st Lt. Edwin S. Green - 0-22330
2nd Lt. Carey O'Brien - 0-22936
2nd Lt. Edgar Whitcomb - 0-409910
Major Luther C. Heigder - 0-205275
S/Sgt. Couts L. McKibbens - 6211554
Sgt. Wilbert A. McClellan - 6569908
Sgt. Bernard F. Strohecker - 6274577
Pfc. Billy D. Templeton - 6938084
Pfc. Robert G. Menzio - 6296374

Crew No. 7
Major David R. Gibbs - 017165
1st Lt. Sig. R. Young - 0-371948
2nd Lt. George Berkowitz - 0-401896
Major Robert F. Fulton - 0-18484
M/Sgt. Albert Stewart - 6225863
Sgt. Joe W. Stevens - 6273566
Pvt. R. F. Morris - 6914318
S/Sgt. Franklin J. Trammell - 6564880
Pvt. William E. Clark - 6574182

Crew No. 8
Captain Edwin D. Broadhurst - 0-20744
2nd Lt. Cuthbert L. Moseley - 0-377814
Avn. Cadet George J. Breinddel - 6940590
Avn. Cadet Edmund D. Benham - 16013180
S/Sgt. Lester M. Brady - 6245404
Cpl. Albert R. Kirby - 6291177
Pvt. Harold P. Phelps - 16027853
S/Sgt. Peter E. Shook - 6658245
Pvt. Vernon L. Ambrose - 19000145

Crew No. 9
1st Lt. Raymond D. Schwanbeck - 0-21567
1st Lt. John E. L. Huse - 0-21777
2nd Lt. John W. Cox - 0-409898

Aviation Cadet James Harris - 15064457
M/Sgt. George Newman - 6074224
Cpl. James J. Mangle - 6914198
Sgt. Robert R. Davis - 6926991
S/Sgt. Frank W. Lytle - 6553898
Pvt. Lloyd B. Whipp - 19050662

Crew No. 10
1st Lt. Jack Adams - 0-22338
2nd Lt. William N. Railing - 0-398588
2nd Lt. Harry J. Schreiber - 0-342137
T/Sgt. John O. Fleming - 6537402
S/Sgt. Thomas J. Crumley - 6203446
S/Sgt. Albert M. Hopkins - 6536596
Cpl. William A. McCool - 6296381
Sgt. James L. Reed - 6914406
Pfc. Edward R. Alsen - 6580736

Crew No. 11
1st Lt. Ray L. Cox - 0-38022
2nd Lt. Richard S. Smith - 0-416359
2nd Lt. Alvino V. Reyes - 0-380564
S/Sgt. William G. Weiss - 6551382
T/Sgt. Charles L. Hunley - R-94744
Sgt. Walter E. Norman - 6291130
Pvt. Frank D. Borchers - 6928053
Cpl. Morris E. Taylor - 6950938
Pfc. Earl R. Christiansen - 6936238

Crew No. 12
1st Lt. Lee B. Coats - 0-22383
1st Lt. Elmore D. Brown - 0-22057
2nd Lt. Walter E. Seamon, Jr. - 0-409906
S/Sgt. Lauton Buchanan - 6555922
T/Sgt. John W. McLaurin - 6307705
S/Sgt. Martin N. Schadl, Jr. - 6663791
Sgt. Lionel L. Lowe - 0-6855137
Pfc. Harry T. Murdock - 6579298
Pfc. Anthony E. Jumia, Jr. - 6911488

Crew No. 13
1st. Lt. Hewitt T. Wheless - 0-323870
2nd Lt. Raymond G. Teborek - 0-397556
2nd Lt. William F. Meenaugh - 0-372623

2nd Lt. Austin W. Stitt - 0-426203
S/Sgt. John N. Gootee - 6268007
Sgt. Bruno A. Katlanz - 6904792
Sgt. Richard D. Dillon - 6268737
Pfc. John E. Maklea - 6579404
Pfc. Andrew V. Slane - 6281875

Crew No. 14
1st Lt. Frank A. Kurtz - 0-22473
2nd Lt. Arthur G. Geary - 0-398704
2nd Lt. Anthony E. Oliver - 0-409904
2nd Lt. Arthur F. Sorrel - 426202
S/Sgt. Wyndolyne Burgess - 6246578
Sgt. Stanley A. Domin - 6915684
Pfc. Herbert Arthur - 6577846
Pfc. William C. Killin - 6934662
Pfc. Everett W. Dodson - 6938453

Crew No. 15
1st Lt. Sam Maddox - 0-21589
2nd Lt. John I. Renka - 0-416595
2nd Lt. Harrold C. Auliff - 0-409902
Avn. Cadet Eugene R. Greeson - 13023197
T/Sgt. Charles R. Shellite - R-6228685
Cpl. Howard V. Harlan - 6580642
Pvt. Kenneth V. Storey - 6291163
Cpl. Frank A. Harvey - 6580257
Pfc. George R. Hall - 6938070

Crew No. 16
1st Lt. Alvin V. H. Mueller - 0-356397
2nd Lt. James E. Colovin - 0-395117
2nd Lt. George M. Markovich - 0-409903
Sgt. Robert W. Schlotte - 6833789
S/Sgt. Adolph Doucet - 6299636
S/Sgt. Clyde W. Anderson - 6269985
Sgt. Lewis D. Wise - 65600334
Sgt. John D. Biff - 6903903
Pfc. George J. McGee - 6298056

Crew No. 17
Capt. Cecil E. Combs - 0-20121
2nd Lt. Jack H. Heinzel - 0-416299
2nd Lt. Harl Pease, Jr. - 0-395206

2nd Lt. M. Rowan, Jr. - 0-396317
M/Sgt. Charles Joyner - R-1114757
S/Sgt. Jacques J. Deckers - 6721138
Cpl. Allan G. Whithead - 6557024
S/Sgt. Ross E. Watkins - 6833782
Pfc. Jack W. Douglas - 6580266

Crew No. 18
Capt. William E. McDonald - 0-20778
2nd Lt. John W. Norvell - 0-23223
1st Lt. John W. Carpenter III - 0-21790
Avn. Cadet William T. Clapp - 19051168
M/Sgt. Richard Olsen - 6047089
Sgt. Elton J. Rose - 6241916
Cpl. Arthur E. Karlinger - 6579249
Cpl. Victor J. Lorber - 6974283
Pvt. William C. Henson - 17010393

Crew No. 19.
1st Lt. James T. Connally - 0-21534
2nd Lt. Milton R. Beekman - 0-416256
2nd Lt. Jack E. Jones - 0-409901
2nd Lt. Maxwell D. Stone - 0-426204
M/Sgt. James Janis - 6620746
Pfc. George F. McGowan - 6578371
Sgt. Milton F. Kelm - 6560806
Sgt. William E. King - 6281545
Pvt. Eugene L. Schmitz - 19050837

Crew No. 20
1st Lt. Morris H. Shedd - 0-21498
2nd Lt. James A. Elder - 0-395144
2nd Lt. Earl R. Tash - 0-374475
Aviation Cadet Cecil R. Gregg - 17014276
T/Sgt. Louis Uliano - 6117425
Cpl. Robert I. Shipe - 6577853
Pfc. Clifton W. Groelz - 6581250
Sgt. Ralph E. Anderson - 6857722
Pfc. Walter S. Rice - 6297760

Crew No. 21
1st Lt. Dean C. Hoevet - 0-22248
2nd Lt. Douglas H. Keller - 0-398623

2nd Lt. Reuben A. Baxter - 0-382722
S/Sgt. Michael Bibin - 67725170
T/Sgt. Lavern B. Barber - 6541993
S/Sgt. John V. Sowa - 6541524
Avn. Cadet Wycliffe H. Malphurs - 18015198
Pfc. Arthur E. Norgaard - 6571986
Pvt. Norman E. Moen - 19050845

Crew No. 22
1st Lt. William J. Bohnacker - 0-22357
2nd Lt. Edward N. Jaquet - 0-398503
2nd Lt. Arthur E. Hoffman - 0-409899
T/Sgt. James A. Wellwood - 6222635
S/Sgt. Robert R. Peel - 6265599
Cpl. Abraham Beerman - 6564699
Sgt. Fred A. Shamblen - 6880537
Pfc. Jean A. Byers - 6291071
Pfc. Benjamin E. Tomerlin - 6578477

Crew No. 23
1st Lt. Walter R. Ford - 0-320271
2nd Lt. Percy N. Hinton - 0-416303
2nd Lt. Charles J. Stevens - 0-409907
Avn. Cadet Melvin R. Hunt - 17025611
T/Sgt. Gerald H. Bloyd - 6493483
Sgt. James W. Hanna - 655009
Cpl. Robert R. Johnson - 6573768
Sgt. Albert H. Collett - 6580825
Pvt. Harold A. Maike - 6568988

Crew No. 24
1st. Lt. Clyde Box - 0-21556
2nd Lt. Vincent L. Snyder - 0-416360
Avn. Cadet Francis R. Carpelletti - 11010513
Pfc. George R. Burke - 6581084
T/Sgt. Charles A. Benner - 6538365
Avn. Cadet Byron R. Work - 18001261
S/Sgt. Max X. Baca, Jr. - 6555898
Pfc. Robert A. Hiron - 6581742

Crew No. 25
1st Lt. Fred T. Crimmins, Jr. - 0-22242
2nd Lt. Phillip H. Ashe - 0-417679

1st Lt. Elliott Vandervanter, Jr. - 0-21989
2nd Lt. Donald C. Miller - 0-398644
S/Sgt. George M. Buffington - 6250163
Cpl. Robert Z. Berlin - 6281699
Sgt. James H. Murray - 6564899
Pfc. Eugene D. Shafer - 6935994
Pfc. Charles V. Hamilton - 6555034

Crew No. 26
1st Lt. Elmer L. Parsel - 0-301750
2nd Lt. Owen R. Graham - 0-398710
2nd Lt. William S. Warner - 0-409909
Cpl. Samuel P. Poole - 6822521
Sgt. Rex E. Matson - 6657964
Sgt. Charles J. Classock - 6571800
Cpl. Harry J. Moss - 6298045
Pfc. Winton J. Long - 6581682
Pvt. Howard S. Peterson - 16006840
will proceed by military Aircraft on or about October 17, 1941, from Albuquerque, New Mexico, via prescribed Air route to destination xxxxxxxx, for permanent change of station.

Upon completion of this duty, the following named personnel will return to the Continental United States and comply with orders to be issued.

1st Lt. Clyde Box - 0-21556
1st Lt. Lee B. Coats - 0-22383
1st Lt. James T. Connally - 0-21534
1st Lt. Fred T. Crimmins, Jr. - 0-22242
1st. Lt. Kenneth R. Kreps - 0-21493
1st Lt. Patrick W. McIntyre - 0-21495
1st Lt. Arthur W. Schmitt - 0-21606
1st Lt. Raymond V. Schwanbeck - 0-21567
1st Lt. Morris H. Shedd - 0-21498

Aviation Cadet Wycliffe H. Malphurs, 18015198 will return to his proper station, Alburquerque, New Mexico, upon completion of this duty.

Duties to be performed at all ports being exceptional will require more than 72 hours for their performance, a delay of not to exceed 15 days is authorized at each place.

In lieu of subsistence a flat per diem of $6.00 is authorized for travel by military Aircraft for officers and enlisted men.

Personnel to be returned to the Continental limits of the United States will return by first available transportation and will proceed by rail from port of embarkation to their proper stations.

The Quartermaster will furnish the necessary rail transportation for Officers and Aviation Cadets returned to the Continental limits of the United States. It being impracticable for the government to furnish cooking facilities for rations, the Finance Department will pay to the above named aviation cadet in advance the monetary travel allowance as prescribed in Table II, par 2a, AR 35-4520, at the rate of $3.00 per day for rations for two days.

The travel directed is necessary in the military service and payment when made is chargeable to Procurement Authorities FD 1437 P 1-06, 3-06, 15-06, 17006, A 0410-2; QM 1620 P 54-01, 54-02, 54-13, 54-07 A 0525-2 "D". Procurement authorities for per diem (Officers FD 1437 P1-06A 0410-2 (Enlisted Men) FD 1437 P 3-06 A 0410-2.

Dependents will not accompany troops. Letter AGO, June 7, 1941, file A.C. 541.1 (5-26-51) MO-D-M, subject: Transportation of Dependents and Household Goods to Overseas Stations, and paragraph 1 c & d, Circular 92, War Department, May 7, 1941 will govern.

By order of Lt. Colonel Eubank:

/s/K. R. Kreps
K. R. KREPS,
1st Lieut., A.C.
Actg. Adjutant

OFFICIAL: /s/ K. R. Kreps
/t/ K. R. KREPS,
1st Lieut., A.C.,
Actg. Adjutant.

A True Copy
E. H. Bruss,
Major, Air Corps,
Adjutant.

Appendix F

Flight Crews of the 14th and 93rd Bomb Squadron at Del Monte on December 8, 1941

B-17[a]
P: Maj. E. O. O'Donnell
CP: Capt. W. E. Horrigan
N: 2nd Lt. P. R. Tarbutton
B: M. Sgt. J. F. Carter
E: T. Sgt. G. A. Head
E: S. Sgt. J. F. Clark
R: T. Sgt. R. W. Stephens
R: S. Sgt. A. L. Richardson

B-17C - 40-2045
P: Capt. C. P. Kelly
CP: 2nd Lt. D. R. Robbins
N: 2nd Lt. J. P. Bean
B: Cpl. M. Levin
E: S. Sgt. J. W. Delehanty
E: Sgt. J. E. Halkyard
R: Pfc. W. L. Money
R: Pfc. R. E. Altman

B-17D - 40-3066
P: 1st Lt. D. M. Keiser
CP: 1st Lt. J. P. Ferry
N: M. Sgt. W.J.P. Griffin
B: 2nd Lt. J. Jamal
E: S. Sgt. W. Partridge
E: Pfc. L. G. Brazelton
R: S. Sgt. J. A. Giardini
R: Pfc. J. W. Kennedy

B-17D - 40-3091
P: 1st Lt. G. E. Schaetzel
CP: 2nd Lt. E. C. Wade
N: 2nd Lt. S. Cottage
B: T. Sgt. E. T. Oliver
E: S. Sgt. F. D. Secrest
E: S. Sgt. J. L. Cannon
R: Sgt. V. Spaziano
R: Pfc. J. A. Rest

B-17D - 40-3062
P: Capt. C. E. Combs
CP: 2nd Lt. P. M. Hinton
N: 2nd Lt. J. E. Jones
B: 2nd Lt. M. D. Stone
E: S. Sgt. J. J. Deckers
R: Sgt. C. G. Hamilton
G: Sgt. A. G. Whitehead
G: Pvt. J. J. Wilfer

B-17D - 40-3074
P: Capt. E. L. Parsel
CP: Lt. J. W. Norvell
N: Lt. F. R. Cappelletti
B: Lt. C. E. Gregg
E: S. Sgt. R. E. Matson
R: Sgt. V. J. Lorber
G: Sgt. H. J. Randall
G: Pvt. W. C. Henson

B-17C - 40-2062
P: 1st Lt. J. T. Connally
CP: 2nd Lt. M. R. Beekman
N: 1st Lt. M. C. Rowan
B: T. Sgt. D. W. Fesmire
E: S. Sgt. J. J. Claud
R: Pvt. L. L. Coburn
G: Pfc. R. A. Hiron
G: Pvt. E. L. Schmitz

B-17[a]
P: 1st Lt. W. J. Bohnaker
CP: 2nd Lt. J. M. Jacquet
N: 2nd Lt. W. M. Carrithers
B: T. Sgt. J. A. Wellwood
E: S. Sgt. R. R. Peel
R: S. Sgt. J. A. Byers
G: Sgt. F. A. Shamblin
G: Pvt. B. E. Tomerlin

B-17[a]
P: 1st Lt. G. R. Montgomery
CP: 2nd Lt. C. J. Holdridge
N: 2nd Lt. R. F. Wasson
B: S. Sgt. S. C. Jackola
E: T. Sgt. A. G. Ramirez
E: S. Sgt. C. O. Jones
R: Cpl. R. D. Johnson
R: Pfc. L. H. Daphron

B-17D - 40-3097
P: 1st Lt. H. C. Godman
CP: 2nd Lt. R. S. Clinkscales
N: 2nd Lt. C. E. Epperson
B: S. Sgt. J. A. Wallach
E: S. Sgt. C. L. James
E: S. Sgt. H. E. Weist
R: Sgt. N. P. Michelson
R: Pfc. S. G. Brooks

B-17D - 40-3078
P: 1st Lt. E. C. Teats
CP: 2nd Lt. T. S. Greene
N: 2nd Lt. F. K. McAllister
B: Sgt. C. R. Payne
E: T. Sgt. R. F. Provost
E: T. Sgt. J. N. Geckler
R: Sgt. L. M. Kramer
R: Pfc. J. H. Hartzell

B-17D - 40-3093
P: 1st Lt. E. J. Vandevanter
CP: 2nd Lt. V. L. Snyder
N: 2nd Lt. R. L. Work
B: 2nd Lt. D. C. Miller
E: S. Sgt. M. C. Baca
R: Sgt. E. L. Hargrove
G: Sgt. B. F. Strohecker
G: Pvt. R. I. Huffman

B-17D - 40-3087
P: 1st Lt. W. R. Ford
CP: 1st Lt. C. L. O'Bryan
N: 2nd Lt. C. J. Stevens
B: T. Sgt. L. B. Barber
E: Sgt. W. A. McClellan

R: Sgt. E. J. Rose
G: Pvt. H. S. Peterson
G: Cpl. H. A. Buller

B-17[a]
P: 1st Lt. M. H. Shedd
CP: Lt. J. H. Heinzel
N: Lt. W. S. Warner
B: Sgt. G. A. Burke
E: M. Sgt. L. Uliano
G: Cpl. R. L. Shope
G: Cpl. G. D. Blanton

B-17[a]
P: 1st Lt. H. Pease
CP: Lt. O. R. Graham
N: Cad. W. N. Carrithers
B: Cpl. S. E. Poole
E: S. Sgt. G. M. Buffington
R: Pvt. R. E. Rennick
G: Sgt. L. J. Long
G: Pvt. C. W. Schmitz

P = pilot; CP = copilot; N = navigator; B = bombardier; E = engineer; R = radio operator; G = gunner.

[a]Documentation failed to identify the airplane or its serial number for this crew.

Source: History of the 19th Bombardment Group.

Appendix G

United States Army Air Forces in Australia

Special Orders)
:
No.........56)

Melbourne, Vic.,
11 March, 1942.

Extract

6. The oral orders of the Commanding General, directing the following named officers to proceed from the Combat Zone to Melbourne, Victoria, by military Aircraft, and authorizing, in lieu of subsistence, for the inclusive dates indicated, a flat per diem of six dollars ($6.00), while traveling, in accordance with existing law and regulations, are hereby confirmed and made a matter of record. Having reported at this headquarters, on the dates last indicated, on temporary duty and pursuant to General Orders No. 13, Headquarters, United States Army Forces in Australia, Melbourne, Victoria, dated February 15, 1942, it having been found impracticable to furnish suitable billets, or quarters in kind, and messing facilities, each of the following-named officers will be paid an

---

Special Orders No. 56, written by General Brett's headquarters in Australia on March 11, 1942, is a partial list of U.S. Army Air Corps evacuees from the Netherland's East Indies.

allowance not to exceed six dollars ($6.00) per day, for actual and necessary expenses, from the last indicated date to March 7, 1942, inclusive. FD 4109 P 1-01, 1-06, 1-07, 1-13 A 0200-2:

5th Bomber Command

Major Cornelius D. Cosgrove, 0-286198, Air Corps, from February 28 to March 4, 1942.

Major Kenneth R. Kreps, 0-21493, Air Corps, from February 28 to March 4, 1942.

Major William E. McDonald, 0-20778, Air Corps, from February 26 to February 28, 1942.

Captain Patrick W. McIntyre, 0-21495, Air Corps, from March 1 to March 1, 1942.

Captain Arthur W. Schmidt, 0-21606, Air Corps, from February 26 to February 28, 1942.

Second Lieutenant James Harris, (ASN Unknown), Air Corps, from February 27 to March 5, 1942.

7th Bombardment Group

Major Earl E. Hicks, 0-1200209, Air Corps, from March 1 to March 3, 1942.

Captain Jack W. Bleasdale, 0-22328, Air Corps, from March 1 to March 2, 1942.

Captain Jacob D. Gottlieb, 0-330588, Medical Corps, from Feb. 28 to March 2, 1942.

Captain Felix M. Hardison, 0-21354, Air Corps, from March 3 to March 4, 1942.

Captain Clarence V. McCauley, 0-22401, Air Corps, from March 1 to March 4, 1942.

1st Lieutenant Edward C. Habberstad, 0-380242, Air Corps, from Feb. 25 to March 1, 1942.

1st Lt. Richard T. Herlund, 0-398607, Air Corps, from Feb. 28 to March 1, 1942.

1st Lt. Maurice C. Horgan, 0-395158, Air Corps, from Feb. 25 to March 1, 1942.

1st Lt. Jack L. Laubscher, 0-398629, Air Corps, from Feb. 7, to March 3, 1942.

1st Lt. Roman T. Schumacher, Jr., 0-398517, Air Corps, from Feb. 25 to March 1, 1942.

1st Lt. Raymond S. Sleeper, 0-23088, Air Corps, from Feb. 26 to Feb 28, 1942.

2nd Lt. Vance L. Beebout, (ASN Unknown), Air Corps, from March 1 to March 4, 1942.

2nd Lt. Jack E. C. Dodd, 0-379447, Air Corps, from March 1 to March 3, 1942.

2nd Lt. Robert W. Elliott, (ASN Unknown), Air Corps, from Feb. 26 to March 3, 1942.

2nd Lt. Gilbert E. Erb, 0-398683, Air Corps, from Feb. 26 to March 5, 1942.
2nd Lt. Sanford W. Hickey, 0-378969, Air Corps, from Feb. 28 to March 2, 1942.
2nd Lt. David F. McCartney, 0-425373, Air Corps, from March 1 to March 4, 1942.
2nd Lt. Ellsworth E. McRoberts, 0-432083, Air Corps, from March 2, to March 3, 1942.
2nd Lt. Albert Nice, (ASN Unknown), Air Corps, from March 2 to March 3, 1942.
2nd Lt. George L. Simmons, 0-416902, Air Corps, from Feb. 28 to March 3, 1942.
2nd Lt. Willis F. Wagner, 0-430637, Air Corps, from Feb. 28 to March 2, 1942.
2nd Lt. Marion L. Wheeler, 0-412742, Air Corps, from March 2 to March 4, 1942.
2nd Lt. Edward R. Yerington, 0-434558, Air Corps, from Feb. 26 to March 5, 1942.

19th Bombardment Group

Major Morris H. Shedd, 0-21498, Air Corps, from Feb. 25 to March 1, 1942.
Captain Jack Adams, 0-22338, Air Corps, from Feb. 25 to Feb. 28, 1942.
Captain William J. Bohanaker, 0-22357, Air Corps, from Feb. 25 to Feb. 28, 1942.
Captain Henry C. Godman, 0-21664, Air Corps, from Feb. 26 to March 3, 1942.
Captain W. A. Marrocco, 0-283009, Medical Corps, from Feb. 23 to March 2, 1942.
Captain Guilford R. Montgomery, 0-22397, Air Corps, from Feb. 26 to Feb. 28, 1942.
1st Lt. Richard T. Carlisle, 0-388886, Air Corps, from Feb. 27 to Feb. 28, 1942.
1st Lt. Morris N. Friedman, 0-401156, Air Corps, from January 25 to March 2, 1942.
1st Lt. Douglas H. Keller, 0-398623, Air Corps, from Feb. 25 to March 3, 1942.
1st Lt. Harold C. McAuliff, 0-409902, Air Corps, from Feb. 25 to March 3, 1942.
1st Lt. Melvin A. McKenzie, 0-374167, Air Corps, from Feb. 28 to March 2, 1942.
1st Lt. William F. Neenagh, 0-372623, Air Corps, from Feb. 27 to March 4, 1942.
1st Lt. Anthony E. Oliver, 0-409904, Air Corps, from Feb. 28 to March 1, 1942.
1st Lt. Walter E. Seamon, 0-409906, Air Corps, from March 1 to March 4, 1942.
1st Lt. Robert A. Trenkle, 0-395138, Air Corps, from Feb. 26 to March 1, 1942.

2nd Lt. Francis R. Cappelletti, (ASN Unknown), Air Corps, from March 1 to March 2, 1942.
2nd Lt. William M. Carrithers, (ASN Unknown), Air Corps, from March 1 to March 2, 1942.
2nd Lt. Stanley Cottage, 0-420870, Air Corps, from Feb. 27 to March 3, 1942.
2nd Lt. C. E. Epperson, 0-420872, Air Corps, from Feb. 26 to March 1, 1942.
2nd Lt. Theodore S. Greene, 0-413592, Air Corps, from March 1 to March 4, 1942.
2nd Lt. Cecil E. Gress, (ASN Unknown), Air Corps, from Feb. 24 to March 3, 1942.
2nd Lt. Percy M. Hinton, 0-416303, Air Corps, from March 1 to March 4, 1942.
2nd Lt. William A. Lorence, Jr., 0-398751, Air Corps, from Feb. 26 to March 3, 1942.
2nd Lt. James R. Smith, 0-393156, Air Corps, from March 1, to March 5, 1942.
2nd Lt. Richard S. Smith, 0-416359, Air Corps, from Feb. 26 to March 3, 1942.
2nd Lt. Vincent L. Snyder, 0-416360, Air Corps, from Feb. 26 to March 3, 1942.
2nd Lt. Austin W. Stitt, 0-426203, Air Corps, from Feb. 28 to March 4, 1942.
2nd Lt. Maxwell D. Stone, 0-426204, Air Corps, from Feb. 28 to March 2, 1942.
2nd Lt. Paul R. Tarbutton, 0-420878, Air Corps, from March 1 to March 4, 1942.

HQ. F. E. A. F.

Major William P. Fisher, 0-20461, Air Corps, from March 1 to March 4, 1942.
1st Lt. James E. Colovin, 0-395117, Air Corps, from Feb. 26 to March 3, 1942.
1st Lt. Dayton W. Eddy, 0-352575, Air Corps, from Feb. 26 to March 3, 1942.
2nd Lt. John F. Gray, 0-430140, Air Corps, from Feb. 25 to March 2, 1942.
(210.482 (AG-0)).

By command of Lieutenant General BRETT:

STEPHEN J. CHAMBERLIN
Brigadier General, U.S. Army,
Chief of Staff.

OFFICIAL:
B. M. FITCH,
Colonel, Adjutant General's Department,
Adjutant General.

Distribution:

Headquarters Commandant. 1
Adjutant General (For Miss Moran) 1
Chief Clerk. 1
Aide-de-Camp. 2
Major Cosgrove 195
Personnel Division. 1
(3 to each officer 189)
G-1. 1
Air Section. 3
G-3. 1
Finance Officer. 126
G-4. 1
Statistical Section. 1
Officers' Section 2

Appendix H

Synthesized Flight Log of the Swoose April 1941 to December 1953

Since no airplane log for the Swoose exists, this is an amalgamation of data from various sources, including the Air Corps Inventory Card, Air Force historical documents, special orders for flight crews and others who participated in those flights, personal diaries, and news reports.

Because this is a synthesis created from limited sources, not all the flights of the Swoose have been identified and it is assumed that there were many others. The nature of some of the source documents prevent identifying a few of the airfields. In those cases the name of the city has been used.

Date	*Pilot*	*Flying Time*	*Destination/Notes*
April 28, 1941	Unknown	7.2	Accepted by U.S. Army Air Corps. Assigned to 19th Bombardment Group and flown to March Field, California.
May 13–14, 1941	Unknown	80.4	March Field, Hamilton Field, Hickam Field (T.H.). Time probably includes

Date	*Pilot*	*Flying Time*	*Destination/Notes*
			hours flown prior to this date.
June 1941	Henry C. Godman	50.4	Training flights in Hawaii
July 1941	Henry C. Godman	34.8	Training flights
August 1941	Henry C. Godman	49.6	Training flights
Sept. 5, 1941	Henry C. Godman	7.2	Hickam Field, Midway Island
Sept. 6, 1941	Henry C. Godman	7.5	Midway Island, Wake Island
Sept. 7–8, 1941	Henry C. Godman	13.0	Wake Island, Port Moresby (Papua New Guinea)
Sept. 10, 1941	Henry C. Godman	6.5	Port Moresby, Darwin (Australia)
Sept. 12, 1941	Henry C. Godman		Darwin, Clark Field (Luzon, P.I.)
October 1941	Henry C. Godman	7.0	Training, reconnaissance
November 1941	Henry C. Godman	24.1	Training, recon (Clark Field)
December 1941	Henry C. Godman	23.7	Training, recon. Transferred to Del Monte (Mindanao, P.I.) on Dec. 5.
Dec. 8, 1941 (Dec. 7 in U.S.)	Henry C. Godman		Recon mission around Mindanao
Dec. 9, 1941	Henry C. Godman		Del Monte, Marivales (Luzon, P.I.), Del Monte. One of three aircraft led by Colin Kelly. The latter was shot down.
Dec. 9, 1941	Henry C. Godman		Second mission on that day. Del Monte to bomb naval forces, San Marcelino, Del Monte.
Dec. 10, 1941	Henry C. Godman		Del Monte to bomb naval forces, Del Monte
Dec. 10, 1941	Henry C. Godman		Del Monte, San Marcelino, Del Monte.
Dec. 12, 1941	Henry C. Godman		Del Monte, Vigan, Marivales. Flight of five landed at Marivales after bombing mission. Stayed here until Dec. 15.
Dec. 15, 1941	Henry C. Godman		Marivales, Del Monte

Date	Pilot	Flying Time	Destination/Notes
Dec. 18, 1941	Henry C. Godman		Del Monte, Batchelor Field (Australia). Bombed Davao shipping en route.
Dec. 22, 1941	Henry C. Godman		Batchelor, Del Monte. Bombed Davao shipping.
Dec. 23, 1941	Henry C. Godman		Del Monte, Davao bombing mission, Del Monte. Engine failure outbound, bombed after dark with feathered engine.
Dec. 23, 1941	Henry C. Godman		Del Monte, Batchelor
Dec. 30, 1941	Cecil E. Combs		Batchelor, Malang (Java)
December 1941		23.7	Total time for the month, according to AAF records
Jan. 2, 1942	Cecil E. Combs		Malang, Samarinda (Borneo), Malang. Mission aborted (weather).
Jan. 3, 1942	Cecil E. Combs	4.0	Malang, Samarinda. Lead airplane.
Jan. 4, 1942	Cecil E. Combs	7.0	Samarinda, Davao bombing mission, Samarainda. Credited with sinking one destroyer and three hits on others. Led mission.
Jan. 5, 1942	Cecil E. Combs	3.7	Samarinda, Malang
Jan. 8, 1942	Cecil E. Combs	4.3	Malang, Kendari (Celebes). Lead airplane.
Jan. 9, 1942	Cecil E. Combs	7.4	Kendari, Davao bombing mission, Kendari. Lead airplane.
Jan. 10, 1942	Cecil E. Combs	6.4	Malang, Tarakan (Borneo), Malang. Bombed target alone, shot down two enemy fighters. Last combat mission.
Jan. 13, 1942			Out of commission, sustained battle damage
Jan. 26–27, 1942	Donald M. Keiser		Malang, Darwin, Laverton (Melbourne, Australia)
January 1942		38.5	Total time for the month, according to AAF records

Date	*Pilot*	*Flying Time*	*Destination/Notes*
March 1942	Weldon H. Smith		Airplane christened "The Swoose"
Mar. 7, 1942	Weldon H. Smith		Laverton, Malang. Lead aircraft for a flight of fighters being ferried to the combat zone.
Mar. 17, 1942	Capt. Arthur A. Fletcher		Returned to Laverton with engines in poor condition
May 6, 1942	Frank Kurtz		Melbourne, Brisbane
Undated	Frank Kurtz		No details or dates available for the following flights: Melbourne, Cloncurry, Darwin; Melbourne, Townsville, Port Moresby; Melbourne, Townsville, Darwin; Melbourne, Charleville; Melbourne, Brisbane, Port Moresby; Melbourne, Sydney, Brisbane.
May 17–30, 1942	Frank Kurtz		Sydney, Wellington (N.Z.), Fiji, Canton Island, Honolulu, and return. Set speed record for the crossing to Hawaii.
June 9–11, 1942	Frank Kurtz		Townsville, Port Moresby, Batchelor
June 11, 1942	Frank Kurtz		Forced landing at Carisbrooke sheep station near Winton with Lyndon B. Johnson on board
June 12, 1942	Frank Kurtz		Winton, Longreach, Melbourne
July 18, 1942	Frank Kurtz		Melbourne, Brisbane
July 28–31, 1942	Frank Kurtz		Tour of bases in Australia and New Guinea with Maj. Gen. George C. Kenney
Aug. 4–12, 1942	Frank Kurtz	36.17	Brisbane, New Caledonia, Fiji, Canton Island,

Date	*Pilot*	*Flying Time*	*Destination/Notes*
Aug. 4–12, 1942 *(cont.)*			Hickam Field, Hamilton Field (Calif.), Omaha (Nebr.), Washington, D.C. (record time)
Aug. 17–?, 1942	Frank Kurtz		Washington, Miami (Fla.), Middletown Air Depot (Pa.)
Aug. 23, 1942	Frank Kurtz		Washington, Langley Field (Va.)
Aug. 26, 1942	Frank Kurtz		Langley Field, Washington, D.C.
Aug. 29, 1942	Frank Kurtz		Washington, Wichita (Kan.)
Sept. 1, 1942	Frank Kurtz		Seattle (Wash.), Sacramento (Calif.)
Sept. 2, 1942	Frank Kurtz		Sacramento, March Field, Los Angeles
Sept. 5, 1942	Frank Kurtz		Los Angeles, Wichita
Sept. 6, 1942	Frank Kurtz		Wichita, Washington
Sept. 9, 1942	Frank Kurtz		Washington, Santa Fe (N.M.), Albuquerque (N.M.).
Sept. 10, 1942	Frank Kurtz		Albuquerque, Tucson (Ariz.)
Sept. 11, 1942	Frank Kurtz		El Paso (Tex.), Duncan Field (Tex.)
Sept. 12, 1942	Frank Kurtz		Duncan Field, Fort Worth
Sept. 13, 1942	Frank Kurtz		Fort Worth, Mobile (Ala.), Eglin Field (Florida)
Sept. 15, 1942	Frank Kurtz		Eglin Field, Panama City (Fla.), Miami (Fla.)
Sept. 17, 1942	Frank Kurtz		Miami, Guatemala City
Sept. 19, 1942	Frank Kurtz		Guatemala City, Albrook Field (Canal Zone)
Sept. 23, 1942	Frank Kurtz		Albrook Field, Trinidad
Sept. 24, 1942	Frank Kurtz		Trinidad, St. Lucia (B.W.I.), San Juan (P.R.)
Sept. 26, 1942	Frank Kurtz		San Juan, Miami
Sept. 30, 1942	Frank Kurtz		Maxwell Field (Ala.), Nashville (Tenn.), Patterson Field (Ohio), Washington, D.C.

Date	*Pilot*	*Flying Time*	*Destination/Notes*
Oct. 2, 1942	Frank Kurtz		Washington, Mitchell Field (N.Y.)
Oct. 5, 1942	Frank Kurtz		Mitchell Field, Washington
Oct. 9, 1942	Frank Kurtz		Washington, Buffalo (N.Y.), Cleveland (Ohio), Scott Field (Ill.)
Oct. 10, 1942	Frank Kurtz		Scott Field, Chanute Field (Ill.), Fort Wayne (Ind.), Detroit (Mich.)
Oct. 11, 1942	Frank Kurtz		Detroit, Fort Knox (Ky.)
Oct. 12, 1942	Frank Kurtz		Fort Knox, Wichita Falls, Albuquerque
Oct. 14, 1942	Frank Kurtz		Albuquerque, Dallas (Tex.)
Oct. 15, 1942	Frank Kurtz		Dallas, Barksdale Field (La.), Biloxi (Miss.) New Orlean (La.)
Oct. 16, 1942	Frank Kurtz		Biloxi, Sebring (Fla.), Miami
Oct. 20, 1942	Frank Kurtz		Miami, Washington, D.C.
Nov. 3, 1942	Frank Kurtz		Miami, Washington
Nov. 5, 1942	Frank Kurtz		Washington, Stewart Field (N.Y.), Washington
Nov. 8, 1942	Frank Kurtz		Washington, Miami
Nov. 9, 1942	Frank Kurtz		Miami, Albrook Field
Nov. 16, 1942	Frank Kurtz		Albrook Field, Jamaica (B.W.I.), San Juan (P.R.)
Nov. 17, 1942	Frank Kurtz		San Juan, Antigua (Leeward Islands), Aruba (Lesser Antilles), St. Croix (V.I.), Antigua
Nov. 18, 1942	Frank Kurtz		Antigua, St. Lucia (Leeward Islands), Trinidad
Nov. 19, 1942	Frank Kurtz		Trinidad, Curaçao (Lesser Antilles)
Nov. 20, 1942	Frank Kurtz		Trinidad, Aruba, Albrook Field

(From September 1 to November 20, the Swoose is reported to have flown 152.5 hours.)

Dec. 3, 1942	Frank Kurtz		Talara (Peru), Salinas (Ecuador)

Date	*Pilot*	*Flying Time*	*Destination/Notes*
December 1942	Frank Kurtz		Flights to Miami, Havana, and Guatemala have been noted for the month but no other details are available
Jan. 9–?, 1943	Martin F. Peterson		Albrook Field, Galapagos Islands, Salinas (Ecuador), Talara (Peru), Lima (Peru), Talara
Jan. 17–?, 1943	Martin F. Peterson		Curaçao, La Guaira (Venezuela), Trinidad, Atkinson Field (British Guiana), Zandery Field (Surinam), Waller Field (Trinidad), Aruba
January 1943	Martin F. Peterson		Flights from Albrook Field to Costa Rica and Quito (Ecuador) are also noted for this month.
Feb. 14, 1943	Martin F. Peterson		Salinas, Quito
Feb. 24, 1943	Martin F. Peterson		Aruba, Curaçao, San Juan, Cuba, Miami
February 1943	Martin F. Peterson		Flights to Peru and the Galapagos Islands are noted for this month but no details
Mar. 21, 1943	Martin F. Peterson		David Field (Rep. of Panama)
Mar. 26, 1943	Martin F. Peterson		San José (Costa Rica)
March 1943	Martin F. Peterson		Galapagos Island, Guatemala, Miami, Caribbean Islands, British Guiana, Belem (Brazil)
Apr. 7, 1943	Martin F. Peterson		Bogotá (Colombia)
Apr. 18–?, 1943	Martin F. Peterson		San Juan, St. Croix, Antigua, St. Lucia, Barbados, Curaçao
May 9, 1943	Martin F. Peterson		Salinas, Talara, Autofagasta (Chile), Santiago, Arica (Chile), Lima (Peru), Galapagos Island
May 31, 1943	Martin F. Peterson		Guatemala City, Batista Field (Cuba), Miami

Date	*Pilot*	*Flying Time*	*Destination/Notes*
June 11, 1943	Martin F. Peterson		Batista Field, Miami, San Juan, Waller Field (Trinidad), Zander Field (Surinam), Curaçao
June 1943	Martin F. Peterson		Flights to the following destinations have been noted, but no details are available: Bogotá, Peru, and Santiago
July 12, 1943	Martin F. Peterson		Aruba
July 20, 1943	Martin F. Peterson		San Juan, Losey Field (P.R.), Borinquen Field (P.R.), Bowen Field (Port au Prince, Haiti)
Aug. 8, 1943	Martin F. Peterson	8.1	No itinerary. Jack J. Crane flew as copilot.
Aug. 17, 1943	Martin F. Peterson		David (Panama), Managua (Nicaragua), Guatemala City
Aug. 18, 1943	Martin F. Peterson	0.9	No itinerary, Crane copilot
Aug. 28, 1943	Martin F. Peterson	5.4	No itinerary, Crane copilot
Sept. 6–15, 1943	Martin F. Peterson	26.1	San Juan, Miami, Ciudad Trujillo (Dom. Rep.)
Sept. 19, 1943	Jack J. Crane	0.4	No details
Sept. 20–23, 1943	Jack J. Crane	15.5	No itinerary
Oct. 2–3, 1943	Jack J. Crane		Miami, Batista Field, Borinquen Field, Antigua, St. Lucia, Zandry Field, Atkinson Field (British Guiana), Hato Field (Curaçao)
Oct. 4–5, 1943	Jack J. Crane	10.1	Salinas (Ecuador), Galapagos Island
Oct. 7–16, 1943	Jack J. Crane	34.5	No itinerary
Oct. 18–22, 1943	Jack J. Crane	14.9	No itinerary
Oct. 27–30, 1943	Jack J. Crane	11.0	No itinerary
Nov. 3–7, 1943	Jack J. Crane	15.9	No itinerary
Nov. 9–15, 1943	Jack J. Crane	19.5	Dakato Field (Aruba), Hato Field (Curaçao), San Juan (P.R.), St. Thomas (V.I.), Miami, Vernon Field (Jamaica)

Date	*Pilot*	*Flying Time*	*Destination/Notes*
Nov. 16–30, 1943	Jack J. Crane	36.4	No itinerary
Dec. 1, 4–6, 1943	Jack J. Crane	14.3	No itinerary
Dec. 7–10, 1943	Jack J. Crane	5.6	Bogotá (Colombia)
Dec. 14–16, 20, 21, 1943	Jack J. Crane	5.0	No itinerary
Dec. 22–29, 1943	Jack J. Crane	21.4	San Juan, Miami
Dec. 30–31, 1943	Jack J. Crane	3.0	No itinerary
Jan. 2–6, 1944	Jack J. Crane	32.0	No itinerary
Jan. 9–29, 1944	Jack J. Crane	75.9	No itinerary
Feb. 1–4, 1944	Jack J. Crane	4.0	No itinerary
Feb. 6, 7, and 10, 11, 1944	Jack J. Crane	19.3	Talara (Peru), Lima (Peru)
Feb. 11–14, 1944	Jack J. Crane	6.6	No itinerary
Feb. 18–23, 1944	Jack J. Crane	6.2	No itinerary
Feb. 24– May 29, 1944	Jack J. Crane		Aircraft out of service. Major overhaul and modification.
May 30, 1944	Jack J. Crane	2.1	Test flight
June 25, 1944	Jack J. Crane	30.1	No itinerary
June 26–30, 1944	Jack J. Crane	26.4	Miami, Batista Field (Cuba)
July 1944	Jack J. Crane	68.0	Batista Field, Cuidad Trujilo, Galapagos Island, Borinquen Field, Beane Field (St. Lucia), Waller Field (Trinidad), Hato Field (Curaçao)
August 1944	Jack J. Crane	93.7	Salinas (Ecuador), Quito (Ecuador), La Guaira (Venezuela), Maracay (Venezuela), Barranquilla (Colombia), Galapagos Island
September 1944	Jack J. Crane	77.1	Medellin (Colombia), Baranquilla (Colombia), Bogotá (Colombia), Lima (Peru), Santiago (Chile), Galapagos Islands, Quito (Ecuador)
October 1944	Jack J. Crane	54.3	Talara (Peru), Arequipa (Peru), Lima (Peru), La Paz (Bolivia)

Date	*Pilot*	*Flying Time*	*Destination/Notes*
November 1944	Jack J. Crane	88.4	Rio de Janeiro (Brazil), Olmstead Field (Pa.)
December 1944	Jack J. Crane	69.3	No itinerary
January 1945	Jack J. Crane	83.4	La Paz (Bolivia), Santiago (Chile). Other destinations unknown.
February 1945	Jack J. Crane	33.1	Guatemala City, Mexico City, San Antonio (Tex.). Other destinations unknown.
March 1945	Jack J. Crane	44.5	Quito (Ecuador), Lima (Peru), La Paz (Bolivia). Other destinations unknown.
April 1945	Jack J. Crane		Salinas (Ecuador), Galapagos Island, Jamaica (B.W.I.), Miami, Havana (Cuba). Other destinations unknown.
May 1945	Jack J. Crane	68.7	Guatemala City, Managua (Nicaragua). Other destinations unknown.
June 1945	Jack J. Crane	85.0	San Francisco for the signing of the United Nations charter. Washington (D.C.), Ft. Worth (Tex.), Prescott (Ariz.), Kirtland AFB (N.M.), Batista Field (Cuba), Albrook Field (Panama), other unknown destinations.
July 1945	Jack J. Crane	60.0	Talara (Peru), Lima (Peru), and other destinations
August 1945	Jack J. Crane	14.2	Destinations unknown
September 1945	Jack J. Crane	9.4	Destinations unknown
Oct. 12, 1945	Charles W. Nall	1.0	Destinations unknown
Oct. 15, 1945	Charles W. Nall	3.8	Albrook to Guatemala City
Oct. 17, 1945	Charles W. Nall	6.7	Kelly Field (Tex.)
Oct. 18, 1945	Charles W. Nall	4.7	Albuquerque (N.M.)
Oct. 19, 1945	Charles W. Nall	3.6	Glendale (Calif.)
		1.9	San Francisco

Date	*Pilot*	*Flying Time*	*Destination/Notes*
Oct. 22, 1945	Charles W. Nall	2.3	Orange County (Calif.)
		1.0	Bakersfield (Calif.)
		1.0	Orange County
		2.2	San Francisco
Oct. 24, 1945	Charles W. Nall	5.2	Albuquerque (N.M.)
Oct. 25, 1945	Charles W. Nall	5.0	New Orleans
Oct. 26, 1945	Charles W. Nall	2.5	Marietta (Ga.)
Oct. 27, 1945	Charles W. Nall	1.1	Smyrna (Tenn.),
		2.3	Akron (Ohio)
Oct. 28, 1945	Charles W. Nall	1.3	Washington, D.C.
Oct. 31, 1945	Charles W. Nall	3.4	Smyrna (Tenn.)
		1.0	Marietta (Ga.)
Nov. 1, 1945	Charles W. Nall	3.3	Miami (Fla.),
		2.3	Tallahassee (Fla.)
Nov. 2, 1945	Charles W. Nall	1.2	Marietta (Ga.),
		2.3	New Orleans (La.),
Nov. 3, 1945	Charles W. Nall	5.6	Albuquerque (N.M.)
Dec. 1, 1945	George H. Brett		Albuquerque, Los Angeles, and return
Jan. 13, 1946			Kingman (Ariz.)
Jan. 18, 1946			Decommissioned
Unknown	Frank Kurtz		March Field (Calif.), Las Vegas (Nev.), Kingman (Ariz.)
Apr. 6, 1946	Frank Kurtz		Los Angeles
Jan. 22, 1949	Frank Kurtz		March Field
Mar. 23, 1949	Frank Kurtz		Los Angeles
Mar. 26, 1949	Frank Kurtz		Hamilton Field (Calif.)
Mar. 27, 1949	Frank Kurtz		Kirtland AFB (N.M.)
Mar. 28, 1949	Frank Kurtz		Offutt AFB (Nebr.)
Mar. 29, 1949	Frank Kurtz		Omaha Municipal Airport (Nebr.)
Mar. 31, 1949	Frank Kurtz		Mines Field (Chicago)
Jan. 11, 1952	Unknown		Flight test
Jan. 17, 1952	Jack Williams		Tinker AFB (Okla.)
Jan. 18, 1952	Floyd O. Bock		Pyote (Tex.)
Dec. 2, 1953	Richard T. Saxe		Laredo (Tex.), Ellington AFB (Tex.)
Dec. 3, 1953	Richard T. Saxe		Maxwell AFB (Ala.)
Dec. 4, 1953	Richard T. Saxe		McGhee Tyson Field (Tenn.)
Dec. 5, 1953	Richard T. Saxe		Andrews AFB (Md.)

Appendix I

Colors and Markings for the Boeing B-17D "Swoose"

Fuselage and Wings

There are a few configurations to consider in defining appropriate colors and markings for this airplane. For the purpose of restoration, none of these schemes can be adopted without considerable compromise. For the record, all authentic possibilities will be discussed, but one configuration is more suitable than the rest.

Although all B-17s were highly polished Alclad before war erupted, the War Department had directed that all such aircraft be camouflaged as soon as possible (Technical Order No. 07-1-1 dated April 8, 1941, "General—Aircraft Markings, Insignia, and Camouflage").

The Swoose was first painted in camouflage colors in December 1941 while at the Del Monte airfield in the Philippine Islands. The pilot at the time described the colors as "brown and swampy green." (Dark brown, olive drab, dark green, and neutral gray were used on aircraft stationed in Hawaii in 1937. According to Dana Bell, the olive drab faded to buff or brown.) Photographic evidence shows that the upper fuselage was painted in a multicolor camouflage scheme. The disruptive pattern included a band of lighter color paint forward of the radio compartment and repeated amidships. The paint had been applied outdoors with brooms and brushes, but the airplane still reflected sunlight. No information is available to define the nature of the camouflage paint used on the under surfaces.

The Del Monte–applied paint scheme remained on the Swoose until early 1944 when it was removed in Panama. However, at various times painted areas were given some touchup applications and there is photographic evidence to show that the rudder was repainted in the United States. Since the doped fabric on the movable surfaces probably deteriorated with time, it can be assumed that those surfaces were refinished or replaced from time to time after the airplane left the Southwest Pacific combat area.

In a photograph taken in June 1943, the airplane is shown in Panama with fourteen flags painted on the right side of the nose under a line of white block letters that read "FLAGS OF THE COUNTRIES WE HAVE VISITED". The airplane was covered with camouflage paint. (The photographs discussed in this section appear in the photo gallery after page 000.)

In early 1944 the camouflage paint was partially removed following a major overhaul when the inboard wing panels were replaced. At that time the paint scheme for the flags changed and four new flags were added. The line of black block letters above the flags read as before. Shortly thereafter, all of the remaining camouflage paint was removed and the airplane hand-polished. Apparently, the flag scheme was removed and replaced at the time since photographs show three rows of eight flags and one row of seven flags under black block letters that read "FLAGS OF THE LANDS THE SWOOSE HAS VISITED."

The airplane was decommissioned in December 1945 and parked out of doors at Kingman, Arizona, in its natural aluminum finish. In preparation for its delivery to Los Angeles in March 1946, the airplane was repainted. In order to restore its appearance as a combat veteran, the Swoose was given a nonstandard coat of camouflage paint.

In a photograph taken in April 1946, before the Swoose was delivered to Los Angeles, the underside of the fuselage appears to be painted black and the upper sides in a light olive drab. The red ball that was added to the fuselage cocarde appears to be makeshift in size and not in compliance with known specifications.

It was in this nonstandard scheme of olive drab and black that the airplane was delivered to the National Air Museum in March 1949. Because of the effects of outdoor storage, this finish has all but vanished, exposing the eroded natural metal finish. The surface of the skin cannot be restored to its original polished appearance with currently available technology.

While the Swoose spent only a few months of its life in combat, it was in that role that it will best be remembered, and it was then that it was christened with a unique, well-publicized name. Accordingly, it should be restored to resemble its appearance as combat aircraft during the early months of World War II.

In the book *Air Force Colors,* volume 1, *1926–1942,* Dana Bell mentions that dark brown paint saw a great deal of use in Hawaii and the Philippines along with olive drab and dark green. From this author's discussions with Bell, the pilot's description of "swampy green and brown" could be accurate reflections of the olive drab and dark green since the former faded into brown and the latter could be described as "swampy."

Investigation aimed at accurately specifying the actual paint and patterns used in the original camouflage scheme have been fruitless. Accordingly, it will not be possible to restore this airplane to its original operational colors and markings. The most logical compromise is to use the color scheme that was the standard for the time of its combat service in 1941 with markings according to A.C. Specification Nos. 98-24102 and 98-24105 (Amendment No. 6 dated December 12, 1941, was not considered because the Swoose had already been painted).

According to Technical Order No. 70-07-1-1 dated April 8, 1941, as amended through Amendment No. 5 dated September 16, 1941, all exterior surfaces, except for insignia and markings should be coated with dark olive drab, Shade No. 41 of Bulletin 41. Two coats of lacquer, Specification No. 14105, should be used or one coat of camouflage enamel, Specification No. 14109. Since the airplane operated over terrain that was predominately green, one coat of medium green, Shade No. 42, A.C. Bulletin No. 41, was authorized to supplement the top camouflage finish.

All undersurfaces except for insignia and markings should be painted with two coats of lacquer, Specification No. 14105, neutral gray, Shade No. 43 of Bulletin No. 41 or one coat of camouflage enamel, Specification No. 14109, neutral gray, Shade No. 43 of Bulletin No. 41.

The dark olive drab should extend downward on the sides of the fuselage and all similar surfaces in such a manner that none of the neutral gray coating is visible when the airplane is in normal flight attitude and is viewed from above in any direction within an angle of approximately 30 degrees from vertical lines tangent to the airplane. The color boundary separating the two shades of paint should be removed as far as possible by blending the colors at the junction lines.

Fabric covered surfaces should be finished with at least two spray coats of dark olive drab or neutral gray, Shade Nos. 41 and 43 of Bulletin 41, fully pigmented, nitrate camouflage dope conforming to Specification No. 14106.

The marking "U.S. ARMY" should be applied with blue, Shade No. 47 of Bulletin No. 41, to the underside of the wing. All other exterior markings should be applied using red, black, or blue, Shade Nos. 45, 44, and 47 of Bulletin No. 41.

One national cocarde, a red circle inside of white, five-pointed stars inside of a blue circumscribed circle, should be applied to the upper surface of the left wing and one applied to the lower surface of the right wing. The design should be in compliance with Specification No. 98-24102. One point of each star should be pointed directly forward.

One national cocarde should also be applied to each side of the fuselage midway between the vertical projections of the trailing edge of the rear window and the leading edge of the horizontal stabilizer. The design should be in conformance with Specification No. 98-24102 and the diameter of the circle should be three-quarters of the length of the projection of the fuselage side. One point of the white star should point upward when the airplane is in normal flight attitude.

The numerals "21" should be painted on both sides of the vertical stabilizer with black, Shade No. 44, camouflage paint. All propeller blades and hubs should be sprayed with one coat of zinc chromatic primer, Specification No. 14080. The final finish should be one light coat of cellulose nitrate camouflage lacquer, Specification No. 14105. The color, except for the tips, should be black, Shade No. 44, Bulletin No. 41. The tips for a distance of four inches from the ends should be yellow, Shade No. 48, Bulletin No. 41.

Swoose Logo

The Swoose logo was designed and painted on the airplane in February 1942. At the time, the airplane was still being used for combat support purposes. Restoration of the Swoose to duplicate its appearance at the time dictates that the logo be included.

The earliest known photograph to include a view of the logo was taken in May 1942 following its first west-to-east crossing to Hawaii. The second photograph, taken shortly after that flight, shows that some effort had already been taken to maintain the logo as it began to deteriorate. However, these efforts did not provide for restoring the logo and changes began to appear.

What is thought to be a sketch of the original logo as drawn by the designer Weldon H. Smith was found among his possessions following his death. He painted a rendition of the design in early 1943 for presentation to "Mother" Tusch's museum in San Francisco. A photograph of that painting is stored in the National Air and Space Museum archives. Of these versions, the sketch is believed to portray most accurately the logo as it was originally painted on the fuselage.

From photographic evidence, the original logo appears to have been altered to some degree at least five times. The logo on the airplane at the time it was delivered to the National Air Museum was applied after all of the camouflage paint was removed in Panama.

Using Weldon Smith's sketch, the colors designated for the logo are: black for the beak, eye, bombsight, (bomb) fins, rudder, propeller, foot, lower leg, wing hinges, and "2,000 LBS." Chrome yellow is specified for the bird's neck and the bomb. "IT FLYS?" was painted red, according to Smith's notes, but the earliest photograph shows the words to be painted black and the question mark in the same color as the name. The question mark could have been altered with the new color paint when the obvious new words "99 - THE —" were added since they appear to be of the same color. Brown is the color specified by Smith for the body, wings, and "THE SWOOSE." Green-gray (probably the original camouflage paint) was specified as the background for the logo.

Flags

The flag motif on the left-hand side of the nose of the fuselage first appeared in a photograph on June 22, 1943. By this time the Swoose was an RB-17 assigned to duty as a passenger transport in Panama. The original flag layout was composed of fourteen flags painted in three rows directly over the camouflage-painted fuselage. Over the years more flags were added. All the flags were repainted following the removal of the camouflage paint. The background was altered, three more flags apparently added, and the words above the flags changed when the Swoose was given a hurried application of new camouflage paint in April 1946 prior to its triumphant delivery to the city of Los Angeles. As the flags did not appear on the Swoose until long after it left the Southwest Pacific Theater of Operations, the flags should not be included in plans for restoration.

Notes

Sources in abbreviated form at first reference appear in their entirety in the bibliography.

Introduction

1. "Swoose Famous B-17, on Way to Museum Here," *Washington* (D.C.) *Times-Herald,* March 25, 1949.

2. *The Flying Times,* Public Information Office, Kelly Field, Texas, December 17, 1953.

3. Boeing Airplane Company, "The Boeing B-17 Flying Fortress"; Paul E. Garber, memorandum to C. W. Mitman, "Subject: Report of Detail to California in Connection with the 'Swoose,' January 19–29 Inclusive," February 4, 1949, NAM662, NASM Archives.

4. War Department AAF Form 1, Aircraft Inspection and Maintenance Record, part 2, for B-17D 40-3097.

5. Morton, *U.S. Army in World War II.*

6. Eugene Eubank, "Wings over Olmsted," Middletown Air Depot, Olmsted Field, Middletown, Pa., August 21, 1942.

7. Editor's note in the "Letters" column, *Air Force Times* 12, no. 51 (July 26, 1952): 4.

8. “Last Parade,” *Time, c.* February 1943.

9. Henry C. Godman, letter to author, January 25, 1988.

10. Henry C. Godman, letter to Bruce D. Hoy, August 2, 1984; Walter M. Male, manager, National Air Museum, letter to commanding general, Pyote Air Force Base, February 27, 1952, curatorial file, National Air and Space Museum, Washington, D.C. (hereafter NASM).

11. Teats, “Turn of the Tide,” installment 8, January 8, 1943; Edmonds, *They Fought with What They Had;* Craven and Cate, eds., *Plans and Early Operations,* 206.

12. Teats, “Turn of the Tide,” installment 5, January 4, 1943.

13. “The Swoose Retires.”

Chapter 1. Birth of a Veteran

1. Craven and Cate, eds., *Plans and Early Operations,* 598.

2. Boeing Aircraft Company, “The Boeing B-17 Flying Fortress.”

3. Bowers, *Fortress in the Sky,* 27.

4. van der Linden, “Struggle for the Long-Range Heavy Bomber.”

5. Ibid., 28.

6. Bowers, *Fortress in the Sky,* 38.

7. van der Linden, “Struggle for the Long-Range Heavy Bomber,” 47.

8. Charles E. Moslander, “First Lady,” *Aerospace Historian* 16, no. 2 (Summer 1969): 21.

9. Bowers, *Fortress in the Sky,* 50, 56.

10. Ibid., 57.

11. Godman, *Supreme Commander,* 25.

12. Craven and Cate, eds., *Plans and Early Operations,* 598.

13. Peter M. Bowers, *Boeing Aircraft since 1916* (Annapolis, Md.: Naval Institute Press, 1989), 257.

14. Boeing Airplane Company, “The Boeing B-17 Flying Fortress.”

15. Jablonski, *Flying Fortress,* 34, 96, 178.

16. Aircraft Inventory Card for B-17D 40-3097, curatorial file, NASM.

17. Bowers, *Fortress in the Sky,* 66.

18. Ibid., 59.

19. Teats, “Turn of the Tide.”

20. Col. John A. Wallach, personal communication with author, January 29, 1988.

21. “History of the 19th Bombardment Group (Heavy), January 1939–February 24, 1942,” Research Studies Institute, USAF Historical Division, Archives Branch, Maxwell AFB, Ala., microfilm frame 1357.

22. Ibid.

23. Copp, *Forged in Fire,* 144.

Chapter 2. Beginning of the Pacific Sojourn

1. Craven and Cate, eds., *Plans and Early Operations,* 171.

2. Copp, *Forged in Fire,* 74; Brereton, *Brereton Diaries,* 7; Prange, *At Dawn We Slept,* 122.

3. Messimer, *No Margin for Error;* Scheppler, *Pacific Air Race,* 5.

4. Horvath, "Bird of Paradise," 27.

5. Scheppler, *Pacific Air Race,* 21.

6. Kingsford-Smith and Ulm, *The Flight of the Southern Cross,* 121.

7. Creed, *PBY, The Catalina Flying Boat,* 38; Mingoes, ed., *Junior Aircraft Year Book for 1935,* 35.

8. P. Davis, *Charles Kingsford-Smith: The World's Greatest Aviator* (Sydney, Australia: Landsdowne Press, 1985), 157.

9. Mingoes, ed., *Aircraft Year Book for 1936,* 135, 142.

10. R.E.G. Davies, *Airlines of the United States since 1914* (Washington, D.C.: Smithsonian Institution Press, 1972).

11. Amelia Earhart, *Last Flight* (New York: Harcourt, Brace and Co., 1937), 70; Doris Rich, *Amelia Earhart: A Biography* (Washington, D.C.: Smithsonian Institution Press, 1989), 257.

12. Creed, *PBY, The Catalina Flying Boat,* 41; Mingoes, ed., *Aircraft Year Book for 1940,* 433.

13. Fourth Air Force Historical Study No. IV-1, *Processing and Ferrying Functions of the Fourth Air Force through the Year 1941:* Vol. 1, *Narrative.* Prepared by the Adjutant General Historical Section of the Fourth Air Force Headquarters, San Francisco 6, California, March 1945.

14. File 452-1A, Box 943, Record Group 18, National Archives, Washington, D.C.

15. Prange, *At Dawn We Slept,* 123.

16. Maj. Gen. Eugene L. Eubank, letter to author, March 12, 1987.

17. Horvath, "Bird of Paradise," 27.

18. T. Sgt. Glenn L. Lewis, "The March Field Story," Office of Information, 22nd Bombardment Wing, NASM Library; Maj. Gen. Eugene L. Eubank, letter to author, January 29, 1987.

19. Lewis, "The March Field Story."

20. The specific crew assigned to 40-3097 could not be identified since aircraft serial numbers were not used in preparing the orders to fly the aircraft; Horvath, "Bird of Paradise," 27.

21. Craven and Cate, eds., *Plans and Early Operations,* 172.

22. *U.S. Air Services* 27, no. 1 (January 1942): 38.

23. Lord, *Day of Infamy,* 48.

24. Godman, *Supreme Commander,* 26.

25. Ibid., 25.

26. Edmonds, *They Fought with What They Had,* 4.

27. Henry C. Godman, letter to author, March 18, 1987.

28. Ibid.

29. Prange, *At Dawn We Slept,* 124.

30. Aircraft Inventory Card for B-17D 40-3097; Wallach, personal communication with author.

31. "History of 19th Bombardment Group," 14th Bombardment Squadron, p. 4; Special Order No. 203, Headquarters Hickam Field, Hickam Field, Territory of Hawaii, September 1941; Haugland, *The AAF against Japan,* 27.

32. Morison, *Rising Sun in the Pacific,* 153; Craven and Cate, eds., *Plans and Early Operations,* 178; Brereton, *Brereton Diaries,* 15.

33. Creed, *PBY, The Catalina Flying Boat,* x.

34. Brereton, *Brereton Diaries,* 15; Prange, *At Dawn We Slept,* 403.

35. Special Order Number 203 of September 2, 1941. See Appendix B.

36. Godman, letter to author; Craven and Cate, eds., *Plans and Early Operations,* 178.

37. Craven and Cate, eds., *Plans and Early Operations,* 179.

38. Godman, *Supreme Commander,* 28.

39. Boyle, "This Dreamboat Can Fly!," 88.

40. "75 Army Men Awarded DFC," *Honolulu Star-Bulletin,* April 25, 1942.

41. Edmonds, *They Fought with What They Had,* 43; Aircraft Inventory Card for B-17D 40-3097; Godman, *Supreme Commander,* 31.

42. Maurer, *Air Force Units of World War II,* 76.

43. Craven and Cate, eds., *Plans and Early Operations,* 178.

44. Edmonds, *They Fought with What They Had.*

45. Ibid., 14.

46. The 14th Bombardment Squadron was officially attached to the 19th on December 24, 1941. See "History of the 19th Bombardment Group."

47. Brereton, *Brereton Diaries,* 39–40, 59; Teats, "Turn of the Tide," installment 1, December 31, 1942.

48. Wallach, personal communication with author.

49. Edmonds, *They Fought with What They Had,* 44.

50. Manchester, *American Caesar,* 233; Brereton, *Brereton Diaries,* 33.

51. Wallach, personal communication with author.

52. Brereton, *Brereton Diaries,* 36; Edmonds, *They Fought with What They Had,* 91.

53. Brereton, *Brereton Diaries,* 36.

54. Birnn, "A War Diary," 200; Craven and Cate, eds., *Plans and Early Operations.*

55. Edmonds, *They Fought with What They Had,* 189.

56. Birnn, "A War Diary."

57. Craven and Cate, eds., *Plans and Early Operations,* 189.

Chapter 3. Combat Operations

1. Diary of the 19th Bomb Group. Enclosure to memo dated October 19, 1943, from Maj. Gustav A. Heuber, Adjutant General, Fort George Wright, to Distribution. The following note appears at the beginning: "All records covering the period December 8, 1941, to December 16, 1941, incl. were destroyed so this part of the journal had to be rewritten from memory." The airmen of the 14th and 93rd squadrons at Del Monte on December 8, 1941, are listed in Appendix F; Diary of the 19th Bombardment Group, December 8, 1941–February 24, 1942; Edmonds, *They Fought with What They Had,* 84; Wallach, personal communication with author.

2. Diary of the 19th Bomb Group.

3. Brett, "The MacArthur I Knew"; Manchester, *American Caesar,* 233.

4. Brett, "The MacArthur I Knew."

5. Statement by Alfred R. Young, CWO, USAF (Ret.), at the time a member of the 28th Squadron of the 19th Bomb Group. From the archives of the Office of History, Clark Field, "Clark Field—From 1939 through 24 December 1941."

6. Gp-19 HI, Aerospace Studies Institute, Maxwell AFB, Ala.

7. Teats, "Turn of the Tide," installment 1, December 31, 1942.

8. Craven and Cate, eds., *Plans and Early Operations.*

9. Ibid., 206.

10. Howard Mingoes, *American Heroes of the War in the Air,* vol. 1 (New York: Lancier Publications, 1943).

11. Morison, *Rising Sun in the Pacific,* 180; Brereton, *Brereton Diaries,* 48.

12. Edmonds, *They Fought with What They Had,* 130.

13. Wallach, personal communication with author.

14. Brereton, *Brereton Diaries.*

15. Wallach, personal communication with author.

16. Diary of the 19th Bomb Group; Godman, letter to author.

17. Weldon H. Smith, personal diary, NASM.

18. Wallach, personal communication with author.

19. Ibid.

20. Edmonds, *They Fought with What They Had,* 179.

21. Ibid., 180, 181.

22. Wallach, personal communication with author; Edmonds, *They Fought with What They Had,* 185.

23. Wallach, personal communication with author.

24. Smith diary.

25. Ibid.

26. Col. John A. Wallach, personal communication with author, August 3, 1992; "Summary of Air Action in the Philippines," 209–10.

27. "Summary of Air Action in the Philippines," 125–26.

28. Interestingly, "Summary of Air Action in the Philippines" (pp. 257–59)

has Pease flying on March 11 and Godman on March 13—further evidence of inaccurate recordkeeping.

29. Henry C. Godman, personal communication with author, January 25, 1988.

30. Godman, *Supreme Commander,* 37.

31. Godman, personal communication with author.

32. The Bataan was outfitted to meet General MacArthur's needs. Except for the machine guns mounted in the nose and tail, all armament was removed. In the bomb bay were two Pullman-type bunks, an electric stove, and an icebox. The radio compartment was used as a sitting room and furnished with a desk and chairs. Extra fuselage windows were installed. The airplane could accommodate thirty-eight passengers. Manufactured as B-17E 41-2593, following the modifications it was redesignated on September 10, 1943, as an XC-108 (a special-purpose transport airplane [C]). Airplane records appear to indicate that the airplane was assigned to General MacArthur on September 18, 1943, when Godman picked it up for the flight to Australia. Godman, *Supreme Commander,* 52; Swanborough and Bowers, *United States Military Aircraft since 1908,* 95; Aircraft Inventory Card for B-17E Serial Number 41-2593, NASM Archives.

33. Haugland, *The AAF against Japan,* 39.

34. Diary of the 19th Bomb Group.

35. "Summary of Air Action in the Philippines."

36. Richard Lipkin, "Stalking the Super Storms," *Insight* (January 9, 1989): 8.

37. Haugland, *The AAF against Japan;* "Summary of Air Action in the Philippines." Regarding the name "Kattary," while the roster for the 19th has no such name, there is a Sgt. B. A. Katlars listed. It is possible this is a typographical error.

38. Edmonds, *They Fought with What They Had,* 263.

39. Haugland, *The AAF against Japan.*

40. Smith diary, entry of January 4, 1942.

41. Haugland, *The AAF against Japan,* 263, 264.

42. "Summary of Air Action in the Philippines."

43. Smith diary.

44. Edmonds, *They Fought with What They Had,* 265.

45. Teats, "Turn of the Tide," installment 8, January 8, 1943.

46. Edmonds, *They Fought with What They Had,* 293.

47. Frank Kurtz, letter dated April 30, 1992, to the director, NASM.

48. "History of the 19th Bombardment Group."

49. Edmonds, *They Fought with What They Had,* 267.

50. Ibid.

51. "History of the 19th Bombardment Group."

52. "General Brett Decorates 23 American Flyers for Pacific Exploits," datelined Gen. Douglas MacArthur's headquarters, Australia, July 9, 1942.

53. "History of the 19th Bombardment Group."

54. Diary of the 19th Bomb Group.

55. Teats, "Turn of the Tide," installment 9, January 9, 1943.

56. Weldon Smith's note on the reverse of a Swoose insignia presented to C. A. "Mother" Tusch. Item 154, NASM690, NASM Archives Cat. No. 1950-0183; also NASM photo 85-17035.

57. Howard Waldorf, "'Unknown Boy, Probably Dead' Found Alive, Laughing Here—Had a Great 16 Months," *Oakland* (Calif.) *Post Enquirer,* May 11, 1943, quoted Captain Smith as stating, "Every time we ["The Swoose"] started out, she developed trouble. An engine would go sour, the oil pressure would drop, or something else would happen to force us back, or down. Each time we snatched parts from some other ship and managed to keep her going. All the while we were trying to decide on a name. Most of the ones the crew suggested weren't printable. Finally she had a rudder from one ship, an engine from another, and it suddenly dawned on me she was a Swoose—half swan, half goose. So that's what we named her, then and there."

58. Smith's note on the reverse of a Swoose insignia.

59. Item 154, NASM690, NASM Archives Cat. No. 1950-0183.

60. Maj. Weldon Smith, as told to George F. Lineer, "The Log of the Flying Fortress Swoose—Half Swan, Half Goose," *San Francisco Chronicle,* April 11, 1943.

61. Aircraft Inventory Card for B-17D 40-3097; no further entries are indicated until August 26, 1942. "History of the 19th Bombardment Group."

62. Teats, "Turn of the Tide," installment 17, January 18, 1943.

Chapter 4. Command Airplane in Australia

1. Courtney, "Born to Fly."

2. Craven and Cate, eds., *Plans and Early Operations,* 115.

3. Letter, George H. Brett to E. A. Goff, February 16, 1960, biographical files, NASM.

4. Craven and Cate, eds., *Plans and Early Operations,* 326; *Air Force Newsletter,* no. 9 (May 1, 1936); Early Birds GAL-1, an obituary in the biographical files, NASM.

5. Craven and Cate, eds., *Plans and Early Operations,* 326.

6. Ibid., 325.

7. Box 899, RG 18, National Archives, Washington, D.C.

8. "U.S. Air Corps Chief in Egypt," *New York Herald Tribune,* September 11, 1941; "American Tribute," *Malta Times,* October 17, 1941; "Gen. Brett Speeding Lease Lend in M.E.," *Egyptian Mail* (Cairo), December 2, 1941; "Axis Attacks Plane Bearing U.S. General," *Washington Times-Herald,* December 2, 1941.

9. John K. Gowen, caption on a photograph in General Brett's scrapbook; Craven and Cate, eds., *Plans and Early Operations,* 326.

10. Leland Stowe, "Brett and Staff Set Mark in Flight from Cairo to Rangoon," *Washington* (D.C.) *Evening Star,* December 22, 1941.

11. Gowen, caption on photograph.

12. Karl Eskelund, "Ditch Sheltered Wavell, Brett during Jap Raid," *Washington Times-Herald,* February 16, 1942; Morton, *U.S. Army in World War II,* 161.

13. Craven and Cate, eds., *Plans and Early Operations,* 226; Lee, *They Called It Pacific.*

14. Brereton, *Brereton Diaries,* 62, 73, 75.

15. Morton, *U.S. Army in World War II.*

16. "General Brett Named Second in Command for Far East," *Cleveland News,* January 3, 1942.

17. Brereton, *Brereton Diaries,* 75; Craven and Cate, eds., *Plans and Early Operations,* 707.

18. Craven and Cate, eds., *Plans and Early Operations.*

19. Edmonds, *They Fought with What They Had,* 434.

20. Ibid., 432.

21. Gowen, caption to photograph.

22. Craven and Cate, eds., *Plans and Early Operations,* 419–20.

23. Haugland, *The AAF against Japan.*

24. Royce, "Combat Notes from Down Under"; Brett, "The MacArthur I Knew."

25. Craven and Cate, eds., *Plans and Early Operations.*

26. George H. Brett, letter to the *Air Force Times,* August 21, 1952; Craven and Cate, eds., *Plans and Early Operations.*

27. Frank Kurtz, "Operation 30," *Boeing Magazine* 19, no. 4 (April 1949): 8.

28. Letter to Frank Kurtz from Hiram Bingham, president of the National Aeronautics Association, February 3, 1942.

29. Moolman, *Women Aloft.*

30. "Flyer Aiming at Washington Hits Brooklyn," *New York Herald Tribune,* October 23, 1935.

31. Frank Kurtz, letter to Martin Harwit, April 30, 1992.

32. *Newark Ledger,* November 4, 1935.

33. From a pamphlet advertising speaking engagements for Col. Frank Kurtz.

34. Ibid.; Frank A. Kurtz, "Randolph Prepares Young Man for Kelly," *U.S. Air Services* 23, no. 4 (April 1938): 12; White, *Queens Die Proudly;* Lee Van Atta, International News Service, with the U.S. Air Force in Australia, March 19, 1943.

35. White, *Queens Die Proudly;* Frank Kurtz, personal communication with the author, September 25, 1989.

36. Brett, "The MacArthur I Knew"; Kurtz, personal communication with author.

37. Kurtz, personal communication with author.

38. White, *Queens Die Proudly.*

39. Gowen, "The Swoose"; Kurtz, personal communication with author.

40. Royce, "Combat Notes from Down Under."

41. Brett, "The MacArthur I Knew."

42. Ibid.; Craven and Cate, eds., *Plans and Early Operations.*

43. Brett, "The MacArthur I Knew."

44. Ibid.

45. Morton, *U.S. Army in World War II;* Brett, "The MacArthur I Knew."

46. Brett, "The MacArthur I Knew."

47. Manchester, *American Caesar.*

48. Brett, "The MacArthur I Knew."

49. Harry Schreiber, letter to author, July 17, 1988.

50. Brett, "The MacArthur I Knew."

51. Frank Bostrom, personal communication with the author, May 24, 1989.

52. Teats, "Turn of the Tide"; Manchester, *American Caesar;* Morton, *U.S. Army in World War II;* Bostrom, personal communication with author.

53. Brett, "The MacArthur I Knew."

54. Manchester, *American Caesar.*

55. Morton, *U.S. Army in World War II.*

56. Manchester, *American Caesar.*

Chapter 5. The Swoose in the News

1. Van Atta, "Springboard to the Skies."

2. Lee Van Atta, "In Tight Spot Call Pilot Kurtz," International News Service, Melbourne, June 10, 1942.

3. Manuscript used by the city of Los Angeles on Army Day, April 6, 1946, as a part of the fact sheet on "The Swoose."

4. Brett, "The MacArthur I Knew."

5. Gowen, "Alexander the Swoose."

6. Kurtz, personal communication with author.

7. "Capt. Frank Kurtz on the Job in Australia," *U.S. Air Services* 27 (August 1942).

8. Kurtz, personal communication with author.

9. Gowen, "Alexander the Swoose"; Kingsford-Smith, *My Flying Life.*

10. Van Atta, "Springboard to the Skies"; Gowen, "Alexander the Swoose."

11. Kurtz, personal communication with author.

12. Brett, "The MacArthur I Knew."

13. Miller, *Lyndon, An Oral Biography.*

14. Kurtz, personal communication with author; Lyndon B. Johnson, World War II diary. Lyndon Baines Johnson Library, Austin, Texas; Birnn, "A War Diary"; Manchester, *American Caesar.*

15. Johnson diary.

16. Lyndon B. Johnson, Australia 1942 Home Movie 6, Lyndon Baines Johnson Library, Austin, Texas.

17. Mission Report, 22nd Bomb Group, as quoted in Henry Sakaida, *Winged Samurai* (Mesa, Ariz.: Champlin Fighter Museum Press, 1985), 44–45.

18. Johnson diary.

19. Sakaida, *Winged Samurai,* 42.

20. Birnn, "A War Diary."

21. Johnson diary.

22. Lt. Cmdr. Lyndon B. Johnson, "Complete Itinerary," Lyndon Baines Johnson Library, Austin, Texas; Johnson diary.

23. Courtney, "Born to Fly."

24. Schreiber, letter to author.

25. Kurtz, personal communication with author.

26. Schreiber, letter to author.

27. Ibid.

28. Kurtz, personal communication with author.

29. Johnson, "Complete Itinerary."

30. Manchester, *American Caesar.*

31. Brett, "The MacArthur I Knew."

32. Ibid.; George C. Kenney, *General Kenney Reports* (New York: Duell, Sloan and Pearce, 1949).

33. Brett, "The MacArthur I Knew."

34. Ibid.

35. Memorandum for General Arnold from George H. Brett dated September 7, 1942, National Archives, Washington, D.C.

36. Freeman, *B-17 Fortress at War.*

37. "Brett Is Relieved of Pacific War Post," *Philadelphia Inquirer,* September 8, 1942; "Flying Fortress Sets Speed Record," Associated Press report, Denver (n.d.); Maj. Charles E. Shelton, "Our Pacific Sky-Lane, *Air Force Magazine,* July 1943; Gowen, "The Swoose."

38. Lawrence Youngman, news clipping from unknown Omaha newspaper, August 22, 1942; "Air Record, General Brett's Pacific Flight," datelined New York, August 30, *West Australian* (Perth, W.A.), September 1, 1942.

39. Aircraft Inventory Card for B-17 40-3097; "Allied Air Chief in S.W. Pacific Changed," *Herald,* Melbourne, Australia, n.d.

40. Aircraft Inventory Card for B-17 40-3097.

41. "Gen. Brett, Air Chief in Australia, Visits Denver," *New York Times,* September 1, 1942.

Chapter 6. Diplomatic Operations

1. Memo for Chief of Staff dated April 2, 1941, File 381, Box 942, Record Group 18, National Archives, Washington, D.C.

2. Maurer, *Air Force Units of World War II,* 338, 339.

3. "Colonel Frank Kurtz," biography prepared by the Treasury Department, New York, in file at NASM.

4. M. Sgt. Boyd S. Hart, letter to the *Air Force Times* 12, no. 51 (July 26, 1952).

5. "Capt. Peterson Named Aide to General Brett," *Star and Herald* (Panama City), February 1, 1943; "LA Ceremonia Deayer En El Aero Club," *El Comercio* (Lima, Peru), January 14, 1943.

6. Jack J. Crane, letter to author, December 4, 1987.

7. "Sturdee to Tour Defenses," *Star and Herald* (Panama City), March 4, 1943.

8. "Brett Presents Merit Emblem to Col. Fabrega," *Star and Herald* (Panama City), June 20, 1943.

9. "Brett Pilots Son from NY to Canal Zone," *Star and Herald* (Panama City), June 7, 1945.

10. "Mascot of 'Swoose' Crew Dies Under Auto's Wheels," *Star and Herald* (Panama City), June 17, 1945.

11. *Panama American* (Panama City), October 27, 1943; "New Pilot for Swoose Is Appointed," *Star and Herald* (Panama City), October 27, 1943.

12. War Department Form No. 5 for Capt. Jack J. Crane, in Crane's personal files.

13. "New Pilot for Swoose Is Appointed."

14. Jack J. Crane, letter to author, January 10, 1987.

15. Ibid.

16. Ibid.; *Star and Herald* (Panama City), November 8, 1944; *Star and Herald* (Panama City), November 13, 1944.

17. Crane, letter to author, January 10, 1987.

18. Ibid.

19. Homer Rogers, letter to author, October 21, 1988; Jack J. Crane, letter to author, November 13, 1988.

20. Crane, letter to author, November 13, 1988.

21. Ibid.

22. Ibid.

23. Bowers, *Fortress in the Sky;* Crane, letter to author, November 13, 1988.

24. Crane, letter to author, November 13, 1988; Gowen, "The Swoose."

25. Jack J. Crane, letter to author, September 28, 1987.

26. Ibid.

27. Ibid.

28. Jack J. Crane, letter to author, November 12, 1988.

29. *Star and Herald* (Panama City), from General Brett's scrapbook.

30. Crane, letter to author, September 28, 1987.

31. *Star and Herald* (Panama City), from General Brett's scrapbook.

32. Crane, letter to author, September 28, 1987.

33. Ibid.

34. Ibid.

35. Swanborough and Bowers, *United States Military Aircraft since 1908*, 557.

36. Crane, letter to author, December 4, 1987.

Chapter 7. The Long Road Home

1. The material in the first part of this chapter is based on information provided by Charles Nall in correspondence dated September 1990 and subsequent conversations conducted at that time.

2. Brett, Letter to *Air Force Times*.

3. Jerry McLain, "Warbirds Swansong," *Arizona Highways*, May 1947 (rpt. December 1988).

4. Philip Chinnery, *Desert Boneyard* (St. John's Hill, Shrewsbury, Engl.: Airlife Publishing Ltd., 1987).

5. Frank Kurtz, note to author, August 1989.

6. Letter from Fletcher Bowron to Russell Hiddelston, Aviation Surplus Division, War Assets Corporation, Washington, D.C., March 2, 1946.

7. Special broadcast of the ceremonies held at the Los Angeles Airport upon the arrival of the Swoose, speech by Mayor Fletcher Bowron, station KMPC, March 3, 1946.

8. Kurtz, personal communication with author.

9. "'Operation 30' Due Tomorrow As Swoose Makes Last Flight," *Washington Post*, March 25, 1946.

10. Kurtz, personal communication with author.

11. "L.A. Salutes U.S. Army Day," *Los Angeles Examiner*, April 7, 1946.

12. "Final Chapter," script for broadcast by KNX, April 16, 1946.

13. Fact sheet for Army Day, Saturday, April 6, 1946; "War-Scarred Swoose Turned Over to City," newsclipping, n.d. curatorial file, NASM.

14. Fact sheet for Army Day, Saturday, April 6, 1946.

15. Ibid.

16. Robert C. Strobell, associate curator, National Air Museum, Memo: "Swoose," January 25, 1949.

17. "'Jet' Flyers Set Records," *Los Angeles Times*, April 7, 1946.

18. Paul E. Garber, letter to Lt. Gen. George H. Brett, February 4, 1949.

19. Strobell, memo; Garber, letter to Brett.

20. Strobell, memo; Kurtz, personal communication with author.

21. Garber, letter to Brett.

22. Ibid.

23. Ibid.; Capt. Rowland A. Boone, letter to Col. Frank Kurtz, December 9, 1948.

24. J. E. Read, assistant regional administrator (CAA), letter to Paul E. Garber, September 30, 1948.

25. Boone, letter to Kurtz.

26. Frank Kurtz, letter to Paul E. Garber, January 3, 1949; Boone, note to Paul Garber, appended to letter to Kurtz.

27. Kurtz, letter to Garber.

28. Kurtz, personal communication with author.

29. Garber, memo to Mitman.

30. Ibid.; Kurtz, personal communication with author.

31. War Department AAF Form 1A, "Airplane Flight Report—Engineering," War Department AAF Form No. 1, "Aircraft Flight Report—Operations," and War Department AAF Form No. 41B, "Maintenance Inspection Record."

32. Garber, memo to Mitman.

33. Speech by Mayor Bowron, March 3, 1946.

34. Garber, memo to Mitman.

35. Ibid.

36. War Department AAF Form 41B, "Maintenance Inspection Record."

37. "A Museum Piece Flying Across the Nation," news clipping from unknown San Francisco newspaper, March 24, 1949.

38. War Department AAF Form 41B, "Maintenance Inspection Record."

39. "A Museum Piece Flying Across the Nation."

40. "Swoose Wartime Pilot Arrives to Check It Out," *Los Angeles Times,* March 24, 1949; "Museum Bound Swoose Starts on Final Mission," *Los Angeles Times,* March 27, 1949.

41. "Ceremonies Start Swoose on Last Flight—to Air Musuem," *Los Angeles Examiner,* March 27, 1949.

42. Vincent X. Flaherty, "The Swoose's Crew Like Smooth Athletic Team," *Los Angeles Examiner,* dateline Albuquerque, March 28, 1949.

43. "Historic Plane on Last Visit," news clipping from unknown Oakland newspaper, March 27, 1949; Kurtz, note to author.

44. "Swoose Off to Smithsonian," Associated Press, Albuquerque, March 27, 1949.

45. "Chicago Set to Honor Swoose"; Karen De Witt, "It's a Girl, It's a Plane, It's a—Swoose," *Washington Post,* June 4, 1977.

46. "Swoose Has Sore Tail Wheel; She Must Sit Down Carefully," *Omaha Evening World-Herald,* March 29, 1949.

47. "Last Old Flying Fortress Reaches Its Museum Site," *New York Times,* April 1, 1949; "Queen of Warplanes Here on Last Flight," *Chicago Herald American,* April 1, 1949.

48. "Kennelly Honors 'Swoose.'"

49. *National Tribune,* April 14, 1949.

50. *USAF Statistical Digest, Fiscal Year 1954* (Washington, D.C.: Department of the Air Force, 1954).

51. AF Form 1, Aircraft Inspection and Maintenance Report, Part 2, dated December 17, 1952.

52. Ibid., dated January 18, 1952.

53. AF Form 1, dated December 2, 1953; *The Flying Times,* December 17, 1953.

54. *Handbook of Operations and Flight Instruction,* T.O. 01-20ED-1, dated October 1, 1941, p. 53; Airplane Weighing Record, November 18, 1953, DD Form 365B. Weight and Balance Clearance Form F, n.d., DD Form 365F.

55. Mueller, "The Final Flight of the 'Swoose.'"

56. Richard S. Saxe, letter to author, June 9, 1987.

57. Mueller, "The Final Flight of the 'Swoose.'"

58. Saxe, letter to author.

59. Aircraft Inspection and Maintenance Record, dated December 3, 1953.

60. Mueller, "The Final Flight of the 'Swoose'"; Air Force Form 510, Aircraft Delivery Receipt.

61. Jack J. Crane, letter to author, January 4, 1987.

Bibliography

Birnn, Lt. Roland R. "A War Diary," part 1. *Air Power Historian* 3, no. 11 (October 1956); part 2, *Air Power Historian* 4, no. 2 (April 1957).

Boeing Airplane Company. "The Boeing B-17 Flying Fortress, Alexander the Swoose." Publication S-1451, January 29, 1949.

Bowers, Peter M. *Fortress in the Sky.* Grenada Hills, Calif.: Sentry Books, 1976.

Boyle, J. M. "This Dreamboat Can Fly!" *Aerospace Historian* 14, no. 2 (Summer 1967): 85.

Brereton, Lewis H. *The Brereton Diaries.* New York: William Morrow, 1946.

Brett, Lt. Gen. George H., with Jack Kofold. "The MacArthur I Knew." *True: The Man's Magazine* (October 1947): 25.

"Chicago Set to Honor Swoose." *Chicago Herald American,* March 30, 1949.

Copp, Dwight S. *Forged in Fire.* Air Force Historical Foundation. New York: Doubleday, 1982.

Courtney, W. B. "Born to Fly." *Collier's* (August 8, 1942): 13.

Craven, Wesley Frank, and James Lea Cate, eds. *The Army Air Forces in World War II.* Vol. 1, *Plans and Early Operations, January 1939–August 1942.* Chicago: University of Chicago Press, 1948.

Creed, Roscoe. *PBY, The Catalina Flying Boat.* Annapolis, Md.: Naval Institute Press, 1985.

"Diary of the 19th Bombardment Group, December 8, 1941–February 24, 1942." Office of Air Force History, Bolling Air Force Base, Washington, D.C.

Edmonds, Walter D. *They Fought with What They Had.* Boston: Little, Brown, 1951.

Freeman, Roger A. *B-17 Fortress at War.* New York: Scribner's, 1977.

Godman, Henry C., with Cliff Dudley. *Supreme Commander.* Harrison, Ark.: New Leaf Press, 1980.

Gowen, John K. "Alexander the Swoose." *Boeing News* 3, no. 9 (September 1942).

———. "It Flies? Alexander the Swoose." *Army Times,* October 24, 1942.

Haugland, Vern. *The Army Air Forces against Japan.* New York: Harper Brothers, 1948.

"History of the 19th Bombardment Group (H), January 1, 1939–February 24, 1942" (BP-19-H1 Bomb). Aerospace Studies Institute, Archives Branch, Maxwell Air Force Base, Alabama.

Horvath, Lt. Col. William J. (USAR, Ret). "Bird of Paradise. The First No-Stop Flight to Hawaii." *Aerospace Historian* 15, no. 2 (Summer 1968): 27.

Jablonski, Edward. *Flying Fortress.* Garden City, N.Y.: Doubleday, 1965.

"Kennelly Honors 'Swoose.'" *Chicago Herald American,* April 2, 1949.

Kingsford-Smith, Sir Charles. *My Flying Life.* London: Aviation Book Club, 1939.

Kingsford-Smith, C. E., and C.T.P. Ulm. *The Flight of the Southern Cross.* New York: Robert M. McBridge and Co., 1929.

Lee, Clark. *They Called it Pacific.* New York: Viking Press, 1943.

Lord, Walter. *Day of Infamy.* New York: Bantam Books, 1957.

Manchester, William. *American Caesar.* Boston: Little, Brown, 1978.

Maurer, Maurer. *Air Force Units of World War II.* Washington, D.C.: Zanger Publishing, 1980.

Messimer, Dwight R. *No Margin for Error: The U.S. Navy's Transpacific Flight of 1925.* Annapolis, Md.: Naval Institute Press, 1981.

Miller, Merle. *Lyndon, An Oral Biography.* New York: G. P. Putnam's Sons, 1980.

Mingoes, Howard, ed. *The Aircraft Year Book for 1936.* New York: Aeronautical Chamber of Commerce of America, 1936.

———. *The Aircraft Year Book for 1940.* New York: Aeronautical Chamber of Commerce of America, 1940.

———. *Junior Aircraft Year Book for 1935.* New York: Aeronautical Chamber of Commerce, 1935.

Mitchell, John H. "The First Bombing Mission of the Air Corps in World War II." *Journal of the American Aviation Historical Society* 34, no. 1 (Spring 1989): 32.

Moolman, Valerie. *Women Aloft.* Alexandria, Va.: Time-Life Books, 1981.

Morison, Samuel Elliot. *History of the United States Naval Operations in World War II*. Vol. 3, *Rising Sun in the Pacific, 1930–April 1942*. Boston: Little, Brown, 1975.

Morton, Louis. *U.S. Army in World War II, Strategy and Command, The First Two Years*. Washington, D.C.: Department of the Army, 1962.

Moslander, Charles E. "First Lady." *Aerospace Historian* 16, no. 2 (Summer 1969): 21.

Mueller, Chuck. "The Final Flight of the 'Swoose' Nearly Kept It from Smithsonian." *The Sun* (San Bernadino, Calif.), July 28, 1985.

Prange, Gordon W. *At Dawn We Slept*. New York: McGraw-Hill, 1981.

Royce, Ralph. "Combat Notes From Down Under." *Air Force Magazine* (January 1943): 15.

Scheppler, Robert H. *Pacific Air Race*. Washington, D.C.: Smithsonian Institution Press, 1988.

Shershun, Capt. Carroll S. "The Man Who Downed Colin Kelly." *Aerospace Historian* 13, no. 4 (Winter 1968).

"Summary of Air Action in the Philippines and Netherlands East Indies, December 7, 1941–March 26, 1942." Army Air Forces Historical Study No. 29A. Prepared by Assistant Chief of Air Staff Intelligence, Historical Division, January 1945. USAF Historical Research Collection, Maxwell Air Force Base, Alabama.

Swanborough, Gordon, and Peter M. Bowers. *United States Military Aircraft since 1908*. London: Putnam and Co., 1971.

"The Swoose Retires." *New York Times,* April 11, 1949.

Teats, Edward C., and John M. McCullough. "Turn of the Tide." *Philadelphia Inquirer*, 17 installments, December 31, 1942–January 18, 1943.

Van Atta, Lee. "Springboard to the Skies." *Cosmopolitan* (October 1942).

van der Linden, Frank Robert. "The Struggle for the Long-Range Heavy Bomber: The U.S. Army Air Corps, 1934–39." M.A. thesis, The Graduate School of Arts and Sciences of the George Washington University, Washington, D.C., September 30, 1981.

White, William L. *Queens Die Proudly*. New York: Harcourt, Brace and Company, 1943.

Index

A

B

C

G

H

I

J

K

L

M

N